RETHINKING ONLINE EDUCATION

Series in Critical Narrative

ᕲ Donaldo Macedo, Series Editor ᕲ

University of Massachusetts–Boston

Now in Print

RETHINKING ONLINE EDUCATION

MEDIA, IDEOLOGIES, AND IDENTITIES

Bessie Mitsikopoulou

Routledge
Taylor & Francis Group

LONDON AND NEW YORK

First published 2015 by Paradigm Publishers

Published 2016 by Routledge
2 Park Square, Milton Park, Abingdon, Oxon OX14 4RN
711 Third Avenue, New York, NY 10017, USA

Routledge is an imprint of the Taylor & Francis Group, an informa business

Mitsikopoulou, Bessie.
 Rethinking online education : media, ideologies, and identities / Bessie
Mitsikopoulou.
    pages cm. — (Series in critical narrative)
 Includes bibliographical references and index.
 ISBN 978-1-59451-966-6 (hardcover : alk. paper) ISBN 978-1-59451-967-3 (paperback :
alk. paper)
 1. Internet in education. 2. Curriculum planning. 3. Critical pedagogy. 4. Iraq War,
2003–2011—Study and teaching. I. Title.
 LB1044.87.M58 2013
 371.33'44678–dc23

                                                              2013002155

Designed and Typeset in New Baskerville by Straight Creek Bookmakers.

ISBN 13 : 978-1-59451-966-6 (hbk)
ISBN 13 : 978-1-59451-967-3 (pbk)

In memory of my father,
Anastasios,
who first taught me
the power of language.

Contents

Figures, Tables, and Boxes

Figures

Tables

Boxes

Acknowledgments

ON MARCH 31, 2003, ALL OF US WHO WOULD BE ATTENDING THE ANNUAL meeting of the European Network on Critical Discourse Analysis (CDA) received a message from Professor Teun van Dijk, who was wondering why we had been silent. It was just a little more than one month since the beginning of the Iraq War. Teun's question motivated a change of theme, and the annual CDA meeting actually attempted to bring together critical perspectives on the Iraq War. It was at that point that I had the idea of systematically studying online educational materials on the war.

In May 2003, I collected a corpus of online educational materials concerning the war's early days, which resulted in a research article that I cowrote with Dimitris Koutsogiannis under the title "The Iraq War as Curricular Knowledge: From the Political to the Pedagogic Divide." The article first appeared in a special issue of the *Journal of Language and Politics* (2005, 4:1) and was later published by Benjamins in a book entitled *The Soft Power of War,* edited by Lilie Chouliaraki (2007). This paper has been the basis for later research, and extracts from it are included in Chapters 1, 2, and 4 of this book.

A year later, shortly after torture at Guantanamo prison was revealed, the corpus of educational materials was enriched with additional resources in order to explore the issue of pain and the ways it was treated pedagogically. Chapter 3, "The Ideology of the Instructional Texts," is a revised version of the article entitled "Representations of Pain in 'War against Terrorism' Pedagogies," which first appeared in *Reconstructing Pain and Joy: Linguistic, Literary and Cultural Perspectives,* 2008, Cambridge Scholars Publishing. I would like to thank the editors of the volume, Chryssoula Lascaratou, Anna Despotopoulou, and Elly Ifantidou, for granting me permission to reprint it. I would also like to thank the Associated Press for granting me permission to reprint the photos that appear in Chapter 3, *PBS NewsHour* for the permission to reprint screenshots from the *NewsHour Extra* homepage on the Iraq War (Figures I.1 and 5.1), and *Rethinking Schools* for the permission to reprint screenshots from their homepage on the Iraq War (Figures I.2 and 5.2).

The theoretical basis for Chapter 4 was initially presented at an international conference entitled "Lived Experience, Metaphor and Multimodality: Implications in Communication, Education, Learning and Knowledge," which was held in Rethymnon, Crete, in October 2008. Finally, the initial corpus was enriched with additional resources in 2010, including later online educational resources on the Iraq War.

I would particularly like to thank Professor Donaldo Macedo for inviting me to present a talk called "Pedagogies of the War against Terrorism" in the Department of Applied Linguistics at the University of Massachusetts–Boston in April 2007, and for encouraging me to proceed with publication of this book. I thank him for including this book in the Series in Critical Narrative. His continuing support has made this book possible, and I am grateful to him for this. I would also like to thank my dearest mentor and colleague, Professor Bessie Dendrinos, for providing valuable feedback on this book and for her constant and generous support. Several people have read earlier versions of the book and helped me considerably to rethink it critically. Special thanks go to Dimitris Koutsogiannis, with whom I have spent several hours discussing this research project. I would also like to thank Mary Drossou, Panayota Gounari, Kia Karavas, and Christina Lykou for their constructive comments. Finally, I am grateful to my family: my husband, Tassos, our children, Ismene and Angelos, and my mother, Ismene, for their continuous encouragement and support.

Preface

IN WRITING THIS BOOK, I HAVE OFTEN WONDERED WHAT KIND OF AUTHOR identity I bring to this text and how my viewpoint has affected its structure and content. This is a book about a specific type of educational discourse that appears in online environments and about related issues of ideologies, identities, and pedagogies embedded and implied in this educational discourse. At the same time, it is a book about how political discourse about the Iraq War is embedded in classroom practices and about how the subject of war is actually taught in American schools.

In this book, I address my readers from my multiple social identity as a European educator and critical discourse analyst, greatly interested in the effects of political discourse, pedagogy, and new media. In fact, it would be useful for potential readers to know what kinds of world experiences have inspired, influenced, and guided my interpretations in this book. The first is a geographical one. Living in Greece, a country in southeast Europe, far away from the United States, yet greatly affected by political changes in the Middle East, I surely did not experience the events concerning the Iraq War in the same way that American people did, nor did I share the same kinds of feelings, fears, and worries as the American people. Consequently, my understanding and interpretation of the geopolitical situation is necessarily somewhat different.

The second type of experience comes from my own educational background. Having studied in two European countries and experienced the effects of a centralized education system, I was intrigued by the wealth of educational materials available through the Internet after September 11, dealing with current political issues and military conflicts. I was also intrigued by the realization that these diverse types of materials may actually be used in the classroom. For instance, the teaching of current events constitutes part of the curriculum of several school subjects and, as a result, American educators are encouraged to select a current event and discuss it in their classrooms. This contrasts sharply with the situation in several parts of Europe, where national curricula outline very specific themes, topics, and issues to be dealt with in the classroom and do not include a component on the teaching of everyday events. Although some of these national curricula may regularly invite teachers to bring the outside world into their classrooms, and to take into account students' experiences, they do not go as far as incorporating into the official curriculum a section that deals with the teaching of current political events.

Another influence comes from my professional experience as an instructor of English in an American higher education institution for more than twelve years, teaching linguistics and freshman composition courses. In fact, it was this classroom experience that gave me valuable insights into the pedagogies that are extensively used in North American institutions and that are analyzed in this book. Most importantly, my teaching practices were greatly influenced by the embedded methodologies found in freshman composition textbooks, readers, and other types of instructional books that position instructors and students alike as specific kinds of social beings and pedagogic subjects.

Finally, my combined applied linguistics and critical discourse analysis backgrounds have positioned me as a specific social subject and analyst, and they have provided me with the theoretical and methodological tools used in the book. Moreover, my interest in political discourse and its effects on teaching, as well as my interest in exploring the online educational environments and their effects on literacy education, have guided both my selection of the topic of investigation in the first place and the research agenda for this project.

In terms of audience, this book concerns educational researchers, educators, and teachers. It could be useful for third- and fourth-year undergraduate students and students attending graduate courses on social studies, curriculum studies, literacy, applied linguistics, educational linguistics, and discourse analysis in education. The book focuses on how political discourse, with the Iraq War as a case study, is taught in schools and on how political agendas (covert or

overt) are related to different representations of reality and the construal of different social subjects. From this perspective, the book
will be relevant to students and academics who deal with the effects
of political discourse in various educational settings. Because of its
particular interest in the Iraq War, the book may seem to address a
mainly American audience. Although this is certainly the case, it also
includes a number of topics and issues that make it relevant to a non-
American audience as well. For instance, the book discusses issues of
pedagogy, pedagogic identities, and discursive ideologies, which makes
it relevant for a European or a non-Western (e.g., Middle Eastern)
audience, because it could function as a starting point for a critical
and reflective comparison. Most importantly, the extensive discussion
of critical thinking—perhaps the most influential pedagogy in different education systems all over the world—and its juxtaposition to
critical pedagogy in different parts of the book would be of interest to
educators all over the world who employ critical thinking techniques
and practices in their teaching. Finally, its focus on digital environments and online educational materials makes the book relevant to
an audience with an interest in media studies.

Introduction

> Today we're beginning to realize that the new media aren't just mechanical gimmicks for creating worlds of illusion, but new languages with new and unique powers of expression.
>
> *Marshall McLuhan, 1960*

A MAJOR TRANSITION IN COMMUNICATION IS OCCURRING WHOSE EFFECTS will be evaluated by historians, social theorists, and educational theorists in the future. Existing literacy practices have undergone major changes as they have moved online, and other, new literacy practices have emerged as a result of the extensive use of new technologies. Confronted by a new communicative order (Street 2000), we have experienced firsthand some initial effects of this transition as the World Wide Web became a worldwide literacy practice environment. Global media networks have greatly affected our experiences as human beings and as educators. For instance, in all parts of the world we witnessed live from our living rooms the beginning of the Iraq War in 2003, becoming spectators of the "shock and awe" military operations. Then, we got continuous updates about the war from the Internet, and we also searched these global media networks, as well as other parts of the Web, for online resources that would help us teach our students about the war.

Online educational materials abound today, and they can be accessed anywhere in the world by anyone with an Internet connection. Teachers and students alike turn to the Internet to locate educational materials and resources. However, these digital environments are not neutral literacy practice environments, as some people tend to think, but are involved in a complex nexus of power structures and relations that need to be explored (Koutsogiannis and Mitsikopoulou 2004).

In addition, although there is an increasingly important body of research that explores the potential of multimodality in the new media

1

(Kress and van Leeuwen 2001) and its effects on students, there is little research on online teacher resources. The impact of the numerous websites that publish materials for teachers of all levels and specializations (e.g., detailed lesson plans, with accompanying handouts and reading texts, streaming videos, interviews, maps, related links) remains to be investigated. Contributing to research that explores online teacher resources as aspects of this complex new communicative order, in this book we will explore the discursive construction of pedagogies, identities, and (explicit and implicit) ideologies that permeate online educational materials made freely available today through the Internet. The educational materials analyzed throughout the book draw from online teacher resources about the Iraq War, which is here treated as a case study of political discourse taught in schools.

Theoretically, this book draws mainly on two fields of study. The first one is **critical discourse analysis**, which "does not only aim to describe discursive practices, but also to show how discourse is shaped by relations of power, and the constitutive effects discourse has upon social identities, social relations and systems of knowledge and belief, neither of which is normally apparent to discourse participants" (Fairclough 1992, 12). Within the tradition of critical discourse analysis that informs this book, discourse has been viewed from two main perspectives. First, discourse is seen as a form of social practice, an interaction, or what people do to or for each other with language. This view relates discourse to other social practices, because it establishes a relationship between the discursive event and the social practice, and it promotes an understanding of discourse as always social and cultural, thus excluding the view of language as a purely individual activity. Second, discourse is viewed as a representation of social practices, a form of knowledge, and an instrument of the social construction of reality. Both understandings of the term have provided valuable insights into the exploration attempted in this book. Drawing on a notion of language as a social semiotic and a meaning-making system (Halliday 1978), the analysis conducted in this book considers the text as the basic unit of analysis, where meaning is negotiated, and analyzes all texts in relation to their social context.

Adopting a critical discourse analytic perspective, we will explore the discursive construction of the Iraq War in online educational resources along the lines of two well-known pedagogies, critical thinking and critical pedagogy. Each of these discursive constructions includes different discourses and genre realizations that have embedded in them specific representations of the world, pedagogic identities, and underlying political ideologies. Each chapter addresses a different aspect of this discursive construction. The purpose of this book is not to argue in favor of one of the two pedagogies, nor to support through its analysis the claim that one pedagogy is better than the other. Nor does it attempt to persuade readers that what it offers is an objective and detached account of some kind of truth. Quite the opposite.

The purpose of the detailed textual analysis of these educational materials is to reveal their deeper political nature (Gee 1996) and, specifically, to illustrate how the recontextualization of different political and media discourses construes different pedagogic identities for both students and teachers. *Recontextualization*, as defined by Bernstein (1990, 1996), is the ideological process in which a text or a discourse is taken away from its original context—it is decontextualized—and then relocated in another context. Bernstein's (1996, 24) famous quote reminds us that "every time a discourse moves, there is a place for ideology to play." As Dendrinos (1992) points out, the relocation of a text to a new site irrevocably changes its nature. She brings up the example of a newspaper article included in an English textbook and suggests that relocation of this text does not trigger the same expectations in the reader when she encounters it in a textbook, when she reads it as a student, or when she reads a similar text in a newspaper. Similarly, when a news report or an editorial about the Iraq War is de-located from its original context (e.g., a political interview, a media broadcast, a newspaper) and through the process of recontextualization is relocated as an instructional text (i.e., a text to be used in the classroom), it undergoes a change of meaning (because meaning is heavily dependent on context), of the communicative purpose of the text, and of the writer–reader relationship. This also implies, according to Bernstein, that the text becomes part of a theory of instruction. Considering that each different theory of instruction "contains within itself a model of the learner and of the teacher" (1996, 49), a question this book addresses is which theories of instruction are embedded in war-related pedagogies, and which models of learners and teachers these theories imply. Most importantly, the view of educational resources as recontextualized discourse requires a research agenda that investigates online educational resources within their broader context: the pedagogies in which they are embedded and their respective theories of instruction.

The second field of study this book draws from is the field of **applied linguistics**, which is here understood to refer to "those areas of language description and analysis which locate language itself within the social world, and which understand language use as a form of social practice" (Seale and Carter 2004, 1). Such an account implies a view of applied linguistics as a social science, and it helps to explain the interaction between social structures, human agents, and language. It also implies the view that some aspects of language use may be more accurately analyzed and interpreted with reference to social scientific work (Pennycook 2001, 3). In addition, applied linguistics is here considered to be in a constant reciprocal relationship between theory and practice. It is this relationship between theory and practice that this book attempts to reveal through detailed textual analysis.

Of particular interest here in this context of understanding applied linguistics is the view of war as curricular subject matter (like, for instance, the American Civil War or Emily Dickinson's poetry), legitimate knowledge, and pedagogic discourse in the context of specific courses. In the case of a history or literature course, for example, educational discourses[1] draw on the discourse of history or literature, respectively. What happens, though, when a current political events issue, such as an ongoing war, is taught in the context of an English or social studies course? What political and educational discourses are selected and recontextualized to "teach" the war? How are media and other discourses transformed into pedagogic discourse during the recontextualization process, and what is their effect on the construed pedagogic subjects? Assuming after Bernstein (1996, 46) that "pedagogic discourse selects and creates specialized pedagogic subjects through its contexts and contents," in this book we will focus on the analysis of the "contexts and contents" of online educational resources covering a current political event, in order to investigate the discursive construction of the war in online pedagogies and the ways they affect the construal of pedagogic subjects.

Consequently, we will look into how broad political issues, such as the Iraq War, may be materialized in more everyday practices, such as the planning, conduct, and evaluation of classroom teaching. "These are in essence ideological questions," Dendrinos argues, and she continues, "The moment we begin to question what type of knowledge is transmitted in schools, how this knowledge is conveyed, and who the legitimate communicator of this knowledge is, we are unavoidably concerned with ideology" (1992, 77).

Pedagogies, Ideologies, and Identities

We have now brought to the foreground the notions of pedagogy, ideology, and identity, three key notions that are addressed in the various chapters. A basic claim of this book is that, from a pedagogical point of view, these three notions constitute part of a whole and unless we investigate all of them together and in combination, exploring the effects of one over the other, we may not be in a position to get the big picture. All three of them are intricately related to each other, and one cannot be adequately explained and interpreted without reference to the others. Educational practice is a complex entity, in which different (often conflicting) discourses and various genres are intermingled and imbued with varying forms of ideology, pedagogy, and identity.

Implicit in this understanding is the view that pedagogies, identities, and ideologies are largely constructed in discourse through a number of culturally available discourses and genres that make available a number of subject positions[2] that social subjects occupy when they enter discourse. As Hall (1997) argues, discursive identities can be seen as points of temporary attachment to the subject positions that discursive practices construct for us. Once we take up a subject position within a discourse, though (and some of them may entail a long-term occupation, such as the subject position of gender), we come to experience the world and ourselves from the vantage point of that perspective, and we arrive at the position of construing and reproducing our discursive identity.

The textual analysis employed in this book analyzes online educational materials for teachers and students to explore discursive identities and ideologies embedded in the suggested pedagogies. *Pedagogy,* as understood in this book, is an active process of learning, a political and moral practice, rather than merely a technique or a set of methods. This understanding of pedagogy draws on Giroux (2006, 69), who argues that pedagogy constitutes both a political and a moral practice. As a political practice, pedagogy foregrounds the relationships among power, ideology, and knowledge, because it influences how and what knowledge and identities are produced within specific sets of social relations. According to this view, classroom teaching should not only be about deconstructing texts and analyzing student experiences, but it should also connect student experiences to specific problems that emanate from the material contexts of their everyday life. Embedded in the notion of pedagogy as a moral practice is the acknowledgment that teachers, as public intellectuals, cannot be separated from the effects of the knowledge they produce, the social relations they legitimate, and the ideologies and identities they offer to students. Consequently, any type of analysis should take these elements into account.

Analyzing Political Discourse

The discourse of war, as this is realized in the analyzed online educational resources, constitutes a particular type of political discourse, and it is, therefore, important that any discussion concerning its different realizations be placed within the broader context of the discourse of politics. The term *political discourse* usually brings into our minds the language used by professional politicians (such as presidents, prime ministers, and other members of a government) and political institutions (such as parliaments and political parties). Studies of political discourse have mainly focused on political speeches (e.g., Chilton 2004; Dedaić 2006; Kyrala 2010; Reisigl 2008), parliamentary discourse (Bayley 2004; Illie 2006; van Dijk 2002; Wodak and van Dijk 2000), rhetorical features and persuasive strategies (Duranti 2006; Fairclough 2000; Musolff 2004), and political marketing and branding techniques (Mitsikopoulou 2008a; Newman 2001; van Ham 2001), among others. More recently, research has expanded to cover other forms of political discourse, including everyday politics (Rollins and O'Connor 2003; Wodak 2009).

However, politicians are not the only participants in the domain of politics, because political activity also involves people as citizens, voters, members of political parties, demonstrators, supporters and dissidents, and members of pressure or issue groups (Verba et al. 1993), who may be actively involved in political discourse. Similarly, discursive political processes include not only official administration (such as governing, legislation, and bureaucracy), but also "the wider field of politics, including propaganda, campaigning, canvassing, media interviews and influencing or being influenced by citizens or 'public opinion'" (van Dijk 1997, 13).

In an attempt to determine which discourse is political and which is not, van Dijk (1997) suggests that analysis should not only be limited to the structural properties of texts, but should also include a systematic account of the whole context in which discourse appears (i.e., communicative events and encounters with their own settings, such as time, place, and circumstances), because, he argues, it is eventually the context that characterizes a discourse as political or not. Locating politics in the public sphere, he turns to define political discourse in broad terms, including official and unofficial political actors, events, encounters, settings, actions, and discourses, as well as, more abstractly, political processes, systems, ideologies, and relations. This contextual definition of political discourse entails that the aims, goals, or functions of these special events or textual practices are "maybe not exclusively but at least primarily political" (1997, 15), having, for instance, political functions or implications.

Taking into account the main theme of this book and elaborating on the previous contextual definition, we would say that political discourse is a matter not only of what we find in the news but also, perhaps more significantly, the ways in which we organize the socialization of children through the massive sociocultural institutions of our society. The book explores a new area—that of the pedagogic instrumentation of online programs for reasons of political information in the context of a war. However, although the focus is on the discourse of war, it is important that we do not miss the bigger picture: How are politics taught in schools? How are different ideological positions treated in educational discourse? To what extent, and in what ways, are current political events included in everyday teaching? Two points of interest should be noted here, concerning the teaching of politics and political discourse in US schools, which will be further discussed in the next section. The first refers to the teaching of democracy, which has a long tradition in US education programs and which is realized through the social studies and civics curricula for elementary and secondary education. The teaching of the Iraq War falls within the aim of this curriculum, which is to inform young Americans about political issues. The second refers to another strong tradition in US education, which concerns the teaching of current events. Both will be further discussed in what follows.

The Teaching of Politics and Current Political Events

Politics and civics are parts of the social studies curriculum in US elementary and secondary education programs. Related research has indicated some common ground in the material that students in US schools cover in these classes (Avery and Simmons 2000/2001; Hahn 1998). In elementary school, where students' political socialization starts, students usually learn patriotic songs, celebrate national holidays, study the need to obey laws, and learn how to be good patriots. According to Journell et al. (2012, 9), the role of the teacher at elementary school should not only be to develop knowledge about civic processes but also to create "emotionally and relationally healthy learning communities—intellectual environments that produce not mere technical competence, but caring, secure, actively literate human beings." Later in middle school, students are introduced to American history and basic principles of the Constitution, and in high school, they take courses on government, which, for Kahne, Chi, and Middaugh (2006), are the part of the formal curriculum that is most explicitly linked to the teaching of democracy in schools. In government courses, students learn how the government functions, the importance of civic participation and voting, and the skills to function as members of a market economy (Patrick 2006).

It seems, however, that most schools consider history as the main course offered in their social studies program, and they only offer a government course as an elective (Niemi and Smith 2001). According to Westheimer (2004, 231), several educators and policy makers consider the main role of civics education to be conveyance of knowledge about important historical facts and a sense of national pride and civic unity. A characteristic example is 9/11. In 2002, a year after the terrorist attack at the World Trade Center, President Bush announced a number of initiatives concerning history and civics education that would aim at enriching students' knowledge of American history and at strengthening their patriotic feelings. Westheimer suggests that these initiatives were applauded by those educators who were uncomfortable about encouraging discussion of current political events in their classrooms and preferred to focus on patriotism through history and civics classes.

Journell (2010) argues that an important component of government and civics courses in secondary education is the teaching of current events. Unlike several European and other countries, in which teaching current events is not a common practice, the United States has a long tradition of teaching such courses in elementary, middle, and high schools. Reference to current events is found in the curricula of several different school subjects. Actually, the editors of the portals that have published online instructional materials on the Iraq War have placed them within the context of teaching current events in the classroom.

However, although there is a general agreement about the usefulness of teaching current events in the classroom, there is disagreement as to its extent and outcomes. In 1955, Hunt and Metcalf suggested that current events, defined as the study of news events presented by the media, bring fresh content into the curriculum and help students to "examine reflectively issues in the closed areas of American culture" (Hunt and Metcalf 1955, 223). They talked about "a current events movement," which promotes democratic values through the use of quality newspaper articles and detailed analysis of controversial issues. However, they warned that there is always a danger of trivializing, or focusing on reporting the events, if the analysis of articles does not focus on critical thinking and interpretation of current events.

Similarly, Clarke and Zelinski (1992) suggest that by their nature, current events are likely to be relevant, meaningful, and of interest to students and hence they may contribute to the development of abilities and dispositions toward critical thinking. More recent publications relate the teaching of current events to the development of twenty-first-century skills, such as lifelong learning, civic literacy, and global awareness (Biser 2008; Pescatore 2007). Specifically, research has revealed that current events instruction is related to five key goals: to engage students in active learning, to draw them into a deeper understanding of the curriculum, to develop critical thinking skills, to learn how to deal with controversial issues, and to teach democratic behavior (Clarke and Zelinski 1992; Haas and Laughlin 2000; Pescatore 2007; Sperry 2006).

Although the teaching of current political events is rarely included in formal government curricula or in textbooks (Journell 2009), government and civics teachers incorporate current events in their instruction on a regular basis, drawing information from newspapers, news magazines, and television programs (Hahn 1998; Niemi and Junn 1998). Similarly, a study of two classes with tenth grade students, which focused on the teaching of controversial public issues, has revealed that the vast majority of students held positive views about in-class discussions of current events (Hess and Posselt 2002). In addition, Kahne and Middaugh (2008) suggest that monitoring current events and political issues, engaging in classroom discussions, and exploring topics of student interest tend to promote commitments to civic participation among high school students. However, there is not a clear picture about the way political events are covered in the classroom or about the factors that influence the way teachers present political information (Journell 2009, 5). In addition, several teachers report that they have not been trained to deal with political and controversial issues, and, as a result, they often find themselves in uncomfortable situations, having to balance students' values with curricular goals (Oulton et al. 2004).

Other literature concerning the teaching of current political events consists of theoretical discussions on how to teach these topics in the classroom (Eaton 2004; Risinger 2007). Turner (1995) summarizes the main techniques used by teachers in the classroom: (1) Students select reading about a current event as homework and report on it in class (e.g., in the form of a debate); (2) teachers select a single news source, which is discussed and analyzed as a classroom activity (e.g., they read an article in class and then write a response to it in an in-class journal); (3) teachers select current events materials, which students read or listen to, and then they are tested on the materials; (4) students study current events in structured, in-class activities, in groups or individually (e.g., they prepare essays or political cartoons based on newspaper and magazine articles about a current topic, such as the results of a presidential election).

Several suggestions have been made for current events instruction. For instance, Biser (2008, 23) argues that current events can be integrated in an overt way, where the main aim of instruction is for students to understand the specific event being covered, or in a covert way, where the main aim of instruction is another class objective achieved through the use of a current event (in which case, the comprehension of the current event is secondary). Similarly, Haas and Laughlin (2000) report that many teachers use current events as contemporary examples to explain abstract historical, social, economic, and political concepts. However, they note that constraints imposed by standards-based curricula have been found to affect current events instructions in American schools in a negative way. Similarly, Pescatore (2007) describes the No Child Left Behind Act as a stumbling block to the inclusion of current events instruction.

Moreover, whereas in the past, students and teachers relied on print newspapers and TV news shows for information about current events, today, the Internet provides access to breaking news, news reports, and stories. It also provides ways to investigate the background of these events and, quite recently, ways to interact with these articles (e.g., by providing online comments on specific articles). At the same time, specifically designed websites for teachers provide access to educational materials and teacher resources for teaching current events. In order to enhance current events instruction, O'Brien et al. (2006) developed a Web-authoring tool to enable students in a social studies class to follow current events and to explore the deeper issues embedded in those events. This online tool enables students to organize current online newspaper articles on a specific event, such as 9/11, and even to create their own newspaper, which includes summaries of these sources on its front page. Although there is a lot of research on the teaching of current events in the classroom, the extent to which online educational materials on current events affect teaching practices remains to be investigated. The research conducted in this book concerning the discursive construction of the Iraq War in online teacher resources may be seen as a contribution in that direction.

The Iraq War as a Case Study of Political Discourse

Following September 11, several academic publications have explored the language of the "war on terror" and the Iraq War from different perspectives. The focus of these publications has been on the symbolic power of war in political and media discourse (Chouliaraki 2007); the discourse of terror (Jarvis 2009; Brecher, Devenney, and Winter 2010); the discursive construction of identities, the shaping of ideologies, and the formation of collective understandings in response to September 11 (Dedaić and Nelson 2003; Hodges and Nilep 2007); the dominant political narrative of war on terror (Hodges 2011); the rhetoric employed to gain support for military action, to justify the Iraq War, and to normalize the abuse of Iraqi prisoners (Jackson 2005); and the analysis of key terms, such as *freedom, justice,* and *terrorism* (Collins and Glover 2002). Fairclough (2006, 141) suggests that the selection of the discourse of the "war on terror" has been motivated by the US government's need to legitimize the shift to "hard power," and he analyzes this discourse around four main themes, each associated with a cluster of discourses, narratives, and arguments. These are (1) the theme of a new era that poses new threats and requires new responses, (2) the theme of unprecedented risks and dangers that Americans face that call for exceptional measures, (3) the theme of the "forces of evil" for the enemies, and (4) the theme of the "forces of good" for Americans and their allies (2006, 144).

Similarly, pedagogic research has also investigated the complex issues related to the "war against terrorism," exploring, for instance, effects on educational practices (Apple 2002) and the role of media in the construal of views and stereotypes (Kincheloe and Steinberg 2004; Steinberg 2007). In addition, other organizations have published instructional materials to help young Americans deal with the complex issues related to the war against terrorism and the Iraq War. Media and educational online portals, such as *National Geographic,* the *New York Times,* Scholastic, and National Council of Teachers of English, made collections of materials available in their teacher resource sections, with the purpose of integrating breaking news into lessons, preparing "lessons on war," and exploring the impact the war had on students. These resources included news and special reports, feature articles, editorials, interviews, and other media texts; maps; video clips; and Internet sources, accompanied by detailed lesson plans that provided information on how to use the resources in the classroom.

American educators have voiced different views as to whether schools should discuss with students the country's involvement in the war. An article entitled "Lesson Plans for Sept. 11 Offer a Study in Discord," which was published in the *New York Times* on August 31, 2002, by Kate Zernike, discusses the controversy over the use of lesson plans on September 11 and on the war against terrorism. The article presents arguments from both sides. Arguments raised by conservatives suggest that these lesson plans spend too much time talking about feelings and not enough time teaching history and civics, that the lessons are too focused on teaching tolerance, and they consequently misdirect attention, and that educators end up being unpatriotic in their attempt to help students understand the ideology behind the attacks. Conservatives seem to support the idea that classroom discussion about the war and terrorism takes schools too far from their traditional business, and they suggest that schools focus on subjects like mathematics and English instead. They are also reported to have written curricula in order to counter "the dangerous idea of moral equivalence" and "the usual pap about diversity." On the other hand, teachers' unions and other groups that have produced curricula on tolerance argue that children are suffering emotionally from the attacks and they need help in identifying and dealing with these emotions. They claim that their curricula on tolerance was a response to requests from parents and teachers, and they support the view that school is for some children the only place where they can find a listening ear. A director of the Health Information Network for the union that prepared lesson plans is said to have commented that the criticism of the lessons on tolerance is thinly veiled bigotry and has to do with the difficulty some people have in dealing with diversity and the "other."

Online Educational Resources

The websites for teachers have become quite sophisticated over the last few years. What started more than ten years ago as single webpages, with poor Web design, including lists of hyperlinks with sources for teachers and very straightforward navigation, has turned into portals, with sophisticated Web design that lead to other pages and sub-pages, each with a complex site map. Online resources for teacher websites in their early days included free lesson plans, downloadable worksheets, teaching tips, and rubrics. The content has been enriched today to include different types of activities for the classroom (e.g., games, projects, simulations and animations, and quizzes and tests); free tools (e.g., lesson plan and activity generators, preformatted rubrics, calendars, and planners of different kinds); and a teacher development section with short tutorials and e-workshops (that can be accessed at no cost or for a fee), teacher articles, reviewed educational websites, online newsletters, teacher forums, and online teacher communities. A number of other services are also offered free for busy teachers who need help, according to the rhetoric used in most of them.

However, the main part of these educational websites is the section with fully developed lesson plans "ready to be used in the classroom." In just one website (www.teach-nology.com), for instance, a visitor can find more than 46,000 lesson plans and 10,200 free printable worksheets that are usually organized by subject area, topic, age group, or level. The same site used to offer a tutorial with specific instructions to teachers concerning how to prepare a complete Web-based lesson plan to be published on the website after being reviewed by website editors. This book draws its materials from two online portals with a wealth of teacher resources: *NewsHour Extra* and *Rethinking Schools,* which are briefly introduced below.

NewsHour Extra

NewsHour Extra (www.pbs.org/newshour/extra; Figure I.1) is an electronic magazine hosted by the PBS portal (www.pbs.org), a private, nonprofit media enterprise, owned and operated by US public television stations. As its mission statement says, "PBS uses the power of non-commercial television, the Internet and other media to enrich the lives of all Americans through quality programs and education services that inform, inspire, and delight." By combining online and television media, pbs.org creates and distributes interactive programming for educational purposes. It hosts supersites for children, parents, and teachers, offering information on subjects such as history, arts, science, and technology, and it includes several online sites with classroom resources, lesson plans, and activities. *NewsHour Extra* is an interactive portal that, according to its mission statement, aims to bring current events and issues into the classroom and to improve students' thinking and analytical skills.

The homepage of the Teacher Resources section, recently renamed Teacher Center, says, "*NewsHour Extra* provides unique current events resources for busy teachers: news stories for a tenth grade reading level, pictures, maps, videos, in-depth lesson plans, stories written by students and more!" In its attempt to "help students understand world events and

Figure I.1 Extract from homepage of *NewsHour Extra* website on the Iraq War.

national issues," it includes news articles especially written for students, with the background and context needed to understand complex topics, as well as free lesson plans and other teacher resources. Individual stories are accompanied by classroom activities and student worksheets, which at the same time might also be included in a lesson plan with other activities for students.

Its lesson plans address current events that are relevant to a variety of high school courses: social studies, civics, journalism, communications, government, US history, language arts, English, geography, economics, religious studies, art, and law.

Articles and reports used for reading texts are primarily drawn from *Online NewsHour,* the online version of a sixty-minute evening television news program hosted by award-winning journalist Jim Lehrer. More recent additions to the program include a daily video with warm-up and discussion questions, a speak-out section for young people to discuss issues important to them by publishing essays, and original audio and video recordings.

Over the years, *NewsHour Extra* has developed a sophisticated database, with a collection of lesson plans, news for students, and student voices sections. Its archive of educational resources includes the following categories and subcategories:

- **World:** Lesson plans here are categorized mainly geographically (*Asia-Pacific, Africa, Europe, Latin America, Middle East, North America,* and *United Nations*).
- **US:** Categories in this section include *government/politics, history, economics, law/Supreme Court,* and *society and culture.*
- **Science:** This section includes categories on *body and brain, Earth/ environment, space,* and *technology.*
- **Economics**
- **Arts and Media**

The **Science** section includes, for instance, lesson plans on vaccines and how they are produced, the H1N1 virus, mental health, the debate over intelligent design, human cloning, alternative energy resources, solutions to clean up the Gulf oil spill, climate change, nanotechnology, and hybrid automobiles. Lesson plans on social media and nonviolent protest, censorship, political cartoons, and political commercials and their role in leading or misleading voters are found in the **Arts and Media** section. Several lesson plans are also listed under more than one category. For instance, a lesson plan on exploring alternative energy resources is found under both the *Earth/environment* and *technology* sections.

Because the portal deals with current events, a great number of its educational resources deal specifically with current political events. Among the various lesson plans that deal with political themes, for instance, are lesson plans on "Afghanistan: People, Places, and Politics," "Archaeological Sites in Peril," "Controlling Nuclear Weapons: Debating the Non-Proliferation Treaty," "Middle East and North Africa Geography," and "How Should the United States Respond to the Demonstrations in the Middle East?" The political nature of the current events is evident in resources found in other categories as well. For example, in a lesson plan entitled "Social Media and Non-Violent Protest," students examine the impact of social media on the 2011 revolution in Egypt.

In addition to lesson plans, visitors to the portal may join the current events teaching community in order to receive email alerts about the portal's new features. The Student Section has also expanded a lot over the last few years. Students take on a more active role, and they are invited to send their essays, personal stories, or poems for online publication.

Rethinking Schools

Rethinking Schools (www.rethinkingschools.org; Figure I.2) is an activist nonprofit, independent publisher of educational materials that advocates reform of US elementary and secondary schools and that views public

Figure I.2 Extract from homepage of *Rethinking Schools* website on the Iraq War.

education as central to "the creation of a humane, caring, multi-racial democracy." The overall aim of its published materials is stated to be the preparation of students for democratic participation and for active citizenship. As a strong supporter of public education, *Rethinking Schools* deals with issues such as critical classroom practice, educational reform, and race and equity in education. It is directed by volunteer editors and editorial associates and has subscribers in the United States, Canada, and other countries. Its online portal includes information about its publications, an online newsletter, an online journal, and educational materials for teachers such as lesson plans and teaching ideas; readings and handouts for students; and various articles for teachers, parents, and students. For Apple (2000b, 245), *Rethinking Schools* has provided a structured space, "an important forum for social and educational criticism and for descriptions of critical educational practices in schools and communities," where critical academics, teachers, and community activists "teach each other" and provide supportive criticism of each other's work.

The online journal is a quarterly publication that holds a prominent position in the portal and includes innovative teaching ideas, teaching resources, and analyses of important educational issues. It includes articles on classroom teaching, curriculum, and other in-school matters, as well as articles on organizing, activism, and policy. In the Writers' Guidelines section, the editors state that they are interested in *how-to* articles on social and ecological topics, with a strong social justice perspective that will be helpful and inspiring for teachers and other education activists. These articles should also include the voices of students, teachers, and parents, and they should acknowledge difficulties and shortcomings. *Rethinking Schools* publications include topical collections and special issues on critical education issues, such as bilingual education, teaching for environmental justice, improving teacher quality, teacher unions, beyond NCLB, war and terrorism, minority students and language rights, climate crisis, marketing American girlhood, stereotypes, and school reform.

Being an educational publisher, *Rethinking Schools* most often presents its teacher resources in resource packs. For instance, *Rethinking Mathematics: Teaching Social Justice by the Numbers* (edited by Eric Gutstein and Bob Peterson) is a collection of thirty articles that, according to its blurb, places emphasis on "real-world math" and "shows teachers how to weave social justice principles throughout the math curriculum, and how to integrate social-justice math into other curricular areas as well." The publication includes lesson plans, teaching ideas, and reflections by classroom teachers on a variety of topics. One of the lesson plans, for instance, is entitled "The War in Iraq: How Much Does It Cost?" and it deals with the mathematics of the war.

In another publication, with a resource entitled *The Line Between Us: Teaching About the Border and Mexican Immigration* (by Bill Bigelow), educational materials include lesson plans, descriptions of role-plays, stories, poetry, simulations, and video that deal with the history of US-Mexican relations and the roots of Mexican immigration, in the context of the global economy. As stated in the introduction of the publication, the purpose of the collection is to teach students how to care about the rest of the world through resource materials that trace "many lines between us. The most obvious are the multiple walls between the United States and Mexico."

Rethinking Schools considers its main purpose to be to build a social justice education movement. Its engagement with politics and political discourse is, therefore, at least twofold: On the one hand, it selects topics related to politics (teacher resources on the Middle East, Islam, 9/11, the Iraq War, and Palestine, among others), and on the other hand, in line with the critical pedagogy it employs, it has a political perspective on all educational matters, whether these include, for instance, multilingual education or school nutrition programs that provide food to schoolchildren. For several years, the archives of online publications and the teacher resources were freely available through their portal as a way to "spread the word." Recently, however, the portal owners have moved to a subscription policy. As they informed their email list members, they were led to this decision in order to ensure their continuation as an independent education-activist journal. A small number of resources are still available for free, but complete access to all of their materials is now given only to subscribers.

The Corpus of Educational Resources on the Iraq War

The online educational resources on the Iraq War that are analyzed in this book come from the two online portals just discussed—*NewsHour Extra* and *Rethinking Schools*—which were selected on the basis of three criteria: First, they both adopted the view that the issue of the war should be explicitly dealt with in the classroom. Second, both of their websites provided a rich collection of resources for teachers, including lesson plans and supporting material such as further websites for exploration, printed articles, maps, and suggestions for additional activities. Third, the two portals adopted different perspectives on the Iraq War: Whereas the suggested lessons in *NewsHour Extra* were supportive of the US government's decision to go to war (at least in the early days of the war), *Rethinking Schools'* lessons openly adopted an antiwar position.

The corpus of online educational materials was collected in three stages. In May 2003, the main body of the data was retrieved from the two portals, whose analysis is reported in a published article (Mitsikopoulou and Koutsogiannis 2005). A year later, shortly after the media revealed the torture at Guantanamo Bay, online resources that focused on the theme of pain and suffering were collected from the two portals. Analysis of this corpus is reported in Mitsikopoulou (2008b). Lesson plans on the Iraq War and the war against terrorism, which were published later in the portals, were added to the corpus during the third stage of data collection in spring 2010. Overall, the *NewsHour Extra* corpus comprises thirty-one lesson plans, and the *Rethinking Schools* corpus comprises fourteen lesson plans and twenty-two readings and teaching ideas (see Appendix I). In addition to the lesson plans, the data include their accompanying materials, such as instructional texts of different types (written, oral, multimodal), student and teacher handouts, links to background readings, various resources for teachers, and other supplementary material to be used in the classroom.

It should be stressed at this point that my interest in these websites is not limited to the different positions they hold about the war. In fact, these two websites may be seen as characteristic examples of two important educational discourses: the dominant and the alternative, critical discourse. Therefore, I also wanted to explore the features of the two pedagogic discourses, the particular features of the pedagogies within which they are materialized, and the extent to which the different positions on the war are related to the construction of different "imagination"/pedagogic subjects (Bernstein 1996, 47).

The materials in the two portals are compared throughout the book. The overall aim, as previously mentioned, is to explore the discursive construction of the war in the two portals. As my colleague Dimitris Koutsogiannis and I have claimed (Mitsikopoulou and Koutsogiannis 2005), both websites have their own agendas and are, thus, inevitably one-sided. It is not, therefore, surprising that the one that adopts the official pedagogic discourse also takes up the official political position, which was then in favor of war, whereas the other, the activist website, aims to turn both teachers and students into activists who take action against the war. A particular interest in this book is to reveal how this ideological positioning is intricately woven into the suggested pedagogies and the construed pedagogic identities.

Online Educational Resources as Informal Curricula

Online teacher resources are generally thematically organized in separate webpages. In the case of these two portals, the educational materials are grouped in distinct websites (see Figures I.1 and I.2), thus occupying their own distinct "discursive space" in their respective portals. The various types of resources in *NewsHour Extra* and *Rethinking Schools* are placed in clearly defined categories from which teachers may draw their educational materials. It is my view throughout the book that, far from being ideologically neutral, the uploaded educational materials in online portals weave together resources that provide a coherent view of a domain, theme, or topic, in this case, the Iraq War, and can thus be seen as constituting a kind of informal curriculum. The treatment of online educational materials as a coherent whole enables the exploration of its pedagogic and ideological implications. Consequently, we will proceed to talk about the *NewsHour Extra* and *Rethinking Schools* informal curricula and engage in an analysis to reveal their embedded pedagogies and teaching approaches, ideologies, and pedagogical identities.

At this point it might be useful to distinguish between overt and informal curriculum and to explain my understanding of the informal curriculum. On the one hand, an overt curriculum has been variously defined as a program of studies, a set of subjects, a set of materials, a sequence of courses, or a course of study (Oliva 1997, 4). It is the curriculum that is taught at schools. On the other hand, an informal curriculum has been broadly defined as the massive, ongoing curriculum of family, peers, media, and other socializing forces that educate people throughout their lives (Cortes 1981, 24). The informal curricula of *NewsHour Extra* and *Rethinking Schools* seem to have some unique characteristics that differentiate them from other types of informal curricula: First, although they do not constitute part of the official agenda to be taught at schools, they are in fact intended for classroom use. Second, they are regularly updated with the latest information on the specific topic and new materials when the circumstances create them. The affordances of the Internet medium facilitate the process of adding new content and updating the materials of these two informal curricula.

In addition, agreeing with Stanley (1992) and Giroux (1988), I understand a curriculum, in this case an informal curriculum, as representing a narrative or a story that is always multilayered and situated within relations of power, and whose interests must be uncovered and critically interrogated. Because of this, I will approach the informal curricula of *NewsHour Extra* and *Rethinking Schools* as representing not timeless knowledge and truth but rather particular ways of understanding the world. Finally, as is the case with other types of curricula, the informal curricula of *NewsHour Extra* and *Rethinking Schools* have implied in them ideologically specific knowledge, skills, meanings, and values (Kress 1996). What is included or excluded in each curriculum is, as we shall see, determined to a certain extent by their adopted pedagogical approaches, and, most importantly in this case, by their assumed positions on the Iraq War.

Overview of the Chapters

Although a curriculum concerns different groups and agents (from administrators and policy makers to teachers and parents), it primarily affects two categories of pedagogic subjects—students and teachers—who are the ones who experience the curriculum. Aiming to reveal the effects of the informal curricula on these pedagogic subjects, the book comprises two main parts. The first part explores instructional materials addressing students. It consists of three chapters that present the adopted pedagogy in each of the two informal curricula, the suggested language activities, and the representations of war in the texts students are asked to read in the suggested lessons. The second part of the book shifts the emphasis and explores materials addressing teachers. A genre analysis of the texts and lesson plans teachers are invited to read is quite revealing of their suggested pedagogic identities. Then focus turns to the ideology of the medium and an exploration of hypertextuality in the two portals.

The Ideology of the Employed Pedagogies

Chapters 1 and 2 deal with the discursive construction of the two distinct pedagogies, critical thinking and critical pedagogy, employed by the teacher resources in the two portals on the Iraq War. Chapter 1 starts with a brief account of the main premises permeating the approach of critical thinking and some main points of the criticism it has received before turning to analysis of *NewsHour Extra* teaching materials along the lines of this approach. Chapter 2 starts with an introduction to critical pedagogy, discussing its main features as well as some points of criticism, and then turns to analysis of the pedagogy adopted in *Rethinking Schools* as a materialization of critical pedagogy.

Both critical thinking and critical pedagogy have been very influential in educational theory and practice over at least the last three decades in the United States as well as other parts of the world. However, although they both invoke the term *critical* as a valued educational goal, and they share some common concerns, they have distinct differences owing to their "historical trajectories, conceptual traditions and ethical and political underpinnings" (McLaren 1994, x). Most importantly, they differ as to the meaning of the term *critical*. As Kaplan (1994, 207) argues,

> The adjective "critical" can be related to the noun "critique" or to the noun "criticism." When someone provides a criticism of my work she or he is giving me information about what is wrong with it, perhaps with the aim of helping me to improve it. When someone provides a critique of my work she or he is giving me information on dimensions of meaning in the work of which previously I might not have been aware. She or he gleans this information by reading with a theory of how meaning is encoded in texts. The critical thinking movement teaches students criticism of arguments, while the critical pedagogy movement teaches students to provide critique as a foundation for criticism of the world around them.

The first two chapters deal with these different understandings of criticality, which educators often misconceive and consider synonymous. Their purpose is to outline the main premises of the two pedagogies, to clarify their different ideological and epistemological bases, and to explore their discursive construction in the two informal curricula about the Iraq War.

The Ideology of the Instructional Texts

Chapter 3 deals with the ideological nature of the instructional texts suggested in the *NewsHour Extra* and *Rethinking Schools* lessons plans. In his analysis of texts used in school textbooks, Apple (2000a, 46) argues that texts participate in constructing ideologies, and, because of this, they can be seen as "messages to and about the future." He maintains that as part of a curriculum, texts "participate in creating what a society has recognized as legitimate and truthful. They help set the canons of truthfulness and, as such, also help recreate a major reference point for what knowledge, culture, belief, and morality really *are*" (2000a, 46). In a similar line of thought, Dendrinos (1992, 152) discusses the ideology of the instructional texts used in English as a foreign language textbooks and suggests that instructional texts "constitute material configurations of discourses which represent the statements of the various social institutions." Through a detailed analysis of instructional texts, Dendrinos shows that selections made concerning the topic and the perspective being discussed in a reading text are ideologically bound, they contribute to the development of different conceptions of social reality, and, ultimately, they determine how the reader as a social and institutional subject will interact with this reality (1992, 170). Most importantly, she argues, instructional texts of any type become pedagogical texts selected to serve purposes of curricular knowledge (1992, 150).

Discussion about the selection process found in Apple's (2000a) and Dendrinos's (1992) work draws on Williams's (1977, 115) notion of "selective tradition," according to which what is selected to be taught (both in terms of content and form) constitutes someone's selection, someone's vision of legitimate knowledge and culture, "an intentionally selective version of a shaping past and a pre-shaped present," which signifies particular constructions of reality and particular ways of organizing the vast universe of possible knowledge.[3] Consequently, the reading texts selected for classroom teaching are revealing of specific ideologies and world representations. With this view as a guiding principle, the analysis conducted in Chapter 3 examines the representations of war found in the assigned readings in the two websites and explores the effects these entail for the construed pedagogic subjects. Therefore, the emphasis in this chapter remains on how students experience the informal curriculum of *NewsHour Extra* and *Rethinking Schools*.

The Ideology of the Materials for Teachers

Following the analysis of the materials addressing students, the next two chapters focus on materials for teachers and explore the ways in which the genre of the lesson plan, the dominant genre for teachers in online educational materials, is realized in the two portals. After Volosinov (1986, 23), viewing genre realizations as not simply moments of the choice, assembly, and reproduction of forms and techniques, but as sites where "differently oriented social interests within one and the same sign community" intersect, contest, and struggle, Chapter 4 approaches the genre of lesson plan as "a nexus for struggles over difference, identity and politics" (Luke 1996, 317). It thus explores the different manifestations of the genre of lesson plans in *NewsHour Extra* and *Rethinking Schools* as articulations of their different ideological positions, which are about the Iraq War as much as they are about wider pedagogical and educational matters.

Chapter 5 explores the ideology of the Internet medium and specifically the new forms of textuality that emerge in Internet-based educational portals, in terms of both informational and design complexity. It starts from the premise that an analysis of digital genres needs to extend beyond analysis of the genre in its print form, in order to take into account the affordances of the Internet medium and the ways the various semiotic modes are brought together in hypertextual and multimodal compositions. Overall, the chapter has two main aims: to identify the particular features of the online genre of lesson plan and to explore the discursive construction of the online genre of lesson plans in the two portals. It employs the notion of *hypermodality* (Lemke 2002) to refer to the meaning-making potential of the interaction between the two defining features of hypermedia texts: their *hypertextuality* and their *multimodality,* that is, the interplay of different modes, which, in the case of websites, goes beyond the conventions of traditional multimodal genres. Chapter 5 also draws on studies of signaling in online environments and hyperlink wording, in order to analyze the types and the function of hyperlinks and their interaction with the main text, specifically their interconnection with content organization and webpage and navigation design. The complementary analysis of the online genre of lesson plan is important in order to fully capture the workings of the genre in its broader online context.

Finally, the last chapter of the book presents an overall account of the construed pedagogic identities for teachers and students and discusses the role of citizenship that is implied in each of the informal curricula.

Part A

Curricular Materials
for Students

Chapter 1

Critical Thinking in
NewsHour Extra

In ANALYZING ONLINE EDUCATIONAL MATERIALS, THE FIRST TASK IS TO discuss the broader context of the pedagogy on which they draw. The educational materials from *NewsHour Extra* draw on a pedagogy of critical thinking, as is often stated in the analyzed lesson plans. Assuming that these educational materials form a kind of informal curriculum, this chapter explores the following questions: How is the pedagogy of critical thinking discursively constructed in these online materials? What is the political and moral agenda of the critical thinking pedagogy that is employed in *NewsHour Extra*? How is the war being taught through these materials? Aiming to position analysis within its broader context, the first part of the chapter begins by analyzing various features of critical thinking and continues with some basic points of criticism that have developed in related literature. The second part of the chapter analyzes the particular ways the critical thinking approach develops in *NewsHour Extra*, and it places particular emphasis on the suggested language activities described in the lesson plans about the Iraq War.

Defining Critical Thinking

Critical thinking has its origins in the positivist tradition of the applied sciences and refers to teaching students how to analyze reading and writing assignments from the perspective of formal logic. Harris and Hodges (1981, 74) define critical thinking as the process of making judgments in reading by "evaluating relevancy and adequacy of what is read." Halpern (2002, 6) claims that critical thinking is more than making judgments and solving problems; she defines it as:

> the use of those cognitive skills or strategies that increase the probability of a desirable outcome. It is used to describe thinking that is purposeful, reasoned, and goal directed—the kind of thinking involved in solving problems, formulating inferences, calculating likelihoods, and making decisions, when the thinker is using skills that are thoughtful and effective for the particular context and type of thinking task.

She argues that the *critical* part of critical thinking denotes an evaluation component that may imply something negative or an evaluation of the thinking process. Critical thinking is often considered synonymous with logical thinking, because, according to its proponents, it is concerned with reason, intellectual honesty, and open-mindedness, as opposed to emotionalism, intellectual laziness, and closed-mindedness (Kurland 1995). It is viewed as careful argumentation, having its roots in classical rhetoric (Billig 1987; Kuhn 1991, 1999), and it involves, among other things, analysis of arguments and evaluation of evidence, identification of author's intent, distinction between facts and opinions, separation of relevant from irrelevant propositions, and identification of faulty reasoning not founded in sound logic and solid evidence (Ellis 1997). For Cottrell (2005, 1), critical thinking is "a cognitive activity, associated with using the mind. Learning to think in critically analytical and evaluative ways means using mental processes such as attention, categorization, selection, and judgment."

The idea of critical thinking as an educational goal dates back several centuries, but it has regained prominence in recent educational discourse (Carr 1988). In the 1980s, some expressed concern that public education in the United States did not prepare students adequately to learn, work, and function effectively in the changing society. Subsequently, a skills-based approach to critical thinking that put emphasis on "the correct assessment of statements" (Ennis 1962, 83) and on "the practice of teaching critical thinking in a stand-alone program, focusing on teaching and learning of content- and context-free micro reasoning skills aligned with discreet and abstract rules of inference in the disciplines of formal and informal logic" (Fung 2005, 13) was developed.

Since then, courses on critical thinking have been offered to students at the college/university level (Browne and Freeman 2000; Garrison 1991; Gokhale 1995) in a variety of disciplines from philosophy (Annis and Annis 1979; Twardy 2004), psychology (King 1995), and economics (Epstein and Kernberger 2004) to engineering (Siller 2001), medicine (Maudsley and Striven 2000), and management (Gold, Holman, and Thorpe 2002) for both undergraduate (Phillips and Bond 2004) and graduate levels (Kaasboll 1998). In fact, Barnett (1997, 2) considers critical thinking "a defining concept of the Western university," whereas Moon (2008, 7) comments: "A simple search on Google shows that critical thinking has a central role in education and this is evident in mission statement information for higher education, professional bodies and programmes."

Curricula have been redesigned around the critical thinking pedagogy for all levels of education, including elementary and high school. Textbooks and manuals (Allen 2004; Bowell and Kemp 2002; Browne and Keeley 2007; Cottrell 2005; Epstein 2006; Fisher 2001) on critical thinking have been published, and standardized tests have been developed that use content- and context-free multiple-choice questions to assess critical thinking skills (e.g., Ennis 2006; Paul and Elder 2007; Yeh 2001). Critical thinking tests have been included in official, often nationwide, schemes of assessment (Mejía 2009). Some of the best-known tests are the *California Critical Thinking Test,* the *Cornell Critical Thinking Tests,* and the *Watson-Glaser Test* (Watson and Glaser 1980).

A typical skills-based course on critical thinking rests on the assumption that argumentation is a central aspect of critical thinking (Kuhn 1999) and that it teaches students two main skills: (1) to identify and (2) to evaluate arguments. First, students practice reading paragraph-length texts in order to identify their main arguments. After a few weeks, they apply "argument analysis" to longer texts. For instance, they are asked to read a passage[1] and identify the main idea of an article, the main argument supporting the main idea, and its conclusions. Then teachers move to the development of a second skill, the evaluation of arguments used in support of claims. Different kinds of argumentative activities are used in the development of critical thinking skills. These include analysis and synthesis of arguments, inferences, interpretation, evaluation, and reasoning (Yeh 2001, 13). Often, students are also given drilling exercises that ask them to focus on analyzing decontextualized statements of different types, as in the following example, which aims to help students distinguish statements that are claims from those that are not (Allen 2004, 13).

Exercise:
Decide which of these statements are claims and which are not. Then write three examples of your own of statements that are claims and three examples of statements that are not.
   a. Why did you do that?
   b. There is a yellow marble on the table.
   c. Get out of here!
   d. Somewhere over the rainbow ...
   e. We should always pay our taxes on time.
   f. Cheese is made from milk.

Similarly, students get practice at good reasoning. A typical activity here gives students a list of logical fallacies, defined as errors in reasoning, and asks them to check the arguments in a reading text and identify the ones with faulty reasoning. As one college textbook states: "A logical argument is based on good reasoning. Your reasoning will be sound if you have enough evidence to support your claim, if you answer opposing claims, and if you avoid the common fallacies that make an argument invalid" (Kanar 1998, 356). Students are also told that critical thinking skills are important in communication, because they enable people to engage in forms of communication that involve arguing, explaining, making decisions, predicting the future, exploring issues, finding answers, and justifying actions (Allen 2004, 5). Textbooks on critical thinking stress its wider significance, which extends beyond the education and professional contexts into various aspects of social life (Moon 2008). For instance, critical thinking is considered to be at the heart of a democratic society, because it enables people to make their own decisions when they vote.

The notion of skills has in fact been a focal point in accounts of critical thinking.[2] At some point, though, it became clear that a skills-alone approach is not adequate, if students are not inclined to use what they have learned. Halpern (2002, 37) argues that "developing a critical thinking attitude and disposition is at least as important as developing the skills of critical thinking. The skills are useless if they are not used. The attitude of a critical thinker must be cultivated and valued." Consequently, in addition to skills for logical analysis, the critical thinker should also develop the disposition to see the world from a critical perspective (Facione 1998, 2000).[3] As Norris (1985, 40) claims, "Students need more than the ability to be better observers; they must know how to apply everything they already know, and feel, to evaluate their own thinking, and especially, to change their behavior as a result of thinking critically." For instance, some of the dispositions include "seeking reasons, trying to be well-informed, taking into account the total situation, open-mindedness, and seeking precision" (Norris and Ennis 1989, 14).

According to the skills-plus-disposition approach to critical thinking, students are expected to use critical thinking skills spontaneously in their everyday life in the same way they practice them in the classroom. For Browne and Keeley (2007, 3), "critical thinking consists of an awareness of a set of interrelated critical questions, plus the ability and willingness to ask and answer them at appropriate times." Paul (1990) conceives of critical thinking in terms of the ability and disposition to critically evaluate beliefs, their underlying assumptions, and the worldviews in which they are embedded. In his account of critical thinking, Paul distinguishes between critical thinking in the "weak sense," which refers to the mastery of the skills that a critical thinker can demonstrate when asked to do so, and critical thinking in the "strong sense," which refers to the disposition of a critical thinker and the incorporation of the developed skills into a way of life.[4] Textbooks on skills and attitudes often stress the benefits of critical thinking. For instance, Allen (2004) suggests that critical thinking helps young people to study, it helps them in their work, and it helps them become active members of their community. Similarly, according to Cottrell (2005, 4) the benefits of critical thinking include:

- improved attention and observation
- more focused reading
- improved ability to identify the key points in a text or other messages rather than becoming distracted by less important material
- improved ability to respond to the appropriate points in a message
- knowledge of how to get your own point across more easily.

As Cottrell claims, these skills of analysis may be employed in a variety of situations. In fact, one of the most contentious issues among theorists is whether critical thinking consists of a generalizable set of skills or is subject-specific. Bringing evidence from a variety of sources that cognitive skills can be learned through instruction, Halpern (2002, 37) suggests that these skills transfer to various settings in real life and that they can be practiced in multiple contexts. Similarly, Ennis (1962, 1987) and Paul (1990), among others, support a view of critical thinking as a set of generalizable skills and dispositions that can be transferred to other areas of knowledge and expertise. They argue that the analytical skills of critical thinking are universal and equally applicable to all knowledge claims, because they are defined by logical rules independent of content, time, and space. Consequently, they can be used in any discourse context as a means of determining logical thinking and justified beliefs. For instance, the same critical thinking skills are applied to freshman composition courses, courses that develop academic study skills (e.g., Ellis 1997), and lessons dealing with analysis of current events and the teaching of the Iraq War, as we shall see in what follows.

McPeck (1981), on the other hand, notes the centrality of subject-area knowledge for critical thinking and argues that, because different fields rely on different epistemologies, using different kinds of reasoning and different types of arguments, what is involved in critical thinking varies from field to field. This view has called for the development of content-specific courses in philosophy, psychology, and many other disciplines, as well as content-specific taxonomies and lists of skills and dispositions.

Moving beyond the skills and the skills-plus-disposition approaches, some theorists have proposed other versions of critical thinking (see, for instance, Bailin et al. 1999; Papastephanou and Angeli 2007; Walters 1994). However, the skills and skills-plus-disposition approaches are still dominant in both traditional and electronic teaching and assessment. Because of the widespread use of new technologies, attempts have also been made to incorporate critical thinking skills in online environments, such as online communities (Buffington 2004), threaded discussions (Greenlaw and DeLoach 2003; Jeong 2003; MacKnight 2000), computer conferences (Bullen 1998; Sloffer, Dueber, and Duffy 1999), teleconferences (Anderson and Garrison 1995), and online bibliographic research (Graham and Metaxas 2003; Oberman 1991; Weiler 2004). In addition, research has also focused on the development of electronic assessment tools for critical thinking skills (e.g., see Garrison, Anderson, and Archer 2001) and on the development of critical thinking through the use of various computer programs, for instance, through the use of databases, spreadsheets, expert systems, hypermedia systems, computer modeling, and visualization tools (Jonassen, Carr, and Yueh 1998).

Critique of Critical Thinking Approaches

Critical thinking in its varying forms has received a lot of criticism. For instance, Atkinson (1997) elaborately refutes the idea that generalized and transferable thinking skills are assumed to be universal and can thus be used beyond their original domains of application. He shows that these thinking skills do not appear to transfer effectively beyond their narrow contexts of instruction.

Martin (1992) criticizes critical thinking for its exclusive and reductive nature, arguing that it is a highly normative and "logistic" model that claims objectivity and rationality. Similarly, Walters (1994) describes critical thinking as "analytic reductionism," whose aim is to teach how to break arguments down to their premises and conclusions and then examine them for their logical inferences. She uses the example of Mr. Spock, the well-known character of the *Star Trek* television series and feature films, who is a member of a humanoid species from the planet Vulcan. All Vulcans, including Mr. Spock, live by reason and logic only, without the interference of emotion, and they are incapable of behaving illogically. Mr. Spock analyzes an argument or a problem into its smallest constituents, by eliminating irrelevant points, checking for informal fallacies, and examining inferential connections between premises and conclusions. He draws conclusions only when there is enough evidence, by closely following the formalistic rules of logical analysis and by refusing to go beyond the limits of logical probability (using famous quotes such as, "Speculate, Captain? Speculation is not logical."). As a result, he is excellent in problem solving and critical analysis, and he represents the epitome of objectivity, which is so much praised by the Western epistemology of the positivist tradition. By equating good thinking to logical thinking, Mr. Spock and other Vulcans leave imagination, insight, and intuition out of their analysis. As a result, their reasoning is always reactive, never innovative.

At this point Walters (1994, 64) uses a powerful metaphor and argues that most conventional instruction in critical thinking leans toward the Vulcanization of students, making them capable of mechanical, Vulcan-like computational analysis of arguments but devoid of any ability to think creatively. This happens, she maintains, because, by equating good thinking with logical analysis, critical thinking concentrates exclusively on the critical examination of already existing arguments and problems. In her discussion of critical thinking at the university level, she suggests that

> mere facility in the logical deconstruction and criticism of propositional arguments, although possessing some pragmatic value in the "real world," is in itself insufficient to prepare students for careers as responsible adults and citizens.... Moreover, the assumption that skill in critical analysis is a necessary condition for effective education is correct but incomplete. The ability to think logically is certainly essential for the comprehension of academic texts as well as initiation into the "rational traditions," but it is not sufficient. The successful student,

in the richest sense of the term, is not one who merely learns how to analyze the ideas of others. He or she also begins to manipulate those ideas creatively, using them as springboards for imaginative leaps from the conventional to the unconventional, the known to the unknown, the orthodox to the heterodox. (68–69)

Along similar lines, Giroux (1994) argues that the limitations of critical thinking lie in what this pedagogy excludes, not what it includes. As he states: "At the core of what we call critical thinking, there are two major assumptions that are missing. First, there is a relationship between theory and facts; second, knowledge cannot be separated from human interests, norms, and values" (201). Concerning the first point, the relationship between facts and values, the argument goes that how information is selected and arranged in order to construct a picture of reality (e.g., in a reading passage or a language task) is not simply a cognitive operation, as suggested by the proponents of critical thinking, but it is actually a process that is intimately connected to our views of the world, assumptions, beliefs, and values. The problem is, according to Burbules and Berk (1999), that both the skills and the skills-plus-disposition approaches place emphasis on the individual, disregarding any considerations of the social context. By focusing exclusively on the logical and evidential strengths of arguments, irrespective of any considerations for its broader context (i.e., sociocultural and historical setting), critical thinking leads to decontextualization of thinking. Moreover, according to Giroux, this relationship between theory and facts raises fundamental questions about the nature of knowledge. In the context of critical thinking, knowledge is seen as *objective* and *decontextualized* and not as an object of inquiry in which facts, issues, and events are presented problematically to students.

Critical Thinking in *NewsHour Extra*: A "Critical Analysis" of War

It is often stated in the *NewsHour Extra* website that the overall aim of the educational materials on the Iraq War is to enable students to analyze some feature stories on current events, in order to help them understand the arguments about the necessity of this war while developing some knowledge concerning aspects of the war. *NewsHour Extra* lesson plans focus primarily on what they call a critical analysis, and their activities are often identified as critical thinking activities that involve students in careful consideration of argumentation.

Overall, the suggested lessons mainly include reading comprehension activities on feature articles (often called stories or reports) published in *PBS Online NewsHour,* the online version of the evening television news program hosted by award-winning journalist Jim Lehrer. The overall aim is to inform young Americans about the Iraq War through an analysis of media texts, such as online articles, reports, and interviews published on their website. The pattern used in the reading comprehension handouts is presented in Box 1.1; it is always the same for all educational materials published in the portal, regardless of the topic that is being discussed. In other words, the same guidelines are followed in the preparation of reading comprehension activities by materials designers on different subjects (e.g., English, journalism, social studies, or history) and on different topics (e.g., the Iraq War, recent scientific discoveries, mental health, or the rescue of trapped miners in Chile). The identified steps (warm-up, main activity, discussion, follow-up, and evaluation) are followed meticulously, ensuring uniform presentation of educational materials and a professional treatment of the feature articles.

Box 1.1 Using *NewsHour Extra* Feature Stories

Overview: *NewsHour Extra* feature stories can help students identify and interpret key issues in current events. This activity anticipates one class period, but the follow-up essay might be assigned as homework, or in another period.

Warm Up: Use initiating questions to introduce the topic and find out how much your students know.

Main Activity: Have students read *NewsHour Extra*'s feature story and answer the questions on the reading comprehension handout.

Discussion: Use discussion questions to encourage students to think about how the issues outlined in the story affect their lives and express and debate different opinions.

Follow-up: Students can write a 500-word editorial on the topic expressing their views and send it to *NewsHour Extra* [extra@newshour.org] for possible publication.

Evaluation: Students are graded on their answers to reading comprehension questions and/or their editorial.

Students are most often involved in exploring a variety of sources that are used as instructional texts. As part of the suggested lesson, students are given good-quality documentation and are invited to read history texts, feature articles, Internet-based sources, and official government documents. For instance, in "The Role of American Embassies," the lesson plan is accompanied by a special report with several sources, including:

- a *NewsHour* article on the opening of the American embassy in Iraq ("U.S. Opens First American Embassy in Baghdad in Over a Decade")
- a Web-based report entitled "African Embassy Bombings: An *Online NewsHour* Special Report," which includes a list of several hyperlinks for related articles
- a two-page article on John Negroponte, the first US ambassador to Iraq since the first Gulf War in 1991
- a website providing information about "the Coalition Provisional Authority"
- a *NewsHour* online article on Saudi Arabian embassies ("U.S. Raises Terror Alert Level; Embassies in Saudi Arabia Close")
- websites of specific embassies worldwide that give information about the services they provide
- two governmental sources ("Diplomacy at Work: A U.S. Embassy" and "State Department: Protocol for the Modern Diplomat")
- a detailed handout and a teacher's version of the handout, with sample answers.

The overall implicit aim of this sophisticated treatment of the subject seems to be to provide students with all those readings from diverse sources to enable them to form personal opinions on the topic.

An important element of the pedagogy employed here is to connect issues concerning the Iraq War to students' prior knowledge and experiences. It is assumed that by drawing connections between current political issues and students' personal experiences, teachers manage to bring complex political issues closer to young Americans' reality, so that they develop a better understanding of the political situation. This is often achieved through the selection of topics and reading questions. For instance, students are asked to read a *NewsHour Extra* feature story entitled "U.S. Forces Capture Eight Iraqis Pictured on 'Most Wanted' Playing Cards" (published on 4/21/03) and to answer the following questions:

Initiating questions:
1. What is the latest information about Iraq? Who is in charge? What is the status of Saddam Hussein's regime?
2. What do you know about playing cards? How are they organized?

Reading comprehension questions:
1. How many Iraqi officials from the "most wanted" list have been captured so far?
2. How are the "most wanted" cards organized?
3. What card is Saddam Hussein? Why?
4. List and explain the ways in which the military has used similar playing cards in the past

Discussion questions:
1. Does this use of cards trivialize the U.S. mission in Iraq? Why or why not?
2. Why might this method be effective in searching for members of the Saddam Hussein regime? Explain.

After the warm-up activity with the initiating questions, which will specify how much students know about the situation in Iraq and about playing cards, students are to read the text and answer the reading comprehension questions. They should report, for example, that eight Iraqis from the most-wanted list are already in American hands (question 1); that the "most-wanted" cards are organized like regular cards, according to importance (the higher the card, the more important the wanted official) (question 2); and that Saddam Hussein is the ace of spades, the highest card in a deck (question 3). Drawing on information about the cards from the feature article, they should also state that this is not a new military technique but one also used in World War II to help soldiers identify enemy tanks, ships, and planes (question 4). In the discussion part, students are to activate their knowledge on playing cards and the information they obtained from the feature article in order to respond to the questions.

In another lesson plan, about the decision made by Eason Jordan, chief news executive at CNN, not to report on the atrocities committed by Saddam Hussein's regime, students are asked to discuss the ethics of this decision by drawing on their school experience as student reporters ("To Report or Not to Report").

Allow students five minutes to brainstorm in their notebooks on the following question: Are there situations in your school that you know about that you would choose not to report on as a student reporter?

You might want to prod their reactions by mentioning some typical (or not so typical) high school newspaper topics: teenage pregnancy in the school, cheating instances, underage drinking, steroid use among athletes, substance abuse, hacking into school records, abuse at home, etc. Do any of these ideas strike students as possibilities for similar decisions such as the one that Eason Jordan made? Why or why not?

As an aid to their comprehension activities, students are often involved in vocabulary activities through handouts especially prepared for vocabulary practice ("Debating Iraq").

In the first exercise, ask students to read the excerpts from the report; excerpts are provided so students may study new vocabulary in context. For each excerpt, students should write synonyms for the underlined vocabulary words or expressions. In the other two exercises, students will match vocabulary words with definitions and write their own sentences. Encourage students to study vocabulary in context; i.e., focus attention on how the vocabulary words are used in the *NewsHour* report.

A Methodology of Balanced Argumentation

A basic element of the critical analysis in *NewsHour Extra* materials is "balanced argumentation," which requires that the same topic be treated from different viewpoints. Based on the premise that sophisticated treatment of an issue involves a consideration of both sides (Billig 1987), critical thinking activities ask students to describe the issue under discussion, give reasons for and against, and draw conclusions related to the main argument. For instance, in one activity, students are given different quotes from a PBS *Frontline* interview with author Said K. Aburish, who worked closely with Saddam Hussein and his government, and are asked to select one and respond to it. Each quote adopts a different perspective. For instance, in the first of the two quotes below, Arabs are presented as people who consider Hussein a hero standing up to the West. In the second one, Hussein is presented as a dictator who lives "by virtue of the Iraqi people's fear" ("A Call to Jihad").

Saddam Hussein is now the only Arab leader who has a following outside his own country.... Saddam Hussein is standing up to the West. He has survived for nine years. He is a hero. He is not winning. But the mere fact that he survives, that he continues, is enough to make him a hero. And (Arab) people like it. They don't live under Saddam Hussein, so they don't suffer from his actions the way the Iraqi people suffer. All they see is the fact that he is standing up to the West, and they like that.

*   *   *

He lives by virtue of the Iraqi people's fear. Once that fear is removed, the Iraqi people will move against him, as they have in the past moved against other dictators successfully, even ones who were very, very closely protected by their followers.

In the process of developing argumentation, students are often asked to identify the advantages and disadvantages of a situation (i.e., in the form of a list). It is expected that by analyzing the positive and negative aspects of an issue, they will approach the issue in an objective and detached way before they come to make an informed decision.

After students have looked at the questions relating to these models, discussing and sharing the pros and cons of the two positions, have them move on to the Iraq discussion. ("Reconstruction of Iraq")

*   *   *

Break the class into groups of three and have each group write a list of pros and cons for each entry. ("Who Should Rule the Interim Government in Iraq?")

*   *   *

Make a list of both the positive and negative aspects of an international organization, such as the U.N., playing a significant role in global conflicts (e.g., Iraq, S. Korea, Kosovo, Somalia). Based on your answers, what conclusions might you draw regarding the involvement of an international governing body in world affairs? ("The Role of the United Nations in Postwar Iraq")

In an activity from another lesson plan ("Iraq's Latest Strategy: Suicide Attacks"), students are given two transcripts from *Online NewsHour*, one that presents the Palestinian perspective ("Making Martyrs") and one that presents the Israeli perspective ("Living in Fear"). They are then asked to explore the articles' argumentation, summarize the perspectives from each side (in outline or essay form), list the political aims and goals for both sides, and analyze them for the rest of the class. We could say that students are prepared to exert criticism, as identified by Kaplan (1994), through an analysis of the "pros and cons" of a situation or an issue.

According to Burbules and Berk (1999, 55), a critical thinking approach does not assume a set agenda of issues that must be addressed, but tends to address issues in an item-by-item fashion. Although the selection of issues themselves is not important (e.g., the issues may or may not be related to one another), the interplay of reasons and arguments concerning the issue is crucial. In *NewsHour Extra* lessons, sometimes it seems that the topic being discussed matters only to the degree that it allows the critical thinker to develop argumentation. The purpose of the following statements, for example, is to provoke reaction on the part of the students, so that good argumentation develops ("Military Women").

> Select one of the following arguments sometimes made to explain why women should not be in combat, or even in the military. Research and analyze the statement. Who makes this argument and what evidence do they offer to support it? Who offers evidence to the contrary? Is it a good argument? Why or why not?
>> Women are not as strong as men. The military should not have to lower its standards.
>> Women may not be able to perform as well as men or survive difficult conditions.
>> Having women in a military force can weaken the group's effectiveness and cohesion.
>> Women have special needs and can get pregnant.

Sometimes it does not even seem to matter what position students develop, as long as they manage to support their point of view with substantial arguments ("Choices in War").

> Assign students to write a position paper stating their opinion on whether coalition forces should have acted earlier to prevent extensive looting and damage to so many Iraqi institutions.... Based on their discussions, their readings of the *NewsHour* article, and other perspectives that they might find during their own research, do they think the coalition forces acted in a timely manner regarding turning their attention to looters or should they have addressed this sooner? Why or why not? Students must defend their positions.

Moreover, the methodology employed within the context of a critical thinking approach invites students to participate in a number of group and pair activities. In the case of group activities, students are often asked to work as a team and then present their conclusion to the rest of the class. In doing so, group members are invited to assume different subject positions and identities and, thus, different perspectives on the discussed issue, for which they have to develop appropriate and relevant argumentation. A number of sophisticated activities are suggested here that take the following forms.

Debates:
Set up a debate between students or have them write op-ed pieces that express their views on the benefits and drawbacks of President Bush's promotion of freedom as stated in his second inaugural address. ("Democracy in the Middle East")

*   *   *

Instructions:
Following the rules of debate, student groups present arguments to convince their classmates to vote for their option. While groups present, other students may take notes for their policy paper assigned after the debate. Instructor acts as mediator. ("Analyzing U.S. Policy in Iraq")

*   *   *

Simulations:
Simulate a press conference in which reporters question military leaders about reports of civilian casualties having been caused by the actions of coalition forces. How should they respond if the reports are true? ("War Expectations")

*   *   *

Role-play activities:
Role Play #1 (U.N. Representative)
Imagine that you are a representative to the U.N. from a country of your choice (e.g., United Kingdom, France, Russia, Turkey, or China). Prepare a short statement expressing your reaction to President Bush's U.N. speech.
Role Play #2 (National Security Council)
Imagine that you are members of President Bush's National Security Council. Write at least four policy recommendations on U.S. national security priorities in the 21st Century. Then, debate the pros and cons of military action in Iraq. ("Debating Iraq")

A common feature of these activities is again the exploration of opposing arguments. However, this methodology, which is widely used in rhetoric classes for the sake of developing sound argumentation, constructs a restricted framework, by placing discussion of complex and rather important issues within a binary logic (e.g., for and against, advantages and disadvantages). In most activities, students are invited to search for the best argument or to identify the opposing positions presented in a text without examining the ideology that lies behind these arguments and without challenging the ideas of the reading text. This restricted framework operating at the level of "either-or" gives students the opportunity to choose the best argument from a limited number of arguments developed in a text. However, it does not enable them to move beyond the reading text, to consider alternative perspectives, and to challenge the necessity of this war in the first place. It merely focuses on unpacking the reasoning of a reading text and discussing the arguments developed in it in the context of what Giroux (2005) has called a "pedagogy of understanding," which aims at making students understand and consequently accept the reality around them. The problem that then arises, according to Kaplan (1994, 205), is that "contrary to the expressed intentions of critical thinking teachers and textbook authors, critical thinking may end [up] encouraging students to accept without question certain political perspectives and discourage students from asking questions about the genesis of these perspectives."

Teaching the War

The homepage of *NewsHour Extra,* which presents educational materials on the Iraq War, includes a list with the suggested lesson plans and has the heading "Teaching the Iraq War," instead of the expected heading "Teaching *about* the Iraq War." Thus, in the heading, the war becomes the goal in a material process (Halliday 1994). Quite interestingly, this is more than just a grammatical construction; in fact, it is a representation of war as a taught subject, like English, history, or geography. By looking at the activities in *NewsHour Extra,* we realize that high school students are actually "taught the war," as if they were students in a military college or in a diplomatic academy. In one activity, they are asked to "devise their own set of rules of war" ("The Rules of Engagement: The Geneva Convention"), and in another, they create an Iraq foreign policy recommendation ("Analyzing U.S. Policy in Iraq"). On several occasions, they are asked to participate in activities in which they take the role of military and political leaders and make important decisions about the war. For instance, they are asked to do the following activities.

Research weapons of mass destruction:
Ask your students what they already know about the weapons of mass

destruction Saddam Hussein is thought to have. Give them the following background as necessary.

mustard gas—blisters/burns exposed tissues, fatal if untreated.

nerve agents (such as sarin and tabun)—can cause convulsions,
unconsciousness, and death if untreated immediately.

Extension Idea: Select a particular weapon of mass destruction
(anthrax, nuclear weapons, nerve agents such as sarin, mustard gas,
etc.). Research its development and/or discovery, its history and usage,
and where it is now believed to exist. ("Weapons of Mass Destruction
in Iraq")

* * *

Create military plans:
Divide students into small groups (call them "battalions" or "divisions"
if you so choose) of three or four. Tell them that they are Field Generals
for the coalition forces and that they must create a plan for assigning
20,000 troops to protect institutions in one city, preferably Baghdad.
("Choices in War")

* * *

Analyze war strategies:
Map activities: In order to determine whether the Doctrine is being
observed, have the students closely examine maps of the region that
highlight the ongoing war strategy, bombing campaigns and troop
deployments. ("The Powell Doctrine")

* * *

Compare military technologies:
Write a report comparing and contrasting the use of military technology in the following conflicts: World War II, the Vietnam War, and the
current war in Iraq. ("War Expectations")

* * *

Select military strategy:
What options do the U.S. forces surrounding Najaf have and what are
the possible results of each?

Cordon off the city—would have to leave troops around the city,
may face attacks from militants inside.

Attempt to take the city—would have to go door-to-door to root out
militants, which is dangerous and could provoke angry responses
from Muslims, especially if holy sites are attacked or damaged.

Ignore the city and continue to move North—the city may contain
many militants and could serve as a base for further attacks by
coalition forces or supply lines.

Break your students into small groups to role-play military leaders
who must decide which of the options they will choose in order to
relay orders to those encircling the city. ("Najaf—A Holy City Caught
in the Crossfire")

✳   ✳   ✳

Decide on a national security strategy:
In your view, what are the strengths and risks of President Bush's preemptive strike policy proposal? Should the U.S. make a preemptive
strike against Iraq if the Iraqi regime refuses to allow U.N. inspectors
in? Why or why not? ("Debating Iraq" Pre-Listening Handout)

✳   ✳   ✳

Make a strategic political decision:
Where does the United States' obligation to the reconstruction of Iraq
end? ("Reconstruction of Iraq")

✳   ✳   ✳

Decide who should be the future leader of Iraq:
Have interested students research the lives of Ahmed Chalabi, Ayatol-
lah Mohammed Bakral-Hakim, Massoud Barzani of the KDP, and Jalal
Talabani of the PUK, and report to the class. Have the class write an
essay on which leader appears to be more qualified to lead. ("Who
Should Rule the Interim Government in Iraq? What Should Be Their
Priorities?")

Overall, regarding the critical thinking approach of *NewsHour Extra,*
the suggested activities treat the topic of the Iraq War in a way similar
to other school topics in terms of the employed methodology of critical
analysis. If we look closely at the content of these activities, however, we
notice that a legitimation issue is at stake. In the context of their everyday
school life, American students at the age of fifteen or sixteen are asked
to decide about complex issues of governmental policy and international
politics. For example, they are legitimated to make a decision about who
should be the next leader of another country.

Another interesting point about the critical thinking pedagogy developed in *NewsHour Extra* materials is the implicit ideological positioning of
the questions students should explore in their activities. Critics of critical

thinking approaches have often discussed the nature of questions posed in the process of developing critical thinking skills and raised doubts about whether these questions actually do what they say they do. Kaplan (1994, 214) argues that "this model of reading may preclude the asking of certain types of politically significant questions about a text" and warns that "the raising of certain critical questions may escape the net of strict logical analysis" (215). Surprisingly, in a pedagogy based on logical analysis and argumentation, a number of questions for students in *NewsHour Extra* are in fact guided questions that lead students toward a preferred answer. For instance, in the following activity, students work individually or in groups to respond to the posed questions, which direct students to provide specific answers. The first question considers the reasons for going to war ("Weapons of Mass Destruction in Iraq").

> Remind students that disarmament was one of President Bush's two main arguments for going to war in Iraq and a goal of the war (the other being regime change). Given this, does it matter if coalition forces find chemical or biological weapons in Iraq?

The selection of the mental process with the use of the word *remind* is important here, because it presents information as obtained knowledge. Students are assumed to already possess this knowledge, and they are simply "reminded" by their teachers. The grammatical selection of this transitivity process (Halliday 1994) contributes to the regulation of students' answers through the use of hypotactic enhancement (i.e., "Given this"), which creates a condition between the two clauses and guides students' answers. A similar condition is used in the next example, which refers to the role of the United Nations in the Iraq War. Students' answers are directed through the use of the phrase *in light of this* (which denotes enhancement), in which the deictic *this* refers to the previous clause. Furthermore, a causal relationship is created in the next nominalized clause: *due to recent complications* ("The Role of the United Nations in Postwar Iraq").

> As Deputy Defense Secretary Paul Wolfowitz recently stated, after the fall of Hussein's regime the U.N. should be more involved in the dispensing of humanitarian aid to the people of Iraq than in the rebuilding of their government (see *Online NewsHour* article). In light of this, should the United Nations primarily be oriented towards humanitarian efforts? Due to recent complications such as those in the governing of Kosovo, should the U.N. be kept out of political or military campaigns altogether?

On another occasion, students are asked about issues concerning Iraq's payment of debts, and their answers are directed through the use of the mental process *keep in mind* and the projected clause starting with *that* ("Reconstruction of Iraq: A Lesson of Historical Precedents").

> Have each group reflect upon the following question for the reconstruction of Iraq: Should Iraq have to pay back billions of dollars in debts incurred by Saddam Hussein? Keep in mind the fact that Iraq has enormous potential economic resources, if the oil embargo is lifted.

In a question about civilian casualties, a directed answer is implied through the subordinate clause starting with *given that,* which denotes condition and creates a causal relation between the two clauses ("War Expectations").

> Given that the U.S. military does not plan to target civilians, but may attack military targets in any area, residential or not, what can we expect in terms of civilian casualties in this war? How should the coalition forces handle the placement of military targets in populated areas or the use of human shields?

In these and other similar activities, high school students, equipped with a few reading texts and some background information provided by the teacher, are invited to discuss and eventually take a position on complex issues of governmental policy and international politics. A careful reading of these activities reveals a strong regulation that directs students' answers. Notice the following examples: "Taking into account Iraq's wealth from oil, should Iraq have to pay back its debts?" and "Due to recent complications such as those in the governing of Kosovo, should the U.N. be kept out of political or military campaigns altogether?"

The War as Episodes in a TV Series

NewsHour Extra lesson plans closely follow the progress of the war from its beginning until its official ending. The war is presented as a kind of TV series that progresses day by day. As stated on the initial webpage, during the first stages of the war, every week two new lesson plans were added that invite students to discuss the most recent events, predict, assess new situations, find analogies with the past, or calculate the cost of the war. This is one of the two key elements of these lesson plans, whose main purpose becomes to construct discursive subjects who are well aware of the progress of war and who vigorously support the government's decision to go to war. In this context, students become spectators rather than agents of history.

This perspective dramatically narrows the context (Chilton 2002) within which discussion can be conducted in class and from which teaching materials are selected. It excludes any discussion about the necessity of the war or its ethics and focuses exclusively on current events. Given that the site presents a positive stance toward the war, the construction of war as a TV series has several effects. First, it shifts discussion from the general to the specific. Thus, any kind of "critical analysis" is inevitably located within this limited context. For instance, discussion of freedom of speech in the press centers around limited themes, such as the ethics of embedded journalists or the ethical dilemma resulting from CNN's decision not to report on Saddam's atrocities before the war. The war is taken as a given, and there is no challenge concerning its necessity. Second, it allows the use of articles from the daily press for educational purposes. In fact, following the progress of the war is largely facilitated by the use of current news articles from the hosting portal.

A second main characteristic of the *NewsHour Extra* lesson plans is the reproduction of the dominant discourse and its argumentation about the necessity of the war and the construction of a national consciousness. The step-by-step following of the war becomes the starting point for class discussion of wider issues. For instance, when discussing the US attempt to establish an "interim authority" in Iraq, discussion also centers on democracy; when discussing "the recent rescue of Private Jessica Lynch," the topic of women in the American army and their invaluable contribution to the nation is introduced. In this context, the teaching material is carefully selected to inspire certainty of a victorious outcome, trust in the justification for going to war, national pride, and a sense of "alertness." Remarkable similarities to traditional patriotic films or TV series emerge.[5] These materials imply that the agenda is already set, leaving little space for alternative explanations.

In this context, the democracy theme is quite popular (i.e., "We have democracy, and we are trying to restore democracy in a nondemocratic country"). In one case, students are given an extract from Thomas Jefferson's first inaugural address and are asked, "Are there aspects of this vision that are uniquely American? Why or why not?" ("Getting to Democracy"). In another lesson plan, through stressing the importance of respecting international conventions in a democratic country, students discuss the Geneva Convention ("The Rules of Engagement: The Geneva Convention").

1. Introduction: Begin by discussing the overview of the Geneva Convention.
2. Next, have the students analyze the Iraqi media's use of images of the prisoners of war (POWs) to determine whether it is contrary to the tenets of the Convention, particularly Article 13.
3. Lastly, ask the students to compare the use of the Al Jazeera images of American prisoners to recent media images of Iraqi prisoners held by U.S. soldiers.

Comparison with previous wars is quite prominent in *NewsHour Extra* and serves two main purposes. First, it is used to stress the positive role of the United States in critical moments in history ("Reconstruction of Iraq: A Lesson of Historical Precedents").

Following the end of WWII, much of Europe, both victor and vanquished, was ravaged. Infrastructure had been destroyed, millions killed, cities leveled. However, rather than punishing the German aggressors with billions of dollars in war reparations, the United States engaged in a massive campaign to rebuild Germany from the ground up. Germany is once again a world leader, and boasts one of the strongest economies and democracies in Europe.

Second, the tactic of comparison is employed to identify differences with previous wars. In the case of the Vietnam War, the focus is on the knowledge gained by the United States and on outlining that war's differences from the Iraq War (e.g., rapid technological developments, the present supremacy of the US army).

Discuss with the class the tenets of the Powell Doctrine. Help them to see that the Doctrine was an outgrowth of US involvement in previous military campaigns (such as Vietnam and Korea) that were ambivalent, tentative and poorly planned. ("The Powell Doctrine")

✳   ✳   ✳

Ask interested students to research the spending in the Gulf War (Budgetary Act of 1990) and the Vietnam War and report to the class their findings. Were there any budget concerns during these wars? Did any laws concerning budgets change because of these wars? What were the issues and changes? ("The Cost of War")

✳   ✳   ✳

Write a report comparing and contrasting the use of military technology in the following conflicts: World War II, the Vietnam War, and the current war in Iraq. ("War Expectations")

The positive role of the United States as a superpower is implicitly stressed in this type of activity. Students are led in particular directions in their discussion and research through teacher guidance (e.g., "Help them to see..."), through the posed questions (e.g., "Did any laws concerning budgets change because of these wars?"), and through a description of technological advances the country has achieved (e.g., by contrasting military technology in different conflicts).

Pedagogic Discourse and Identities

This book's introduction states that the suggested lessons in *NewsHour Extra* about the Iraq War, which include lesson plans, with their suggested activities and accompanying available resources (newspaper articles, interviews, historical and political texts, graphs, maps, etc.), comprise a kind of informal curriculum on the subject of the "war against terrorism." As is the case with other types of curricula, this informal curriculum has implied in it meanings and values that are ideologically specific and that contribute to the construction of discursive pedagogic identities. It then becomes important to examine the effects of this informal curriculum on the "imagined pedagogic identity" (Bernstein 1990, 1996) and the future lives of the students. Kress defines a curriculum as a design for a future social subject and a future society, because it puts forward knowledge, meanings, values, and skills that students will be encouraged to use as models in the future (1996, 16). The *NewsHour Extra* curriculum on the Iraq War can, thus, be seen to put forward a particular set of cultural, social, and linguistic resources that students will have available in the (re)construction of their subjectivity. The questions thereby raised concern about which resources will be available to the students who experience this curriculum, how specific representations will affect students' future active (re)construction of reality, and what vision of the future the informal curriculum implies.

Let us for a moment try to obtain a vision of the future by considering what seems to be the imaginary ideal student-subject in the pedagogy employed by *NewsHour Extra*. The curriculum students experience is based on a critical thinking approach that deals with the development of rational and argumentative skills. Activities ask students to identify and evaluate authors' intent, main arguments, supporting evidence, facts versus opinions, logical fallacies, and solid evidence. However, according to those who have criticized the approach, these skills do not engage readers in active reconstruction of the reading text, nor do they equip them with the tools necessary to negotiate with the text and to challenge its underlying assumptions.

The analysis conducted in this chapter suggests that students who experience the *NewsHour Extra* curriculum and its associated pedagogy will most probably become informed adults who try to understand the reality around them, who have learned to analyze facts, and who approach an issue from its opposing sides. However, because they have not learned to challenge governmental decisions, as good American patriots they will most probably align themselves with the official view of things, because the lessons in *NewsHour Extra* clearly attempt to manage pedagogic discourse within official US policy on the war.

Consequently, today's students will become citizens who will probably approach the world around them as something they need to understand but not change, because the pedagogy they experience today does not prepare them to become active agents who intervene in their environment. In moments of crisis, like war, they may develop a technical approach, such as "our country decided to go to war; let's try to analyze and understand why we had to do it." This "pedagogy of understanding," as Giroux (2005) has called it, prepares students to argue or engage in rigorous dialogue, but it does not give them the tools that will enable them to consider changing the world and making it a more meaningful and just place. The problem for Giroux (2005) is that, although educators

> believe in practices that open up the possibility of questioning among students, they often refuse to connect the pedagogical conditions that challenge how and what students think at the moment to the next task of prompting them to imagine changing the world around them so as to expand and deepen its democratic possibilities.

Chapter 2

Critical Pedagogy
in Rethinking Schools

THIS CHAPTER DISCUSSES THE PEDAGOGY EMPLOYED IN *RETHINKING SCHOOLS* data along the lines of a *critical pedagogy*. It raises similar questions to the ones posed in Chapter 1, concerning the educational materials from another website on the Iraq War. It particularly explores how critical pedagogy is discursively constructed on the *Rethinking Schools* website and how war is taught in the context of the specific informal curriculum. On another level, it aims to reveal the political and moral agenda of critical pedagogy, as it is realized in the specific context. The first part of the chapter outlines the main features of critical pedagogy, then presents some basic points of criticism that have come up in related literature. Through this analysis, the differences between critical pedagogy and the pedagogy of critical thinking become obvious at theoretical, epistemological, and methodological levels. The second part of the chapter analyzes the particular ways in which critical pedagogy develops in *Rethinking Schools*. Particular emphasis is placed on the suggested language activities described in the lesson plans about the Iraq War and the overall pedagogy of lessons as it unfolds in the lesson plans. As in Chapter 1, the analytic focus is on the students who experience the informal curriculum of *Rethinking Schools*.

Defining Critical Pedagogy

Monday morning a child brings a stray dog into the classroom. The traditional teacher sees that it is removed immediately.

The progressive teacher builds on the students' interest; perhaps measures and weighs the animal with the children, has the children draw and write about the dog, and eventually calls the humane society.

The Freirian [critical] teacher does what the progressive teacher does, but more. She asks questions, using the dog as the object of reflection. "Why are there so many stray dogs in our neighborhood?" "Why are there more here than in the rich suburbs?" "Why do people have dogs?" "Why doesn't the city allocate enough money to clean up after the dogs and care for the strays?" (Peterson 2003, 365)

Peterson uses this narrative account to illustrate differences among the traditional, progressive or liberal, and critical pedagogies. He suggests that, whereas the first pedagogy emphasizes getting the right answers and preparing students for participation in criterion-referenced exams, the progressive pedagogy builds on students' interests, yet in a limited (and rather local) way.[1] The critical pedagogy focuses on asking questions that engage students in reflective dialogue on topics of their interest and lead them into an analysis of the social situation with the ultimate purpose of changing it.

Critical pedagogy has its origins in critical theory, the sociological and philosophical theory of the early twentieth century, which drew on Marxism, phenomenology, and psychoanalysis, and flourished mainly in the 1960s and 1970s. Developed by German intellectuals who formed the Frankfurt School, critical theory took from Marxism "an orientation toward maximizing human freedom from political and economic domination," from phenomenology "an emphasis on observing and articulating the structures of lived experience," and from psychoanalysis "a push to decode cultural forms" (Kaplan 1994, 207). In addition to critical theory, critical pedagogy also draws on American progressive education (from John Dewey to George Counts, Harold Rugg, and Theodore Brameld) and social reconstructionism. Acknowledging that education is aligned with the capitalist marketplace mentality (Apple 2000a, 2000b, 2001) and that schools often reproduce the dominant culture, critical pedagogy comes to argue that there is a possibility for transforming culture and social institutions through educational practice (Stanley 1992).

Critical pedagogy is a strand in education developed in the United States in the 1980s. Giroux first linked education with concepts from critical theory: He termed it "critical foundation for a theory of radical pedagogy" (Giroux 1983a, 1). In his book *Theory and Resistance in Education* (Giroux 1983b), he talked about a theory with a radical view of knowledge that would try to put schools and pedagogy on the map and diffuse other disciplines with the pedagogical, making the pedagogical political and the political pedagogical.

Inspired by the work of Paulo Freire, the most renowned critical educator, critical pedagogy theorists developed a critique of formal education that stressed its sociopolitical and historical character. A central point in critical pedagogy is that education is not neutral but inherently political, and that schools are sites of contestation and struggle. According to McLaren (1989, 1998), critical pedagogy examines schools both in their historical context and as part of the existing social and political fabric that characterizes the class-driven dominant society. It critiques the purported neutrality of education promoted by conservatives and liberals alike, under which right-wing conservatives and neoconservatives are trying to impose a reactionary agenda on schools and universities (Macedo 2006). Moreover, critical pedagogy challenges the view of schools as neutral institutions designed to equip students with the knowledge and skills they need to successfully integrate into society and the labor force, because that view of education theory looks at schools and classroom pedagogy in a way that separates power from knowledge while simultaneously abstracting culture from politics. Critical educators further challenge liberal notions of schools as the great social and cultural equalizers. The interrelationship among school, culture, and power, according to critical pedagogy theorists, has long been ignored, because conservative and progressive educators are unwilling to view schools as political sites that both repress and produce subjectivities. For Aronowitz and Giroux (1991), schools not only constitute subjectivities through language, knowledge, and social practices, they also function in a related fashion to discredit, disorganize, and dismantle specific ways of experiencing and making sense of the world.

Different definitions and conceptualizations have given rise to different versions of critical pedagogy,[2] yet they all agree on the political character of education and its important role in developing students' capacity for critical reflexivity (Biesta 1998, 499). Shor (1992, 129) defines critical pedagogy as

> habits of thought, reading, writing, and speaking which go beneath surface meaning, first impressions, dominant myths, official pronouncements, traditional clichés, received wisdom, and mere opinions, to understand the deep meaning, root causes, social context, ideology, and

personal consequences of any action, event, object, process, organization, experience, text, subject matter, policy, mass media, or discourse.

Moreover, Giroux (1983, 1988b, 1988c) suggests that the term *critical* in critical pedagogy refers both to the development of *a language of critique,* which raises students' awareness of dominant ideologies, and to the development of *a language of possibility,* which enables the construction of counterhegemonic discourses and practices in schools. By using a language of critique, Giroux (1997, 220) argues, teachers may problematize how different subjectivities and identities are positioned within historically specific social practices and ideologies that inscribe students in particular modes of behavior. They may also analyze with their students how differences between social groups are discursively constructed and maintained. By using a language of possibility, teachers may explore how knowledge and power relations are constructed in various social practices, in order to provide students with an opportunity to consider alternative perspectives and possibilities of change. Giroux particularly notes that radical education has often abandoned the language of possibility for the language of critique, and he stresses the importance of developing a language of possibility as part of what makes a person critical. Embedded in this language of possibility is hope, conceived as a theoretical construct, which could provide alternatives for a better future, "for a different, less-ugly world" (Freire 1974, 91). Benesch (2001, 132) notes that by overlooking hope as a theoretical construct, some theorists were led to view critical pedagogy as a negative and depressing pedagogy.

Another important notion here is the notion of *voice,* understood not as liberal humanistic expression of free will, but as the opening up of a space for those who are marginalized by the structures of society to speak, "so that the voicing of their lives may transform both their lives and the social system that excludes them" (Pennycook 2001, 101). Being the focal point for a critical theory of education, the concept of *voice* here means more than just speaking; it means developing the possibility for articulating alternative realities. In addition, the notion of voice has been seen as an attempt to understand students' social life in and out of school and to explore the ways it affects their learning.

Related to the notion of voice is that of *difference.* According to Giroux, critical pedagogy concerns "a politics of difference" that is much more than simply a celebration of plurality. In the context of critical pedagogy, the argument goes, "student voice must be rooted in a pedagogy that allows students to speak and to appreciate the nature of difference as part of both a democratic tolerance and a fundamental condition for critical dialogue and the development of forms of solidarity" (1988a, 72). This notion of difference allows critical teachers to frame their understanding of student identities as constructed through multiple and often contradictory subject positions (Giroux and McLaren 1989). It also provides a tool to help both students and teachers analyze how social groups are constituted in the ways they are and to analyze "historical differences that manifest themselves in public struggles" (Giroux 1997, 220).

Critical pedagogy theorists have also drawn attention to the *hidden curriculum* in schools, "the tacit teaching to students of norms, values and dispositions that goes on simply by their living in and coping with the institutional expectations and routines of schools day in and day out for a number of years" (Apple 2004, 13). These unspoken values, norms, and dispositions, concerning issues such as competition, success and failure, work and play, discipline, stereotype, and gender and class division, among others, are passed on to students as common sense (Kanpol 1999, 34). The point is, for Apple (2005, 99), that as students learn to accept as natural the social distinctions that schools implicitly teach and reinforce, they also internalize visions of the ways social institutions are organized and the ways they fit in these institutions. Consequently these everyday school practices—which tend to be invisible, because they are not stated in official documents as educational objectives and goals—contribute to the reproduction of dominant ideologies that support existing structurally based inequalities and maintain the ideological hegemony of the most powerful classes in society. In the context of critical pedagogy, Giroux (1983, 61) argues that the notion of the hidden curriculum should not be limited to uncovering implicit and underlying assumptions that shape school experience. It should also be related to the notion of liberation, so that it can contribute to the development of a theory of schooling concerned with both reproduction and transformation.

The Notion of Literacy in Critical Pedagogy

Luke (1997, 143) refers to critical pedagogy as another orientation to critical literacy. He argues that all critical approaches to literacy "are characterized by a commitment to reshape literacy education in the interests of marginalized groups of learners, who on the basis of gender, cultural and socioeconomic background have been excluded from access to the discourses and texts of dominant economies and cultures."

The concept of *critical literacy* developed in the 1970s, when Paulo Freire used the term to mean the critical capacity to use language as a means for people to decode and demythologize their own cultural traditions and the inequitable structures of their society. For Freire (1974, 1985, 2005), education should focus on the development of critical consciousness (*conscientization*), which enables teachers and students to make connections between their individual experiences and the social contexts in which they are embedded. The development of this critical consciousness is the first step of *liberatory praxis,* an ongoing reflective approach to taking action. In fact, for Freire, change in consciousness and concrete action are linked. The role of critical pedagogy is then to empower students and to lead them to emancipation, which will help them change their lives.

In Freire's account, literacy is not a technical skill. Most importantly, the ability to read and write is tied to developing an enhanced sense of individual and collective self-esteem and a desire to change the circumstances of one's social group (Burbules and Berk 1999, 52). Therefore, critical literacy is oriented to the development of a critical citizenry capable of analyzing and challenging the oppressive characteristics of society. Freire suggests that in "reading the word" people are always engaged in a "reading" of the world around them (Freire and Macedo 1987, 35). He argues that "the reading of the world that omits the reading of the text implies a rupture of the inherent cycle that involves thinking, action, language, and world" (Freire 2006, ix), and he warns that the problem with illiteracy is that it limits people's capacity to read the world, to write about its reading, and ultimately to rethink their reading of the world.

Therefore, for Freire, literacy is an act of knowing, an act that views learners as subjects in the reading process and not as objects of the teacher's action. Most importantly, within his pedagogy of inclusion, literacy should provide "the possibility for participation, the possibility for different languages and cultures and forms of knowledge to be allowed a pedagogical role" (Pennycook 2001, 103). In this context, the traditional teacher and student roles change, because they are both actively and collaboratively engaged in analyzing the socially constructed nature of knowledge and because "the classroom becomes a context in which students analyze their reality for the purpose of participating in its transformation. They address social problems by sharing and comparing experiences, analyzing root causes, and exploring strategies for change" (Auerbach 1995, 12).

Lankshear (1997, 156) suggests that this concept of critical literacy requires that students know and do things *and* that they know these things for what they are and for their social effects. He outlines four educational goals for classroom learning that derive from such an inclusive pedagogy:

a. Enable students to make explicit the relationship between *word* and *world*.
b. Provide students with opportunities to explore social and discursive practices as historical rather than natural and fixed.
c. Encourage students to explore the effects of discourse and explore how the use of different language may produce different outcomes for individuals and groups.
d. Provide students with opportunities to enhance their appreciation of the vast range of actual and possible ways of doing and being.

He particularly notes that two focal points of critical literacy and critical pedagogy refer to the development of a critical perspective of texts and of the wider social practices that are "mediated by, made possible, and partially sustained through reading, writing, viewing, transmitting, etc., texts" (Lankshear 1997, 44).

In this context of critical literacy, the role of teachers is to enable students to become knowledgeable about their histories, their experiences, and the culture of their everyday environments and to discern the dominant culture's codes and signifiers, in order to escape their own environments (Macedo 2006, xiii). Consequently, in an educational context shaped by a critical literacy pedagogy, Macedo argues that teachers must constantly teach a dual curriculum: a curriculum that empowers students to make sense of their everyday life, and a curriculum that enables students to obtain the tools for mobility valued in the dominant culture (ibid.). These tools of mobility often include, for instance, the development of specific skills. McLaren (1989, 188) acknowledges that skill development may be important, yet he stresses that in the context of critical pedagogy, "schooling for self and social empowerment is *ethically prior* to a mastery of technical skills, which are primarily tied to the logic of the marketplace." He suggests that attention should be paid to the purpose to which the skills are to be put (187). For instance, skills such as critical thinking, according to Benesch (1993, 546), should focus not only on higher-order thinking skills but also on "a search for the social, historical, and political roots of conventional knowledge."

Critique of Critical Pedagogy Approaches

Freire's work and other forms of critical pedagogy have been criticized over the years on many grounds. Pennycook (2001, 133) identifies three main points of critique. The first refers to the political nature of this pedagogy. Critical pedagogy could be alienating for some teachers, owing to its abstractions and political posturing, according to Johnston (1999). In fact, critical pedagogy has been criticized for remaining at the level of grand theorizing oriented to critical discussion of schooling rather than providing outlines for specific teaching practices. Usher and Edwards (1994, 218) talk about a "curious silence on concrete educational practices," and Gore (1993, 110–111) argues that the problem with critical pedagogy lies "in the juxtaposition of its abstract metatheoretical analysis of schooling with its abstract dictates and declarations for what teachers should do," which may lead to a prescriptive kind of pedagogy. However, as Johnston (1999, 558) suggests, critical pedagogy should be seen as a theoretical framework rather than a teaching method whose microlevel pedagogical elements will have to be developed by individual teachers, according to their specific teaching situations. Similarly, Bartolomé (2003) warns about the risks of domesticating critical pedagogy by turning it into a method of instruction. She claims that critical pedagogy is a political project, not a method, and she argues against the "fetish of method" and the conceptualization of the critical curriculum as a series of steps for teachers to follow (a view also shared by Brady 1994).

The second main point of critique refers to the notion of voice and inclusion. It has been suggested that the concept of dialogic pedagogy is perhaps one of the most confused ideas of critical literacy, with voice and dialogue (the engagement with voice) being treated trivially, because "at a simplistic level it has been taken as a process within which a student 'voice' is 'taken seriously' and in this respect is counterposed to a transmission pedagogy" (Simon 1992, 96). It has also been suggested that critical pedagogy tends to romanticize the notion of voice as the writing and speaking of marginalized people (Luke 1996), that its notion of voice includes an inability to escape a North American individualistic idealism (Cope and Kalantzis 1993), and that its theory is often unclear about how the possibility of using one's voice is related to empowerment and social change (Pennycook 2001). Similarly, in his critique of critical approaches to literacy, Luke (1996) suggests that the North American critical pedagogy has failed to provide an account of how power relates to language and literacy.

This leads us to the third main point of critique identified by Pennycook (2001), which is related to the transformative vision of education. Some strands of critical pedagogy have been criticized for a rationalist view of education, in which students are expected to arrive logically at an understanding that they have a right to freedom from oppression, whereas critical teachers take the position as the ones who know the universal truth (Ellsworth 1989; Lather 1992). Moreover, Gore (1993, 39) talks about lack of reflexivity, or the inability of critical theorists to become critical of their own work.

There have also been different answers to the question posed by several educators: *How critical can one teacher be?* It is generally acknowledged that critical pedagogy has to deal with deeply rooted institutional practices that dominate language and other classrooms and that support inequality. At this point, critical pedagogists offer alternative practices, which include discussing and negotiating with students specific effective pedagogies, suggesting optional reading materials from which students may choose what to read, introducing alternative forms of assessment, assigning students responsibility for their own learning, involving students in course design decisions, and preparing meaningful assignments (Benesch 1999; Lin 2004).

Similarly, Johnston (1999, 557) argues that "more than anything else, perhaps, critical pedagogy offers a way of combining a trenchant critique of previously unquestioned practices in education with concrete ways of introducing change—that is, with a belief in the transformative power of the individual teacher." Considering the outcomes of a critical pedagogy, Auerbach and McGrail (1991, 105) conclude that "change takes many forms, both inside and outside the classroom, and may not be packaged in discrete actions but rather in the gradual, cumulative building of confidence, validation of experience and change in perspective." After all, they argue, critical pedagogy allows changes in the social relations within the classroom and the critical examination of everyday reality.

Critical Pedagogy in *Rethinking Schools*

As frequently stated in the data, the purpose of the *Rethinking Schools* educational materials is to develop an alternative perspective on education. We read in one lesson plan, "Our pedagogy has to be more political. We need to invite students to consider alternatives—we need to invite them to become part of making alternatives" ("Defeating Despair"). Discussing the design of an alternative curriculum, Bill Bigelow of *Rethinking Schools* states in a lesson plan on the Iraq War:

> We don't feature classroom activities that present full-blown, worked-out alternatives to corporate-driven globalization.... The distant and utopian feel to imagining the Good Society can unwittingly make fundamental change seem less attainable, and more dream-like.... To

provide a sense of alternatives, we have focused more on highlighting concrete examples of past and present resistance to the dire threats posed by profit-driven globalization.... But unless teachers make these examples explicit, students may ... fail to recognize the glimpses of hope along the way.... Over the course of a school year, we can also help students recognize how much their own global awareness has grown, and perhaps their commitment to act for justice. This too can be a source of hope.

To raise students' critical awareness, the authors of the lesson plans often point out the need for developing relevant teaching materials. In the words of one teacher, "As I sat down recently to figure out how I was going to teach about the impending war against Iraq, I was struck by how much information was available and yet how little curriculum" ("Teaching Gulf War II").

The lesson plans and student activities do not follow the systematic presentation in *NewsHour Extra* lesson plans (see more in Chapter 4), which have full instructions for teachers and detailed handouts for students. The aim in *Rethinking Schools* seems to be on sharing the experience but leaving to teachers the initiative to develop their own lessons. The personal element is also very important in this pedagogy, with teachers bringing in their own experiences and subjectivities. In fact, a teacher's subjectivity is linked to her agency, because this pedagogy views the teacher as a transformative intellectual. One of the lesson plans identifies the main elements of the alternative curriculum, according to which educators need to nurture student empathy so that they can become multicultural and antiracist, ask the deep "why?" questions, and enlist students in questioning the language and symbols that help frame how we understand global events ("Sept 11 and Our Classrooms").

New technologies are extensively employed in the suggested lessons. In addition to antiwar documentaries and war films, the Internet is regularly used as an information source for both teachers and students, because, it is argued, "the Internet makes it possible for us to seek out different perspectives from non-corporate, alternative media, and from media of other nations" ("Drawing on History to Challenge the War"). The texts used are primarily drawn from literary discourses (antiwar literature, such as poetry, novels, short stories, and songs), historical discourses (particularly concerning the first Gulf War, Vietnam, and Afghanistan), and political discourses.

For assigned activities, students are directed to find information on various Internet sources, such as the Citizens for Tax Justice site ("House

Stimulus Money Grab"), the Ban Mines website ("The World Up Close"), and the Foreign Policy in Focus website, for background readings in foreign policy issues ("Drawing on History to Challenge the War"). The suggested activities generally encourage students to think about "the frameworks that the media fashions for us—the purely bad guys and the purely good guys, the cleansing role of violence, the contempt for non-Western cultures, etc." ("Teaching Gulf War II"), to "think about social events as having concrete causes, constantly asking 'Why?' and 'In whose interests?'" ("Rethinking the Teaching of the Vietnam War"), and to "look back at the history of U.S. relations with Iraq in order to better understand U.S. objectives today" ("Predicting How the U.S. Government Will Respond to the Iraqi Government").

Overall, the pedagogy employed in the *Rethinking Schools* curriculum deals systematically with posing questions. Often the aim of the suggested lesson is not to provide answers to students' questions but to invite students to pose the questions. One teacher reports:

> The lesson ended with more questions than answers, but that didn't bother me. Early in the year, it's less important to "answer" such questions than to raise them. ("The World Up Close")

In some cases, the aim of an activity may be to have students share their fears and worries about the war. As stated in several lesson plans, through the questions students ask, teachers develop a better understanding of students' feelings and positions and can then frame their lessons accordingly. From the lesson descriptions, it becomes clear that students are systematically encouraged to raise their own questions and that teachers are quite flexible in the ways they treat these questions and incorporate them into their lessons. Overall, although the ways to treat student questions vary, there is a consensus that the questions constitute an important part of the employed pedagogy. We see this in the class in which a special notebook entitled "Questions That We Have" records student questions ("The World Up Close").

> It was Sept. 12 when Rafael, one of my fifth graders, pointed out the window and asked, "What would you do if terrorists were outside our school and tried to bomb us?"
>
> Clearly, the tragic events of the day before had left my students confused and fearful. Such questioning continued when the United States started bombing Afghanistan in October. "Will they bomb us like we are bombing them?" one student asked.

Sometimes we stop and immediately talk about such questions. Other times we postpone them until the day's lesson on "current events." I often have students write their questions in a spiral notebook, labeled "Questions That We Have," that sits in front of the class.

Often student questions become the output of language activities. In one case, for instance, students are asked to write a poem, using questions in order to make the reader "see" the war. On another occasion, they work in groups to raise questions on a particular topic about the war. Questions are also used by teachers not as a form of checking student answers, as is often the case in a traditional classroom, but as a way to unpack commonsense assumptions and to question the official story on Iraq. The way this is conducted is also of interest. Rather than dealing locally with the necessity of the war, these questions look at the "big picture" in their attempt to locate present events within their broader historical, sociocultural, and economic contexts ("Entering History Through Poetry").

In teaching students about the potential war with Iraq, they need facts, statistics, video clips, history. They need to tackle big ideas: Why is the U.S. government pushing so desperately for war? What is the cost of war?

✳   ✳   ✳

What happened to the veterans after they returned home? How did these men and women learn to live normal lives again after their experiences?

Clearly, the aim of the *Rethinking Schools* curriculum on the Iraq War is to prepare informed students who will speak out against the war and make their voices heard ("Drawing on History"). This pedagogy does not approach the war in a neutral and "objective" way, nor does it attempt to make students understand the necessity of this war. It invites them to take a negative stance, through a pedagogy that is a political project (McLaren 1994). To do so, it often draws on students' personal experiences. In one lesson, a teacher wants his students to behave as allies. After they analyze ally behavior from the historical and literary characters of "Warriors Don't Cry," students are to focus on the four categories of ally, victim, perpetrator, and witness and to brainstorm, drawing on their personal experience to identify times when they themselves acted as allies, victims, perpetrators, or witnesses. Next, students write down their experiences and read them aloud in class. After listening, the rest of the students write on some prompts related to each story. For instance, they could write about what can be learned from the piece, form questions to ask the storyteller, in order to get more details, write about a similar experience in their lives, or consider alternative courses of action for the particular incident. In the next part of the activity, students choose one story from their group to act out, assign character roles, and decide how to stage the story. The lesson plan states that the aim of these activities is to make students see oppression in other students' stories and be in a position to stand up against it ("Acting for Justice" in "Entering History"). Cho (2010, 313) reminds us that critical pedagogy relies on experiences against the claims of hegemonic truth. She refers to Zavarzadeh and Morton (1994, 22), who support the idea that focusing on personal experiences frees students "from oppressive cultural frames of knowing by providing them with new ways of claiming authority for their own experience." Most importantly, personal experiences are not viewed as self-evident or self-explanatory here. Critical pedagogy does not stay at the level of personal experience but attempts to theorize it by giving students both a language of critique and a language of possibility.

This emphasis on students' personal experiences also enables teachers to build student empathy—another important part of the critical curriculum—and help them process the events of the war. Several activities focus on encouraging students to express their frustration and anger. As a teacher put it in "The World Up Close," "I want my students to be comfortable expressing their fears about war and terrorism. This allows for emotional release and also provides insight into my students' thoughts." Different types of activities are used to build empathy. For example, in "Letters to the Universe," an English teacher drew on student experiences with losing a loved one to help them cope with the September 11 tragedy.

> My lesson plan was based on the idea of the guided freewrite—students are given a topic and given time to write whatever they want. I passed out a sheet that asked students to "share a time in your life when you lost someone, and offer advice from your experience and what you learned." The students were to write their response on the back of the sheet.
> When I called "time's up," we folded up our letters and dropped them into the "Letters to the Universe" box. Then, I opened the lid and students passed around the box, each picking out an anonymous letter. The students began to read.

Visual material is used extensively to raise student empathy. In "Drawing on History," a teacher uses a documentary on the history of US attempts to control oil in the Middle East. As stated in the lesson plan, the video raises questions about the current war rhetoric and possible motives behind the call to war.

> To engage students' empathy, I began the unit with the last seventeen minutes of the sixty-four-minute video, because this segment on war disabilities is emotionally compelling. It shows both U.S. veterans and Iraqis made ill from depleted uranium, which the U.S. military uses to harden bullets, tanks, and missiles. After seeing video images of Iraqi children dying of leukemia caused by depleted uranium, it was hard for students to see Iraqis as "the enemy." One student said, "I had no idea children were dying."

Interestingly, the pedagogy employed in *Rethinking Schools* does not discursively construct the enemy negatively, as usually happens during wartime; instead, it tends to humanize the enemy, to bring young Americans closer to young Iraqis, and to reveal the ugly face of war. Poetry is also used to build student empathy, in order to develop antiwar consciousness. In the following extracts, teachers discuss the importance of poetry.

> Poetry is only a piece of a much broader social justice curriculum that aims to critique injustice and build empathy. But at this moment in our nation's history, poetic intimacy seems an especially valuable strategy to invite our students to touch the lives of others—others who may be in urgent need of allies. ("Poetry in a Time of Crisis")

> ✳   ✳   ✳

> Poems are not a substitute for information. Students need to investigate why this war is happening. Poetry is not social analysis. Students' poems won't help them figure out the role of oil in this war. It won't help them figure out why Iraq and not North Korea. However, poetry will help students understand the human consequences of those decisions. And by humanizing the war, students may care enough to join our investigation into its causes. ("Entering History Through Poetry")

It seems, therefore, that the overall aim extends far beyond helping students understand the current situation and the decision to go to war. The present war is placed in a much broader context, which critically investigates the roots of the problem, its causes and effects, and more general concepts, such as injustice and discrimination. In this context, students are invited to write their own poems and sometimes combine them with visual images, as in the following examples.

We told students that they would be writing a poem about discrimination or injustice. To prepare for this, we encouraged them to highlight incidents that created a visual image for them, that created a visceral reaction or helped them understand the current crisis from a personal point of view. ("Poetry in a Time of Crisis")

*   *   *

Ask students to brainstorm metaphors that capture their understandings of the aftermath of Sept. 11. Students can make metaphorical drawings or use the metaphors as the basis for poems. ("New World Disorder")

The poems students write as a result of their class and home activities often become the topic of class discussion. They are presented in class, analyzed, and posted on the class bulletin board. They are also included in some lesson plans. For instance, the following poem was written by a girl, who said she supported the US bombing of Afghanistan when it began, but later felt differently ("The World Up Close").

> Twisting
> Turning
> Turning
> Twisting
> Twisting and Turning
> My feelings are burning
> Like the Twin Towers
> My heart is broken
> from all the hating
> All the killing in Afghanistan
> has made my brain to start
> twisting, My feelings are burning
> My heart is broken.

A noticeable element of the critical pedagogy employed here is the use of different types of texts as instructional tools. In addition to print materials, teachers also use a variety of resources such as songs, photos, and videos. Songs, like poetry, are considered powerful tools to build consciousness and solidarity, and, for this reason, they are extensively used ("Songs for Global Conscience"). According to one teacher, "the lyrical metaphors, rhythms, and stories in many songs motivate and educate students" ("Teaching with Protest Songs"). Videos are often used to present issues for discussion, usually extracts from films and documentaries on current and historical topics. Photos and pictures are also extensively used. In one instance, a teacher used a Sept. 16 photo of a demonstration in Pakistan, with a banner reading "Americans, Think! Why You Are Hated All Over The World!" ("The World Up Close"). Following Searle (1977), Peterson (2003, 369–370) stresses the importance of taking children out into the world and bringing the world into the classroom. He refers to speakers, movies, poetry, and music as bringing the world into the classroom. In fact, we could say that the *Rethinking Schools* curriculum on the Iraq War brings the outside world into the classroom, by employing a variety of authentic resources as teaching materials.

However, students are not only exposed to a variety of monomodal and multimodal texts, but they are also asked to produce a variety of genres. For instance, they are asked to prepare their own postcards; a bulletin board with photos, maps, and student writing; and a poster on land mines, with pictures of victims, maps, essays, and facts. Although they are rarely asked to respond in writing to typical reading comprehension questions, students are often asked to write essays and papers on issues discussed in class. Most importantly, they are invited to analyze the language of their reading texts.

> I pointed out the mechanics of Priest's use of questions, followed by a list of images. Students underlined the images that made them see or hear war. ("Entering History Through Poetry")

> ✳   ✳   ✳

> They were to clip articles about Iraq from the local newspaper, and I handed out a list of alternative media websites. After several weeks of following the news, they would write a paper analyzing contrasts between the two types of media.... They were to look closely at such things as loaded language, plays on emotion, historical context (or lack of), and depth of investigative reporting. ("Drawing on History")

Other types of activities involve group work, role-plays, simulations, and action research projects, as in the following example ("The World Up Close").

> In late September, we read in a news article that there are 10 million land mines in Afghanistan. After explaining what a land mine was, I mentioned there was an international campaign to end the manufacture and sale of land mines. Out of this discussion, a few students

formed an "Action Research Group." After a few recess sessions on the Internet (www.banmines.org), they made a poster with pictures of victims of land mines, maps locating the world's 110 million land mines, an essay and facts about land mines.

As stated in "Rethinking Our Classrooms"[3] from the *Rethinking Schools Journal* (fall 2003), the critical curriculum should be "a rainbow of resistance," and its main aim should be to prepare students to challenge social reality: "Through critiques of advertising, cartoons, literature, legislative decisions, foreign policy choices, job structures, newspapers, movies, consumer culture, agricultural practices, and school life itself, students should have opportunities to question social reality." However, it is also noted that a critical curriculum should encourage students to "see themselves as truth-tellers and change-makers," because "part of a teacher's role is to suggest that ideas have real consequences and should be acted upon, and to offer students opportunities to do just that." In this context, the main purpose of the suggested lessons is to change students' attitudes toward the war. This may be the reason that changes of students' views are so frequently reported:

> When the video ended, they jumped right into an angry critique of the rhetoric surrounding the present war. One indignant student asked, "If our companies gave Hussein weapons of mass destruction, why are we going to bomb him because he might still have some?" ("Drawing on History to Challenge the War")

> * * *

> One student wrote, "To me, this cartoon is saying that we (the U.S., portrayed by Popeye) can do whatever we want to other people in other cultures, because we're always right. Violence is alright and gives you power and control." ("Teaching Gulf War II")

Elsewhere, students prepare an educational session to teach their fellow students about Iraq, and in the same lesson a student is reported as actively attempting to persuade others: "I was so proud to know how to argue with my dad. I told him, 'I'm telling you realities. You think what they want you to think'" ("Drawing on History to Challenge the War").

An interesting account of how a student resisted the dominant curriculum is recorded in a reading included in the materials for teaching about the Iraq War. The extract that follows is part of a speech delivered at a peace rally in April 2003 by twelve-year-old Charlotte Aldebron, who holds a strong antiwar position. Charlotte describes the types of activities she engaged in in two classes and how she resisted the ideology of the activities conducted in her classroom. Interestingly, the first activity is similar to those we found in *NewsHour Extra* lesson plans ("Free Speech: Concept versus Reality").

> After the invasion, our class focused on combat. It was like a game: we got a hand-out on the Persian Gulf countries, called "The Players"; we were given photos with short bios of top Iraqis, the team we had to beat; we got a map of the Gulf region with the size and location of all the armies, and the weapons each possessed; we read an article about the threat of Iraq using chemical weapons against our troops.
>
> My mother complained to the principal and the Commissioner of Education that we were being taught to glorify war, admire military strategy, and objectify the killing and maiming of human beings. The Commissioner responded that each school's curriculum was its own business. The principal answered that he thought the social studies lesson plan was "balanced and comprehensive." Yes, my mom was free to speak—in fact, she could scream her head off for all they cared. It wouldn't change a thing.
>
> Meanwhile, in science, we had to answer questions like, "what are the advantages of biological weapons?" I said there weren't any advantages because biological weapons kill people. How can death be an advantage? I was asked to give two examples of biological weapons. I said one was the smallpox on blankets we gave to Native Americans to kill them. The other was *E. coli* bacteria that have been found in McDonald's hamburgers. I said we could close the gap between the threat and the capability of biological weapons by signing the U.N. Chemical Weapons Convention, and by hiring more meat inspectors. Somehow, our assignments never got corrected.

These two instances could be seen as an attempt to resist the dominant curriculum. Resistance here is realized in two ways: In the first activity, a student's mother makes an official complaint to school authorities, and in the second, the student herself resisted the question posed in class, by providing unexpected answers to the teacher.

It should be noted at this point that in these and other instances, the preoccupation with developing an alternative pedagogy focuses on the presentation of antiwar argumentation and not on a multifaceted and disinterested presentation of the Iraq War. The projected and "objective" account of war that we met with in *NewsHour Extra* lesson plans is not found here. Instead we find activities that encourage students to adopt a critical stance on the decision to go to war, or, as we saw in the previous extract, to resist the dominant curriculum. As a result, argumentation of the opposite side is often left out of discussion. This may be because it is assumed that students are already immersed in mainstream discourse and press. The analysis of lesson plans conducted in this book turned up only one instance in which students were asked to research both mainstream and alternative press, in order to record both sides' arguments. Even then, however, the ideological context was given to students, because the purpose of the analysis was to show that the opposite position was wrong. In most other instances, the attempt to develop students' critical awareness generally ignored the arguments of the opposite side, perhaps assuming that, because this was the prevailing view, it was well known to all students.

Challenging the War

Thematic analysis of the lesson plans and activities has revealed that the critical curriculum in *Rethinking Schools* actually contextualizes current events in two ways: by comparing this war to previous wars and by exploring this war in relation to other political issues that raise global inequalities. The first historicizes the war and aims to equip students with background knowledge and to raise antiwar consciousness. The second humanizes the war and aims to sensitize students to issues concerning the brutality of war, raising a much broader discussion of current issues.

The importance of history is stressed in all types of critical curricula as a way to provide alternatives for the future. As Darder, Baltodano, and Torres (2003, 12) put it, through critical pedagogy, "students come to understand themselves as subjects of history and to recognize that conditions of injustice ... can also be transformed by human beings." History plays an important role in *Rethinking Schools*' curriculum on the Iraq War. A connection is often made between this and the previous Gulf War. For instance, one lesson "looks back at the history of U.S. relations with Iraq in order to better understand U.S. objectives today" and the "real possibilities of creating a different policy" ("Predicting How the U.S. Government Will Respond to the Iraqi Government"). In another lesson, students watch a video about how the first President Bush persuaded the United Nations to support the invasion and are then asked to draw parallels to the present situation ("Drawing on History"). Another attempted connection is between this war and previous wars in recent American history ("Rethinking the Teaching of the Vietnam War").

A video I've found useful in prompting students to explore a bit of the history of Vietnam and the sources of U.S. involvement ... offers an overview of Vietnamese resistance to French colonialism (which began in the mid-19th century) and to the Japanese occupation during World War II.

Analogies between past and current situations are frequently drawn to encourage students to challenge the war, not to justify it. Role-play activities are prominent here. In one case, students get involved in an activity simulating members of Congress in 1964. In another case, they become members of the Viet Minh and the French government invited to a meeting with President Truman to present their position on the question of Vietnamese independence. Students also read a text by Martin Luther King and are then asked to write the speech that he might deliver today if he were alive, covering the events of September 11, "terrorism" of all kinds, and the war ("When Silence Is Betrayal"). Through these activities, students are expected to develop an alternate perspective on historical events and are encouraged to search for deeper reasons and motives.

Overall, we could say that rather than attempting to make students understand the reasons for going to war, the *Rethinking Schools* pedagogy invites students to challenge war rhetoric. For instance, the term *coalition,* so frequently used in *NewsHour Extra,* is avoided in *Rethinking Schools,* and the United States is presented as a superpower with financial and geopolitical interests. A great number of the lesson plans aim to illustrate the United States' powerful position and to answer the question "why war?" by closely examining the wars the country has been involved in since World War II.

In *Rethinking Schools* lesson plans, the day-by-day progress of war is ignored. Topics focus on challenging the war's necessity and calling for the investigation of its deeper causes. Instead of dealing with current events, these lessons focus on the general, the underlying, and the global. This is probably related to the lessons' preoccupation with the larger issue at hand and not with the fragmentation of knowledge that necessarily disarticulates it from a larger context and loses sight of the important issues. As one teacher put it, "Teachers have a special—and difficult—responsibility to help students extend their circle of caring beyond the victims of Sept. 11 to all of humanity" ("Teaching about Sept. 11"). Sometimes the topics discussed in the classroom do not relate directly to the current war, the name of which is systematically avoided in the lesson plans. For instance, in the opening page of the website, in the early days of the Iraq War, the collection of lesson plans was placed under the heading "The War," with no reference made to Iraq. In addition, although four of the suggested lesson plans were posted before the war (i.e., winter 2000/2001, winter 2001/2002), they were included in the selection that originally appeared in spring 2003, because they were studying September 11 and its possible outcomes.

Furthermore, the war is discussed relative to other important issues that lead to global inequality, according to *Rethinking Schools* lesson plans. For instance, in one activity students "examine the current U.S. policy and how interest in oil is a factor" ("Predicting How the U.S. Government Will Respond to the Iraqi Government"), and in another, they explore how oil has influenced previous US foreign policy ("The Geopolitics of War"). Economic factors are explored, as students list all the groups of Americans hurt by the September 11 attacks on the Pentagon and World Trade Center and examine which of these groups will benefit by the "stimulus" tax-cut bill, which was designed to stimulate the US economy after September 11 ("House Stimulus Money Grab"). Other topics discussed in lessons related to war include land mines and children, child labor, and poverty. As a teacher states, "While I have always done such lessons, after Sept. 11 they became more useful in helping students understand why some might resent the United States. While our attention currently is focused on the U.S. war in Afghanistan, I frame such involvement in broader issues of global exploitation" ("The World Up Close").

Pedagogic Discourse and Identities in a Pedagogy of Intervention

It is often stated in the website on the Iraq War that *Rethinking Schools* is informed by a critical pedagogy perspective that historicizes knowledge, views education as a political act, and stresses the importance of students and educators as active agents. As also mentioned in one of the resources in the data, *Rethinking Schools* aims to develop an alternative perspective on education, raise students' critical awareness, and teach them "that ideas have real consequences and should be acted upon."[4] The informal curriculum on the Iraq War involves students in multimodal analysis and critique of media texts (such as articles, advertisements, newspaper reports), poems, photos, videos, songs, and other genres, by emphasizing the bigger picture and by having students ask questions and examine the deeper causes that have led to war. In short, it is "a curriculum which enables students to read the media" (Steinberg 2007, 313) and reflect on them critically.

Turning now to examine the effects of this informal curriculum on the "imagined pedagogic identity" (Bernstein 1990, 1996) and on the future lives of the students who experience it today, we can draw some interesting conclusions from the analysis conducted in this chapter. The students who experience the *Rethinking Schools* curriculum and its associated pedagogy will most probably become adults who have been trained to ask questions, challenge the reality constructed for them in the media, search history in order to understand the present, connect present events to their sociohistorical contexts, and in moments of crisis, such as a war, confront important issues directly and with empathy. Trained through a pedagogy that adopts a self-reflective perspective, they will probably become critical readers of the world around them, and of themselves. Most importantly, they are trained to view themselves not within strict national boundaries, but as citizens of the world, as "cosmopolitans" (Mitsikopoulou 2007; Silverstone 2007), showing understanding of the difference of the "other." The socially driven approach of the *Rethinking Schools* curriculum is intended to prepare them for a life of democratic participation and active citizenship, accordingly affecting their ways of being and acting.

An account such as the one just presented does not wish to draw deterministic conclusions about the curriculum as a one-sided process, with students as passive recipients of a pedagogy. This approach would oversimplify a much more complex issue. Acknowledging that pedagogies may be resisted, negotiated, and challenged, it merely draws attention to the effects of curricula that are often overlooked by both educators and policy makers, or cannot be predicted, as the following extract from a *Rethinking Schools* lesson account eloquently put it ("Sept.11 and Our Classrooms").

No teacher education program could have prepared us to confront the emotionally shattering events of Sept. 11. We began school that morning in one era, but left that evening in a different era—one filled with sorrow, confusion, and vulnerability. No matter what age student we work with, we found ourselves rethinking and revising our lesson plans, if not our life plans.

After all, as Street (1995, 125) wrote, a curriculum "becomes an organizing concept around which ideas of social identity and value are defined; what kinds of collective identity we subscribe to, what kind of nation we want to belong to."

Chapter 3

The Ideology of
the Instructional Texts

THE PREVIOUS TWO CHAPTERS HAVE EXPLORED THE WAYS IN WHICH
critical pedagogy and the pedagogy of critical thinking are materialized
in the educational materials of *NewsHour Extra* and *Rethinking Schools*.
Analysis of the suggested language activities has revealed the systematic
employment of two distinct pedagogic discourses that are ideologically
and politically grounded. They reflect the wider political conflict and the
different ways educators may organize the socialization of children on
current events. Elaborating on these findings, this chapter continues to
investigate how students experience the curriculum. The focus here is
on the ideological nature of the instructional texts used in the suggested
lessons; the representations of war, pain, and suffering in the texts; and
the effects they entail for the pedagogic subjects.

The underlying assumption here is that the various texts selected for
students to read at school, often for reading comprehension purposes,
constitute part of a selective tradition that constructs specific versions of
reality for them. "But always the selectivity is the point," Williams (1976,
205) argues; "the way in which from a whole possible area of past and
present, certain meanings and practices are chosen for emphasis, certain other meanings and practices are neglected and excluded." As part
of the broader social training students receive within the institution of
school, the reading of selected texts that are part of a curriculum involves
students in a continual making and remaking of a specific reality and

ultimately in what will be considered as official knowledge (Apple 2000). The role of texts in this process is important, according to Inglis (1985, 22), because as part of a curriculum, they participate in creating what a society recognizes as legitimate and truthful.

To reveal the ideologies embedded in the texts, Kress (1989, 7) argues that we may start by asking three basic questions: (1) Why is the topic being written about? (2) How is it being written about? (3) What other ways of writing about the topic are available? By emphasizing the "how," this chapter proceeds to an analysis of the ideologies embedded in the instructional texts in *NewsHour Extra* and *Rethinking Schools*, by looking into their different "ways of writing" about war and pain. These different ways of writing are related, as we shall see in what follows, to different representations and ideological positions about the war and, ultimately, to the construction of different versions of reality for the students.

The theme of pain and suffering has been explored by media research (see, for instance, Chouliaraki 2006 and Silverstone 2007), discourse analytic research exploring the September 11 attacks and the Iraq War (see, among others, Chilton 2002, 2004; Fairclough 2005; Graham and Luke 2005; Silberstein 2004; van Dijk 2005), and linguistic research that analyzes the language of pain (Bacini 2008; Halliday 1998; Kövecses 2008; Lascaratou 2003, 2008). Contributing to this body of research, this chapter focuses on how the notions of war and pain are treated pedagogically in times of crisis.

Analyzing Representations of War

In her seminal work *The Body in Pain*, Elaine Scarry (1985) argues that war belongs to two larger categories of human experience: It is a form of *violence*, whose activity is injuring, and it is a form of *contest*, whose goal is to out-injure the opponent. However, she notices that quite often war as injury is omitted or holds a marginal position in policy and historical documents and accounts of war. Her analysis reveals how injuring disappears from the surface of discourse (by being completely omitted or by being renamed) or how, through the use of metaphors, it holds a marginal position, according to which injuring is a by-product of war (the "production" metaphor); it occurs on the road to another goal (the "road" metaphor); it is transformed into freedom (the "cost" metaphor); or it is a continual act of extension, as in the continuation of peace by other means (the "extension" metaphor).

In addition, according to Scarry (1985, 87), war is a kind of contest in which participants "arrange themselves into two sides and engage in an activity that will eventually make it possible to designate one side the winner and the other side the loser." It is this activity of reciprocal injuring, whose goal is to out-injure the opponent, that actually identifies a winner and a loser. Therefore, Scarry argues, the language of contest is crucial here, because it registers the central fact of reciprocity.

Combining Scarry's work with a critical discourse analytic perspective, this chapter explores representations of pain in the pedagogic discourses of *NewsHour Extra* and *Rethinking Schools*. Assuming that social events are represented in texts, we look at the types of representations selected to represent war and pain. However, when we represent a social event, we also recontextualize it, because we are incorporating it into the context of another social event. Drawing on Bernstein's (1990) work, Fairclough (2003) argues that social events are recontextualized according to specific principles, known as *recontextualizing principles* (Bernstein 1990, 139), which "underlie differences between the ways in which a particular type of social event is represented." He further suggests that social events are selectively "filtered" according to four main principles: (1) *presence* (which events are excluded or included), (2) *abstraction* (how abstractly or concretely events are represented), (3) *arrangement* (in what order events are represented), and (4) *additions* (to the representation of events, such as explanations, legitimations, evaluations). Whereas the purpose of this chapter is not to investigate thoroughly all types of representations in the data, and emphasis is particularly placed on the first of the principles, that of *presence,* Fairclough's account of representations provides the necessary analytic tool for analyzing pain in the two pedagogic discourses. Assuming with van Dijk (1998) that discourse structures may be used in the production and reproduction of ideologies, and taking into account the different ideological positioning of the two websites, we expect the two pedagogic discourses to draw on different representations and employ different linguistic resources and modes of meaning (van Leeuwen 1996, 34). In what follows, analyses of representations are attempted on the basis of the two angles identified by Scarry: war as *injury* and war as *contest.*

Representations of War and Pain in *NewsHour Extra*

The data analyzed from the *NewsHour Extra* portal come mainly from one thematic area entitled "The Rights of Detainees at Guantanamo Bay" and consist of a detailed five-page lesson plan for teachers, handouts with reading comprehension questions for the articles students are invited to read, teacher's keys with suggested answers, and more than twelve related readings (articles, editorials, reports, and interviews published in the *NewsHour Extra* portal). These materials were retrieved in spring 2004, when the media revealed torture at Guantanamo Bay and other prisons abroad, which caused heated debate in the United States and the rest of the world. Videos and pictures circulated through the Internet, and various feature articles; news reports; editorials; analytic articles; and interviews with prisoners, journalists, and US officials appeared in the press.

The Backgrounding of Human Suffering

Scarry (1985) argues that war as injury may disappear from the surface of discourse, through omission of human suffering and through active redescription and renaming. Concerning the latter, *NewsHour Extra* readings employ a technical language to refer to the war. For instance, they generally talk about "casualties" to refer to people dying. In one reading, interrogations are called "interviews" that have to be "equal and not unpleasant," without the use of some of the "usual psychological techniques of a police interview" and without anything insulting, according to the Geneva Convention ("Update: The Detainees"). In addition, several readings emphasize technical aspects of the war. For instance, students read legal details about Guantanamo in feature articles, such as "War and Liberties" and "Supreme Court Hears Guantanamo Case," which describe why, according to the US government, prisoners at Guantanamo should not be able to argue their cases in US courts. Abstract language is also used to refer to interrogation, as in the extract from "Inside Guantanamo" that follows. Interesting here is the use of words such as *mining* and *valuable intelligence*, and expressions such as *it's still working* and *they're getting good stuff from them*:

> NEIL LEWIS: General Jeffrey Miller, who is the commander of the joint task force that runs the prison, in an interview that day, before I left, said, "we don't want to keep any of these people a day longer than is necessary."
> However, he said they are still **mining** them for **valuable intelligence**. I would point out that's kind of a controversial point. They've been there for eighteen months; they're still getting interrogated, and whatever portion of them have **valuable intelligence** is sort of open to debate. But he says **it's still working; they're getting good stuff from them**.

However, the most outstanding characteristic of the articles students are invited to read in *NewsHour Extra* lessons is the omission of any reference to human suffering and ill treatment of the prisoners held at Guantanamo Bay. Significantly, this omission is replaced by positive accounts of Guantanamo. At a time when extensive media coverage revealed torture and bad living conditions for the prisoners, the readings for students mainly focus on the satisfactory living conditions of the prisoners, the good quality of food and medical care offered to them, the care for the prisoners' religion, and the special treatment of teenagers. A few of the texts present an idealized view of Guantanamo Bay that resembles a recreational place rather than a prison camp. First, Guantanamo Bay is represented as a "slice of America" ("Inside Guantanamo").

> M. W.: Now tell us about the camp itself. I gather security is incredibly tight.
> REPORTER: Remember, this is a strange place anyway, the naval base at Guantanamo Bay. It's on the southeastern part of Cuba.... And like a lot of military bases, it's a little slice of America, with McDonald's and a Subway and a PX.[1] But the camp, the prison camp is kept in one remote corner. It's behind these mountains.

Details are also given of the prisoners' living conditions. We are informed that when prisoners arrive, they are "issued an orange jumpsuit, a pair of sandals, towels and personal grooming items such as soap and shampoo" and stay in cells that are approximately 8 feet by 7 feet and contain a flush toilet, a small washbasin, a metal bed, a mattress, sheets, and blankets. The experienced commander of the prison is said to pay attention to details, "right down to the toothpaste" ("Update: The Detainees"). Reference is made in several articles to the "recreational period": "for two or three fifteen-to-twenty-minute periods a week they are let out individually for showers and some simple exercise in a little ... just a little area, and they usually kick around a soccer ball" ("Inside Guantanamo"); "they can go out and walk around and do calisthenics and anything that they might want to do inside the recreational center" ("Update: The Detainees").

The texts stress the prison authorities' degree of consideration for the prisoners' religions.

> And the military is very eager to demonstrate tolerance of Islam, so each cell, the inmate has a copy of the Koran ... beads, oils, for prayer. And it's the only military base in the nation or abroad in which the

Muslim call to prayer rings out five times a day from the loudspeaker. ("Inside Guantanamo")

✳ ✳ ✳

The Americans have gone to considerable lengths to provide only food deemed to be halal under the strict requirements of Islam, and each cot is etched with an arrow to indicate the direction of Mecca, which Muslims face in prayer. ("Guantanamo Bay on Trial")

Positive accounts of American soldiers are presented that create feelings of sympathy toward their case.

[The camp] is ringed by several layers of fencing and perimeters. And around it also there are soldiers who patrol in small groups usually of four, on hot, miserable Guantanamo days with green camouflage paint on their faces. ("Inside Guantanamo")

Extensive reference to the good quality of food focuses on the types of meals offered to prisoners, the effects of good meals on malnourished prisoners, and changes of the prison feeding schedule during fasting periods.

REPORTER: The food distributed to the inmates is prepared according to Muslim religious requirements. The diet is Middle Eastern.
J. K.: This is fish stew that will go on rice, plus the vegetables. They will also get a baguette, a French baguette, a small roll, bread. They'll get milk, they'll get a piece of fruit, and there will be additional cake served as well.
REPORTER: Because of the diet, officials say, detainees, many of whom arrived malnourished, have gained an average of thirteen pounds. Navy Commander T.C.D. is the base supply officer. He says it was his idea to serve the detainees culturally appropriate meals. ("Update: The Detainees")

✳ ✳ ✳

M. W.: You talk about trying to be culturally sensitive in terms of what they had in the cells. What about the food?
REPORTER: Well, they're served three meals a day, two of them hot . . . they're pretty good meals by some standards. The camp went out of its way during Ramadan to serve them breakfast quite early before

dawn, because they ... most of them fast, and something of a larger meal or a feast later. ("Inside Guantanamo")

NewsHour Extra articles also stress the special care taken of the underage prisoners. We are informed that three prisoners, ages thirteen to sixteen, are kept in a special unlocked house, and they live there communally, taking lessons in their native language, Pashto ("Inside Guantanamo"). A fourteen-year-old who was released from Guantanamo is reported to say, "I am lucky I went there, and now I miss it. Cuba was great." He describes his typical day as including watching movies, playing football with the guards, and going to classes for Pashto, English, Arabic, mathematics, science, and art. As stated in the text, "He was fascinated to learn about the solar system, and now enjoys reciting the names of the planets, starting with Earth" ("Cuba? It Was Great.").

Similarly, prisoners are reported to have good-quality medical care, probably for the first time in their lives. According to the texts, there is a traditional patient-caregiver relationship, in which "the same doctors and nurses who treat the general base population also provide medical care to detainees," who are said to be "very appreciative of the care they receive" ("Update: The Detainees").

Moreover, in addition to the overall positive picture of Guantanamo prison, there is also an exclusion of any suspicion concerning prisoners' mistreatment.

> REPORTER: Yes, I actually interviewed the head of the Washington Office of the International Committee of the Red Cross.... [He] said publicly that the conditions at the camp were just unacceptable.
> M. W.: But I gather he wasn't so much talking about physical conditions as the ... what—the sort of uncertainty of their condition?
> REPORTER: Indeed. He had no public complaints about the physical conditions—torture, food, any of those kind of things that the Red Cross usually deals with. His complaint, and the committee's complaint, is a far broader and in a sense more subtle complaint that these people are being held indefinitely with no sense of what the legal process is. ("Inside Guantanamo")

Prisoners, on the other hand, are represented as passive entities, "detainees," as the stative verb *remain* indicates in the following extract from the lesson plan: "After the terrorist attacks of 9/11 and the war in Afghanistan, the U.S. moved about six hundred captured prisoners to Guantanamo Bay. Most have remained there for the past two years without being charged with crimes or being given hearings." Notice also in the previous clause that the lack of agent, concerning who made them "remain," suggests it was their choice to stay there. A very different representation would result, for instance, through the use of the word *keep* instead, as in, "Most have been kept there for the past two years." Overall, systematic exclusion of any representations of pain characterizes most *NewsHour Extra* texts, which instead choose to focus on describing the good conditions at Guantanamo Bay. This selection is highly ideological and important, considering the time period that these texts appeared: shortly after videos showing torture were made available worldwide. Reassurance about the good conditions comes from a high-ranking military officer: "I would hope that should any of our soldiers, sailors, airmen, Marines, coast guardsmen be held as detainees, that they would receive the same kind of humane care and humane detention that we are putting on the ground every day here at JTF Guantanamo" ("Update: The Detainees").

Interestingly, the systematic omission of war as injury and of any suffering of the human body from the surface of discourse is consistent with Scarry's (1985, 64) account:

> One can read many pages of a historic or strategic account of a particular military campaign, or listen to many successive installments in a newscast narrative of events in a contemporary war, without encountering the acknowledgement that the purpose of the event described is to alter (to burn, to blast, to shell, to cut) human tissue, as well as to alter the surface, shape, and deep entirety of the objects that human beings recognize as extension of themselves.

The Foregrounding of War as Contest

On the one hand, *NewsHour Extra* texts background injuring and omit any reference to human suffering, while on the other hand, they foreground the element of war as contest. They do so in several ways. First, they emphasize the importance of out-winning the opponent through contest vocabulary, in which naming is important. Positive evaluative words are attributed to American soldiers, who are repeatedly called "freedom fighters," whereas negative evaluations are attributed to prisoners, who are called "enemy combatants," "noncitizens" ("War Liberties"), "unlawful combatants," "terror suspects" ("Military Tribunals"), and "illegal combatants" ("Update: The Detainees"). War as contest is thus emphasized through the systematic construction of polarizing subject positions of *us*

("U.S. troops," "innocent people") versus *them,* "our enemy," as in this extract from "Guantanamo Bay on Trial."

> Images of 9/11 abound at Gitmo. In the room guards use to send e-mails home, a poster showing the World Trade Center cautions, "Are you in a New York state of mind? Don't leak information—our enemy can use it to kill U.S. troops or more innocent people."

Here we often find what Scarry (1985) has identified as "road" and "cost" metaphors, which are employed in projecting the contest element of war and in inspiring patriotic feelings. According to these metaphors, war is the cost we have to pay to achieve peace, or it occurs on the road to peace. As one member of the intelligence service at the camp said to a reporter, "We are developing information of enormous value to the nation," and, "We think we're fighting not only to save and protect our families, but your families also" ("Guantanamo Bay on Trial").

These accounts contain a few negative representations of the prisoners as savages or "spoiled brats," who are in need of discipline.

> REPORTER: Guards say that in the early days, when prisoners first arrived, detainees spat, yelled at, and threw urine at them, but that now a cool and correct relationship prevails. ("Update: The Detainees")

> ＊　＊　＊

> In the camp's acute ward, a young man lies chained to his bed, being fed protein-and-vitamin mush through a stomach tube inserted via a nostril. "He's refused to eat 148 consecutive meals," says Dr. Louis Louk, a naval surgeon from Florida. "In my opinion, he's a spoiled brat, like a small child who stomps his feet when he doesn't get his way." Why is he shackled? "I don't want any of my guys to be assaulted or hurt," he says. ("Guantanamo Bay on Trial")

Negative representations of the enemy, however, come in second, after positive self-representation. The following extract is characteristic of this tendency ("Update: The Detainees").

> REPORTER: There are probably people listening right now who are cringing. These guys are accused of being terrorists. Why are we catering to their dietary needs?
> CMDR. T. C. DOWDEN: I don't believe that we're catering. I think that we would be doing the same thing that we would expect from them if

they were … if the shoe were on the other foot. If we have people who are going … who could end up being captives someplace, we would expect that our cultures, our traditions would be followed by them as well. We don't ask our staff to throw compassion out the window. We're providing medical treatment, and when you provide treatment for someone who is ill or injured, compassion is part of that.

Both the reporter ("why are we catering to their dietary needs?") and the prison authorities ("we would be doing the same thing that we would expect from them") maintain the polarizing positions. Noticeable in this last example is the use of the hypothetical *would* and *if they were* to refer to the possibility of US soldiers becoming captives of the enemy. What prevails in this extract and in several other texts is the positive representation of *us*. Treating the others the way you want others to treat you (e.g., "I think that we would be doing the same thing that we would expect from them"), respecting other cultures ("we would expect that our cultures, our traditions would be followed by them as well"), showing compassion (mentioned twice in the last extract), treating them on equal terms ("the same doctors and nurses who treat the general base population also provide medical care to detainees") all work toward a positive self-construction. Even interrogations are said to be "conducted humanely and legally," with no complaints from detainees ("Detainees at Base in Cuba Yield Little Valuable Information").

Positive attributes for the Americans, however, come not only from the American side. A released fourteen-year-old teenager is reported in one of the readings to have said, "Americans are great people, better than anyone else," "Americans are polite and friendly when you speak to them. They are not rude like Afghans," and, "If my father didn't need me, I would want to live in America" ("Cuba? It Was Great."). These positive evaluations, coming from a variety of sources (e.g., reporters, prison authorities, prison guards, prisoners themselves) portray a positive image of America. In times of war, they reinforce patriotic feelings, while maintaining the climate of polarization.

Moreover, there are instances in which the two sides are presented and the opposite perspective is considered. Even then, however, the contest element is present. An article used for reading comprehension entitled "Two Different Wars: Comparing Arab and U.S. Coverage of the Iraq War" begins by suggesting that "there are differences between the way the Arab media is reporting this war and the way it is covered by U.S. media organizations." The text continues with "neutral" and "objective" accounts: "While most U.S. media sources use the term 'coalition forces' to describe the troops, many Arab media outlets instead choose the word 'invaders.'" Interesting from the contest perspective is the description of reactions to media coverage from the same article.

> Criticism of the Arab media's war coverage has streamed in from American and British officials. British Prime Minister Tony Blair ordered a campaign last week to counteract what he calls negative coverage of war in the Arab media. American officials called the coverage of the war **inflammatory**.
>
> "I am afraid many in the Arab press have been **misconstruing** things and inflaming things. All we ask is that ... we get a fair hearing, that they look at the facts, that they not jump to conclusions," said the U.S. State Department spokesman Richard Boucher.
>
> On the other side, some Arab-Americans have criticized American coverage for being too sanitized.
>
> "There is a feeling in our newsroom that you need to be as realistic as possible and carry the images of war and the effect that war has on people," said Hafez Mirazi, Washington bureau chief of Al-Jazeera. "If you are in a war, your population shouldn't just eat their dinner and watch sanitized images on TV and video games produced by the technological whizzes in the Pentagon and say, 'This is war.'"

The voices chosen to be presented are quite revealing for their ideological positioning. Despite the attempt at an "objective" account of both sides in the first part of the text, the previous extract brings to the fore the contest element by polarizing *us* and *them*, with *them* being negatively represented as "misconstruing things and inflaming things" and *us* being positively represented as asking only for "a fair hearing." *Us* is also related to rational thinking ("look at the facts ... not jump to conclusions"), consistent with the rationality promoted through the critical thinking approach in *NewsHour Extra* (see Chapter 1). Interestingly enough, whereas the people whose voices are represented in the previous extract are on the one side American and British officials, British Prime Minister Tony Blair and US State Department spokesman Richard Boucher, the opposite side is given voice only through an Arab-American, Washington-based chief of Al-Jazeera, Hafez Mirazi. That is, the criticism of the American/British side comes from an Arab-American located in Washington and focuses on urging American media to become more realistic and abandon a sanitized coverage of the war.

Moreover, another way in which war as contest is foregrounded in *NewsHour Extra* data is through the engagement of students in contest types of activities. Specifically, students are often invited to participate in role-plays and debates, involving groups of students supporting opposing sides of an issue. As stated in the lesson plan "The Rights of Detainees at Guantanamo Bay," one of the lesson objectives is for students to "understand the clash between civil liberties and national security during wartime." Students read in one of the articles, "The administration contends that they are dangerous enemy combatants being detained and interrogated legally and humanely during the ongoing war on terrorism." They are then invited to participate in the following simulation ("Supreme Court Hears Guantanamo Case" Handout with Discussion Questions).

> Pretend you are the President of the United States. You have a suspected terrorist in custody, who may have information leading to the capture of a ring of terrorists believed to be responsible for a recent bombing. Do you, a) hold him indefinitely until you get the information you think he has, or b) give him access to a court trial where he may go free without providing any information? Explain your rationale.

One wonders what types of arguments students are likely to develop concerning the prisoners' civil liberties after reading these texts when the readings systematically avoid any reference to the constitutive elements of civil liberties, such as freedom from torture, and when they instead merely focus on the provisions offered to prisoners. Moreover, when the dilemma is between safety and security on the one hand and civil liberties on the other (which, according to the readings, are guaranteed and even graciously offered to the prisoners), then students are implicitly guided to argue in favor of national safety and security. The use of such activities point toward the adoption of a particular point of view, one that is in agreement with governmental decisions, and reinforce the foregrounding of the contest element in *NewsHour Extra* texts. Overall, here, too, in contest types of activities and in other representations of war as contest, representations of pain are missing from the texts.

Representations of War and Pain in *Rethinking Schools*

The Foregrounding of Human Suffering

In the context of developing a critical curriculum, texts in *Rethinking Schools* foreground pain and injury by emphasizing the human suffering that war brings. Instead of the technical documents students read in *NewsHour Extra* lessons, in *Rethinking Schools,* students read texts that foreground human suffering and emphasize war's actual effects on people. The agenda of *Rethinking Schools* concerning the "war against terrorism" is clearly illustrated in the following extract from an editorial addressing American teachers.

> Editorial: Teaching Against the Lies
> Summer 2004
> *By the editors of* Rethinking Schools
> As the horrifying photos and reports of U.S. military personnel abus-
> ing Iraqis at Abu Ghraib prison have made their way into the public
> eye, a clearer picture of the occupation is emerging. Even before the
> scandal broke on *60 Minutes II* in late April, Amnesty International
> warned that U.S.-led forces have "shot Iraqis dead during demonstra-
> tions, tortured and ill-treated prisoners, arrested people arbitrarily
> and held them indefinitely, demolished houses in acts of revenge and
> collective punishment." ... The question before educators is whether
> or not we are equipping students with the tools to think critically
> about our government's policies.... Some of our former students are
> coming home maimed or in body bags, while the military continues
> to step up recruiting.

Acknowledging that "it's important that a critical curriculum does not itself become propaganda, simply offering conclusions and handing students anti-war positions," the overall purpose of the published materials, according to the editors of *Rethinking Schools,* is to equip students with the thinking skills they need "for a life of democratic participation, of active citizenship." The pedagogy developed in this context is not one that focuses on technical aspects, but one that deals explicitly with the dark side of war, by illustrating the destruction war brings.

In fact, the analysis has revealed that the foregrounding of suffering in *Rethinking Schools* lessons takes place in two distinct ways: through the "reading" of visual and multimodal texts, including pictures, photos, and posters, that students are invited to analyze in class, and through the reading of feature articles and other types of texts that describe the ugly face of war.

First, students in *Rethinking Schools* are often asked to "read" and analyze different types of photos and pictures. In a lesson account entitled "Images of War,"[2] part of which is reproduced in what follows, a bilingual elementary teacher describes her teaching on images of war that her students see and don't see in the US media. In this lesson, pictures from newspapers become pedagogical texts to be analyzed in class.

I felt compelled to help students examine photos of the war on Afghanistan because, especially in those early days of bombing, the media did not portray with either words or pictures the suffering that must have been occurring in Afghanistan as a result of the U.S. attack. Through our discussion, I hoped to help students develop a critical perspective on the stories and images that they and their families are consuming everyday.

Even though the images of Sept. 11 were almost a month old, when I asked students about images from that day, an animated conversation ensued. Native speakers of Spanish and Spanish language learners shared their memories in Spanish.

"*Yo via las personas saltando de los edificios,*" said one student ["I saw the people jumping from the buildings"].

"*Yo vi la gente en la calle corriendo y tratando de escapar,*" said another ["I saw people in the streets running and trying to escape"].

"*Vi los bomberos que se murieron tratando de salvar a las personas,*" remembered a third student ["I saw the firefighters who died trying to save people"].

After several comments about people, I asked if they remembered images that did not involve people. More hands.

"*Los edificios cuando el avión chocó*" ["The buildings when the plane crashed into them"].

"*Los edificios cuando se cayeron*" ["The buildings when they collapsed"].

"*Los zapatos de una mujer que se quedó atrapada*" ["The shoes of a woman who was trapped"].

I then asked the students if they had seen any of the people in Afghanistan since the attacks began. No hands. I asked if they had seen any pictures of Afghanistan. One student raised his hand and mentioned something about a bomb dropping in the middle of a barren field. "Keep this in mind as you watch the news in the next few days. Look closely and see if you see any people," I said.

Students in this account are not mere consumers of media texts to which they respond by expressing their opinion after they have identified opposing arguments on a specific subject. The pedagogy employed here operates rather differently. It activates students by drawing on their personal experiences, by urging them to recount these experiences and talk about their feelings, and by guiding them to investigate issues for themselves (e.g., "Keep this in mind as you watch the news in the next few days. Look closely"). In addition, it foregrounds human suffering, pain, and injury, as well as physical destruction (examples of buildings collapsing), as is illustrated in the description of the following activity ("Images of War").

> That Friday, five days after the bombing began, I brought all the newspapers I had received since the U.S. attacked Afghanistan. In groups of four, students studied the *Milwaukee Journal Sentinel* or the *New York Times*. Their task was to look at all the images and pick out one image of the war in Afghanistan that impressed their group.
>
> One group found a page which had two different pictures of planes: one plane that dropped bombs and another that dropped food. One student offered a thoughtful response: "After they bomb, they will need to send food in for the children who lost their parents in the bombing."
>
> We finished looking at the pictures. "Is there anything we're not seeing?" I asked. A few hands went up slowly. Rosana said: "We're not seeing the people from Afghanistan who are dying." Roberto spoke next. "We're not seeing the war."

The pedagogy that unfolds in these extracts involves students in critical reading of the texts, a critical unpacking of the reality being constructed in the media texts. At the same time, it urges students to consider not only what is included but also what is excluded from media texts ("Is there anything we're not seeing?"), in an attempt to develop further their critical awareness and to point to an important issue concerning what is reported and what is not reported in the media texts.

Moreover, critical reading involves reading the verbal as well as the visual. Students are invited to "read" images of war and to respond to them by trying to analyze their feelings. Thus, the foregrounding of pain and suffering in *Rethinking Schools* texts is also achieved through the dramatic effect of photos showing images of war and destruction, such as wounded people, people in despair, destroyed buildings, and other scenes of injury. In a picture from a lesson about the September 11 attacks (Figure 3.1), human absence from the picture implicitly refers to human loss and death. This photo, taken on the day of the attacks, shows a tennis shoe, debris, torn documents, and correspondence coated with dust.

Human suffering and pain are not considered only from the American point of view, however. On the contrary, *Rethinking Schools* texts emphasize the horror of war for both sides. Photos play an important role here, by projecting the destructive effect of war on Americans as well as on the people on the other side. Figure 3.2, placed next to the title "Whose 'Terrorism'?" in another lesson account, illustrates the destruction brought to an Afghan family by US troops. The picture depicts residents of Kabul

**Figure 3.1 A photograph taken on September 11, 2001,
one block from the World Trade Center.**
Source: "Teaching about Sept. 11" (AP Photo/Mark Lennihan, 2001)

removing their belongings from a house damaged from bombardment. Eight civilians, including four children, are reported to have been killed when an allied bomb hit the house.

In fact, the pattern of showing in parallel the effects of war and injury is repeated in several parts of the *Rethinking Schools* materials. For instance, on the front cover of a Special Report entitled "War, Terrorism and Our Classrooms" (www.RethinkingSchools.org/special_reports/ sept11/index.shtml), there are two main photos in the center of the page, placed one below the other: The first (Figure 3.3) shows survivors fleeing the World Trade Center on the day of the attack, and the second (Figure 3.4) shows Afghan refugee children at a refugee camp set up by the Iranian Red Crescent Society in Taliban-held Afghanistan territory two kilometers from the Iranian border.

Rethinking Schools texts support the view that "education must be about developing the skills and disposition to question the official story, to view with skepticism the stark us-against-them (or us good, them bad) portrayal of the world and the accompanying dehumanization of others" ("Teaching about Sept.11"), while acknowledging that this can be especially difficult "when textbooks and pundits alike use *us, we,* and *our*

Figure 3.2 Residents of Kabul, Afghanistan, remove belongings from a house damaged from bombardment Sunday, October 21, 2001.
Source: "Whose 'Terrorism'?" (AP Photo/Amir Shah, 2001)

Figure 3.3 A woman walks with other victims amid debris near the World Trade Center on September 11, 2001.
Source: "War, Terrorism and Our Classrooms"
(AP Photo/Gulnara Samoilova, 2001)

Figure 3.4 Afghan refugee children play in the dust at the Makaki refugee camp two kilometers from the Iranian border.
Source: "War, Terrorism and Our Classrooms"
(AP Photo/Hasan Sarbakhshian, 2001)

to promote a narrow nationalism" ("Sept. 11 and Our Classrooms"). In fact, language activities and reading texts for students in *Rethinking Schools* systematically avoid polarizing positions of *us* versus *them* in which the "enemy" is negatively constructed—something found in most accounts of war, according to Scarry (1985). Instead, as we have seen, they foreground the pain and suffering that war brings to both sides.

In Figures 3.5 through 3.7, originally placed one below the other, pain is dramatically marked on the faces of all the women. The close-up of an Afghan refugee who arrived in Pakistan, having lost both her son and her husband in US air raids, and the picture of the two American women in despair, holding each other as they watch the Twin Towers burn after the terrorist attack, convey the meaning that war has the same impact on both sides. The picture of the Twin Towers burning behind the Empire State Building, placed between the two other pictures, stands symbolically in the middle as the event connecting the other two.

This symbolism constitutes a basic element of the pedagogy outlined in *Rethinking Schools* texts: It focuses on developing students' empathy, their ability to feel others' emotions as if they were their own, and realizing the

Figure 3.5 An Afghan refugee.
Source: "Sept. 11 and Our
Classrooms" (AP Photo/
Shabbir Hussain Imam, 2001)

Figure 3.6 The Twin Towers of the
World Trade Center burn behind the
Empire State Building.
Source: "Sept. 11 and Our Classrooms"
(AP Photo/Patrick Sison, 2001)

Figure 3.7 Two women hold each other as
they watch the World Trade Center burn.
Source: "Sept. 11 and Our Classrooms"
(AP Photo/Ernesto Mora, 2001)

effects of war destruction on both sides. As one teacher put it, "I want to help my students to move beyond the compassion they felt for those who died in the Sept. 11 attacks, and develop a sense of the tragedy the U.S. government is imposing on many innocent Afghani people" ("Images of War").

In his multimodal discourse analysis of photographs of the Iraq War that appeared in the European and American press in 2005 and 2006, Machin (2007) has found that civilians are mainly shown en masse, with the exception of children and women, who may be shown in close-ups. In his data, though, those close-ups seem to foreground the element of contest, indexing some kind of difference, showing, for instance, a child holding an automatic weapon. As he states, "Those women and children are not presented as enemies themselves but as part of the corruption of normality caused by the enemy, which can be restored by the humanitarian acts of the Western forces" (130). The foregrounding of the element of contest is also shown in the photos of enemy soldiers, who are depicted as badly dressed, badly armed, and lacking order and discipline. These pictures are different from the ones found in *Rethinking Schools,* in which civilians from both sides are shown to suffer equally.

Powerful war images that foreground human suffering are also conveyed through vivid descriptions in print that students are invited to read in the classroom. Following is the beginning of a speech delivered at an antiwar rally in February 2003 by Charlotte Aldebron, an American student from Maine, who asks American children to put themselves in the place of the Iraqi children ("What About the Iraqi Children?"). This speech, which is suggested as a class reading with accompanying language activities, has received worldwide attention and has been translated into many languages. As stated in the editor's note before the speech, it is an excellent example of how someone may take a different perspective.

> When people think about bombing Iraq, they see a picture in their heads of Saddam Hussein in a military uniform, or maybe soldiers with big black mustaches carrying guns, or the mosaic of George Bush Sr. on the lobby floor of the Al-Rashid Hotel with the word criminal. But guess what? More than half of Iraq's 24 million people are children under the age of fifteen. That's 12 million kids. Kids like me. Well, I'm almost thirteen, so some are a little older, and some a lot younger, some boys instead of girls, some with brown hair, not red. But kids who are pretty much like me just the same. So take a look at me, a good long

look. Because I am what you should see in your head when you think about bombing Iraq. I am what you are going to destroy.

If I am lucky, I will be killed instantly, like the three hundred children murdered by your smart bombs in a Baghdad bomb shelter on February 16, 1991. The blast caused a fire so intense that it flash-burned outlines of those children and their mothers on the walls; you can still peel strips of blackened skin, souvenirs of your victory, from the stones.

But maybe I won't be lucky and I'll die slowly, like fourteen-year-old Ali Faisal, who right now is on the death ward of the Baghdad children's hospital. He has malignant lymphoma cancer caused by the depleted uranium in your Gulf War missiles. Or maybe I will die painfully and needlessly like eighteen-month-old Mustafa, whose vital organs are being devoured by sand fly parasites. I know it's hard to believe, but Mustafa could be totally cured with just $25 worth of medicine, but there is none of this medicine because of your sanctions.

A characteristic feature of this extract is the powerful images it constructs. First, the text builds on the images that students are exposed to through the media, such as images of soldiers in military uniforms with black mustaches carrying guns. Then it turns to subjectifying the war: "Take a look at me.... I am what you should see in your head when you think about Iraq. I am what you are going to destroy." The text presents detailed descriptions of Iraqi children who are real people with real names and who were seriously hurt by American weapons. Charlotte Aldebron's speech is not a detached presentation of the war in an objective way but a political text that invites its audience to develop an alternative to the official perspective. Her words do not merely connect *us* with *them* on the same side; *I* is put in the place of *they* as a victim of a terrible death: *If I am lucky, I will be killed instantly. ... But maybe I won't be lucky and I'll die slowly. ... Or maybe I will die painfully and needlessly.*

In another text entitled "What War Looks Like,"[3] included in the *Rethinking Schools* collection of reading texts on the Iraq War, historian Howard Zinn describes the destructive effects of the (then) coming Iraq War.

In all the solemn statements by self-important politicians and newspaper columnists ... there is something missing.... What is missing is what an American war on Iraq will do to tens of thousands or hundreds of thousands of ordinary human beings who are not concerned with geopolitics and military strategy, and who just want their children to live, to grow up. They are not concerned with "national security" but with personal security, with food and shelter and medical care and peace.

I am speaking of those Iraqis and those Americans who will, with absolute certainty, die in such a war, or lose arms or legs, or be blinded. Or they will be stricken with some strange and agonizing sickness that could lead to their bringing deformed children into the world (as happened to families in Vietnam, Iraq, and also the United States).

The article continues with vivid descriptions of human suffering from previous wars. Zinn refers to the John Dos Passos novel *1919,* in which the author describes the death of John Doe in World War I: "The blood ran into the ground, the brains oozed out of the cracked skull and were licked up by the trenchrats, the belly swelled and raised a generation of bluebottle flies, and the incorruptible skeleton, and the scraps of dried viscera and skin bundled in khaki." Zinn also refers to the Vietnam War, painting pictures of women and children huddled in a trench as GIs pour automatic rifle fire into their bodies and a Vietnamese girl running down a road, her skin shredding from napalm. He contrasts the freakish details of deformed bodies with technical accounts of war casualties as they are presented in the discourse of Pentagon officials.

Ten years ago, in that first war against Iraq, our leaders were proud of the fact that there were only a few hundred American casualties (one wonders if the families of those soldiers would endorse the word "only"). When a reporter asked General Colin Powell if he knew how many Iraqis died in that war, he replied: "That is really not a matter I am terribly interested in." A high Pentagon official told *The Boston Globe,* "To tell you the truth, we're not really focusing on this question."

War as injury is systematically stressed throughout the readings in *Rethinking Schools,* thus urging the readers of the text to adopt an antiwar position and resist the dominant curriculum.

The Backgrounding of War as Contest

In her analysis of war as contest, Scarry (1985, 89) argues that what differentiates war from other types of contests is that in war, "participants must work to out-injure each other" and "although both sides inflict injuries, the side that inflicts greater injury faster will be the winner." It is in this context that different types of texts on war have worked to raise patriotic feelings and a strong national identity, often by construing polarizing positions. As Scarry (1985, 87) put it:

> In consenting to enter the war, the participants enter into a structure that is a self-cancelling duality. They enter into a formal duality, but one understood by all to be temporary and intolerable, a formal duality that, by the very force of its relentless insistence on doubleness, provides the means for eliminating and replacing itself by the condition of singularity.

Working systematically against such an account of war constructions, *Rethinking Schools* texts position their pedagogy against the element of contest. They do so by either backgrounding the element of war as contest or by actively involving students in readings that deconstruct such well-settled views. One way to achieve this is by working on students' empathy, which involves caring for the other side as well as their own and going against narrow nationalist views. As one teacher said, "I also wanted to help my students understand the power of empathy, and how people gain strength by coming together in times of crisis" ("Letters to the Universe"). In the words of another teacher, active citizenry entails that "children locate themselves in widening circles of care that extend beyond self, beyond country, to all humanity" ("Sept. 11 and Our Classrooms").

Consequently, the stories students read about the "war against terrorism" are not ones that raise feelings of hatred and fear (e.g., "our national security and safety are in danger"), which justify the decision to go to war. On the contrary, readings focus on themes such as world peace and an understanding of the "other" not as an enemy but as a human being suffering the consequences of war. In a lesson account entitled "Not in Our Son's Name," students are asked to read a letter (provided in the following excerpt) written by the parents of one of the World Trade Center victims before the bombing of Afghanistan began.

By Phyllis and Orlando Rodriguez
Our son Greg is among the many missing from the World Trade Center attack. Since we first heard the news, we have shared moments of grief, comfort, hope, despair, fond memories with his wife, the two families, our friends and neighbors.

We see our hurt and anger reflected among everybody we meet. We cannot pay attention to the daily flow of news about this disaster. But we read enough of the news to sense that our government is heading in the direction of violent revenge, with the prospect of sons, daughters, parents, friends in distant lands, dying, suffering, and nursing further grievances against us. It is not the way to go. It will not avenge our son's death. Not in our son's name.

Our son died a victim of an inhuman ideology. Our actions should not serve the same purpose. Let us grieve. Let us reflect and pray. Let us think about a rational response that brings real peace and justice to our world. But let us not as a nation add to the inhumanity of our times.

Although they lost their son in the September 11 attack, Phyllis and Orlando Rodriguez call for peace and an understanding of what has happened within a much broader context. War here is not understood as a contest in which *we* should out-injure the opponent. Students who read this letter are then asked to adopt the Rodriguezes' perspective and write an editorial responding to the policies of the US government in the weeks after the Rodriguez letter.

Elsewhere, students read and respond to a poem by Lucille Clifton entitled "We and They."[4] The poem concludes:

> and "we" and "they" is just a game
> and the wind is a friend that
> doesn't fuss
> and every They is
> actually Us.

As we saw in Chapter 2, poetry is widely used in *Rethinking Schools* lesson plans, in order to build students' empathy. In this poem as well as other readings, war as contest is completely backgrounded. Students are not invited to consider the "other" as an enemy or to out-injure the opponent; *we* and *they* are on the same side: *us*.

Pedagogies of War

Scarry (1985, 63) argues that the essential structure of war resides in the *relation* between collective casualties that occur *within* war and the verbal issues that stand *outside* war: the various discourses before, during, and after the act of war. Her analysis of the interior content of war as constituting a form of violence, whose activity is injuring, and as a form of contest, whose activity is to out-injure the opponent, provides a useful theoretical and analytic tool in exploring representations of pain and suffering in two pedagogic discourses dealing with the "war against terrorism." Elaborating on Scarry's model, Table 3.1 summarizes the findings.

Table 3.1 War as Injury and as Contest in *NewsHour Extra*
and *Rethinking Schools*

	War as Injury	War as Contest
NewsHour Extra	Backgrounded	Foregrounded
Rethinking Schools	Foregrounded	Backgrounded

Scarry argues that it is in the relationship between the two (war as injury and war as contest) rather than in either individually that the nature of war resides. Based on this claim, it becomes clear that if we want to engage in a deeper understanding of the war pedagogies outlined in the previous sections, we need to approach the model suggested in Table 3.1 across both the horizontal and vertical axes. In other words, what differentiates the two pedagogies relies not simply on the foregrounding of pain in *Rethinking Schools* and the backgrounding of pain in *NewsHour Extra.* The pedagogy employed by *NewsHour Extra* also obtains its meanings by the foregrounding of war as contest, whereas the pedagogy outlined in *Rethinking Schools* is considerably affected by the backgrounding of the contest element of war.

Furthermore, analysis of representations in the data has revealed other important elements that permeate the categories of war as both injury and contest. For instance, *NewsHour Extra* texts have been found to systematically build on the creation of a positive self-presentation. Elements of the *Rethinking Schools* pedagogy include critical reading of what is there (and of what is not there) in the texts, reading of the verbal and the visual, and building of students' empathy.

An important difference between the pedagogies concerns the student needs they address. The critical thinking pedagogy employed in *NewsHour Extra* places particular emphasis on helping students develop thinking and analytical skills, in order to "understand a current events issue happening right now and why it's important" in their life. It assumes that the students already have the intellectual resources they will need in order to develop an authentic voice and express themselves, using language to tell the truth as they perceive it. A special section in the *NewsHour Extra* website, *Speak Out,*[5] hosts student writings, such as *editorials,* where students express personal opinions on important current events; *stories,* where students share experiences that have affected them personally;

debates, where students outline different perspectives on an issue; and *poetry,* where students create their own poems. In this account, students should be creative and take chances, let their "natural voices speak out," and produce writing that is fresh and has integrity (Grabe and Kaplan 1996, 88).

In the context of a critical pedagogy, *Rethinking Schools,* on the other hand, seeks "to respond to students' emotional and intellectual needs," yet in a different way from the one employed in *NewsHour Extra* pedagogy. The purpose here is to equip students with "habits of skepticism" and tools to reflect on the world around them. It also employs the systematic use of a meta-language, which shows how "a critical perspective on the world differs from what they might encounter in their textbooks or on the nightly news" ("Teaching against the Lies").

At this point, a connection can be made between the pedagogies of war employed in the two websites (which includes the specific combinations of foregrounding and backgrounding of pain) and the ideological positions of the two websites on the "war against terrorism." Students are presented with different aspects of reality in the two sites, aspects that are consistent with the implicit or explicit ideological positions of each site and the pedagogies each promotes. One supports the US decision to go to war (at least in its initial stages), thus objectifying the war and treating it as a technical issue from a detached point of view. The other challenges the decision to go to war, thus subjectifying the war, by raising students' empathy and by emphasizing the destruction that accompanies war activities.

Part B
Curricular Materials for Teachers

Chapter 4

The Genre of Lesson Plans

THE PREVIOUS THREE CHAPTERS FOCUSED ON THE WAYS STUDENTS experience the informal curriculum comprising the body of suggested lessons in the *NewsHour Extra* and *Rethinking Schools* portals. Chapters 1 and 2 presented the pedagogies that the two informal curricula draw from and analyzed the language activities in the suggested lessons. Chapter 3 analyzed the embedded ideologies in the media and other texts that function as reading texts in the suggested lessons. The emphasis in this and the next chapters shifts from students to teachers and the ways teachers experience the curriculum through their engagement with the lesson plans. This chapter starts with a conceptualization of lesson planning as a historical and cultural practice and a suggestion for reading lesson plans within their sociohistorical context. It provides a brief review of related research concerning what we call the *traditional lesson plan* and moves to an analysis of the genre of lesson plan in *NewsHour Extra,* by illustrating its organization. I suggest that *NewsHour Extra* lesson plans constitute a sophisticated version of traditional lesson plans, which are descriptive and procedural, follow a strict format resembling that of a technical document, and have formal and "objective" language. The second part of the chapter presents a brief account of the *reflective lesson plan,* which I describe as an alternative to the *traditional lesson plan.* The analysis that follows explores *Rethinking Schools'* lesson plans as retrospective versions of the *reflective lesson plan,* because they have been written after a particular class has been conducted, and they use personalized language addressing colleagues and describing their personal experience, including personal evaluations, uncertainties, failures, and successes.

This chapter shows that the genre of lesson plans is differently realized in the two portals. However, these generic differences go beyond differences in style and format. Like Volosinov (1986, 23), who saw genre realizations not simply as moments of the choice, assembly, and reproduction of forms and techniques, but as sites where "differently oriented social interests within one and the same sign community" intersect, contest, and struggle, I approach the genre of lesson plan as "a nexus for struggles over difference, identity and politics" (Luke 1996, 317). From this perspective, the differential manifestations of the genre of lesson plans in *NewsHour Extra* and *Rethinking Schools* are explored as articulations of their different ideological positions, which, as we shall see, are about the Iraq War as much as they are about wider pedagogical and educational matters.

The Lesson Plan as a Historical and Cultural Practice

Lesson planning has been variously approached by educational researchers, who have generated considerable discussion concerning its features, format, and use in the educational process. This book focuses on the different manifestations of the lesson plan genre and their ideological underpinnings. We will, thus, approach lesson planning as a historical and cultural practice that is "handed down through the institutional practices of teacher education and professional development programs" (Tasker et al. 2010, 130). Analyzing the lesson plans within their sociocultural and historical contexts is important, if we take into account that dominant forms of pedagogical processes develop within specific educational and sociohistorical contexts. Therefore, although lesson plans can be seen as texts that mediate the actions of the teacher, at least in print, these actions are neither purely personal nor incidental. They are rooted in well-established institutional practices, theories of language, learning, and teaching that constitute the dominant paradigm of the time. When a paradigm shift takes place, practices change, and so do the ways we use to record them. It is in these cases that genre changes may be noted. In this sense, we may conceive of lesson plans as symbolic texts that, at least externally, mediate teaching processes.

At the same time, it is important to consider that, although a lesson plan is not a real lesson, it is, however, a way of getting close to what is expected to take place in the actual teaching process (Linne 2001, 135). It is also a way of identifying elements of the dominant classroom discourse in a particular educational context. In her analysis of late nineteenth- and early twentieth-century lesson plans, Linne (2001) explores how the lesson as pedagogical text was structured in the early periods of modern compulsory schooling in Sweden. Her analysis captures genre changes that, as she suggests, are indicative of wider educational and social changes. She also argues that the lesson plans at the beginning of the twentieth century reflect dominant themes in the curriculum code and the mentality of the period (145), and she claims that

> the formation of classroom discourse, as historically and socially constructed, is reflected in the lesson plans. Both what is said and the rules of how it is said—the discursive rules—contribute to the creation of the meaning of the text. (140)

To illustrate her point, Linne describes the ritual of reading a text found in the lesson plans, which, she suggests, is characteristic of the specific classroom discourse: First the teacher reads a biblical text, then one or all of the pupils read it, and next it is divided into pieces and read again. Reading aloud in the classroom, so that everyone can hear and the teacher can correct possible mistakes, is a core part of this ritual. Such an account also indicates the teacher's and students' role in this classroom discourse, she argues. The focus is clearly on the teacher, who takes the leading role, and students are not participants in a conversation but rather represent an abstract collection of silent voices.

Linne argues that relating lesson plans to classroom discourse enhances their understanding within their sociohistorical context. If we take into account that a lesson plan is a text that stands for something else—the lesson—then we may explore its embedded and implicit assumptions about the elements of a good lesson and the legitimate ways of recording them in a document. For instance, today many templates are available for lesson plans; these are often presented as objective and universal tools to be used in different educational contexts. Many of them are online environments produced by software companies that claim to make teachers' lives easier (see Chapter 5) and that promote the lesson plans in the market as effective tools in the service of educators. In this context, writing a lesson plan is considered mainly a technical skill to be mastered by teachers of different educational contexts and cultures. However, as Lave and Wenger (1991, 76) state, any tool or technology "is intricately tied to the cultural practice and social organization with which the technology is meant to function." This does not seem to be the case with these market templates, which, far from being neutral, are reflective of a particular type of educational professionalism. Koutsogiannis (2004) brings the example of templates that are translated almost verbatim from English into other languages and are promoted as ideal solutions to the problems of various local settings, regardless of language and cultural context. He argues that the noted tendency toward uniformity is particularly problematic for the less-spoken languages, mainly because these semiotic resources are alien to the history and culture of these societies.

Attempting to approach lesson plans within their sociohistorical context (both at a broader sociocultural level and at the more specific educational context in which they appear), the following analysis focuses on the structure of the lesson plans, their discursive patterns, the narrative in which these texts involve both teachers and students, and the effects on the pedagogic subjects they discursively construct. As we shall see, the lesson plans in the two portals are involved in the formation of two different types of classroom discourse at a critical historical time, not only for the American nation but for the whole world. By inquiring into the forms and content of these texts, which represent classroom discourses from two different pedagogical paradigms, we will also look into the pedagogic identities discursively constructed for both teachers and students.

The Traditional Lesson Plan

This section offers a brief review of related literature and looks into the genre of lesson plan. Placing the genre in its broader historical and cultural context and examining the various tensions and trends around the genre will help us understand how the dominant generic structure of the lesson plan has come to take its present form and what its underlying ideological, epistemological, and theoretical bases are.

What is widely known today as the typical lesson plan has its origins in Tyler's (1950) model of curriculum planning, which identifies four main steps: (1) specify objectives, (2) select learning activities, (3) organize learning activities, and (4) specify evaluation procedures. Most importantly for this model, which has been recommended for all levels of education (Clark and Peterson 1986), planning progresses logically from one's goals and objectives. Although the model was first formulated in the 1950s, it gained greater prominence in the 1960s and 1970s, during curriculum reforms. Yinger (1980) notes that this model of curriculum planning, known as the *rational model*, was originally adapted from models of economics and national and city planning. Because of the "rational and scientific appeal" that it attributed to educational curriculum, Yinger (1980, 108) continues, this model has managed to affect all types of educational planning, from curriculum to teachers' daily planning. John (2006, 485) argues that much of the attraction of the rational model to lesson planning lies in its "elegant simplicity." He also claims (487) that four main reasons account for why the rational model has become the dominant model and has maintained its popularity for several decades. The first reason is a well-established view that inexperienced teachers need to learn how to plan in a rational way first, before they develop more complex lesson structures. A second argument that is often made is that students need to follow the same model required by official documents. This means, however, according to John, that students are prepared for teaching as required by policy makers, not as required by the needs of classroom teaching. A third argument is that the use of a commonly agreed upon model helps communication among teachers and other personnel. Finally, it is argued that when all teachers follow the rational plan, it is easier to manage, assess, and direct their work. In this account, the use of the lesson plan was mainly viewed as a way to monitor (inexperienced) teachers' work, to achieve some kind of uniformity when discussing a lesson, and to provide a conventionalized way of recording classroom experience.

John (2006) identifies four sequential steps in the genre of the rational lesson plan, which for presentation purposes are described in Table 4.1. A problem with this model is that it isolates means and ends as successive steps and that it views planning and teaching as linear processes that proceed from preplanned opening to predetermined ending (Doyle and Holm 1998). Important aspects of planning and teaching are lost

Table 4.1 The Genre of the Rational Lesson Plan

Step 1	Selection of the topic to be taught.
	Student age and ability range are major factors in the early consideration of aims and objectives.
Step 2	Exemplification of aims and objectives.
	Learning objectives and goals are specified.
Step 3	Consideration of the teaching methods and learning experiences: The lesson plan is broken down into activities (type of activity, time, and materials are specified).
Step 4	Assessment process: Efficacy of the teaching methods and activities are measured against the set objectives.

when students have to conform to rigid templates and wrestle with the technical aspects of a lesson plan in which "teaching and learning are broken down into segments or key elements, which are then sub-divided into tasks, which are further broken down into behaviors and assessed by performance criteria" (John 2006, 487). Consequently, the rational lesson plan, with its variations, may look good on paper, but it is, to a great extent, predictive and prescriptive.

Zahorik (1970) was perhaps the first to conduct empirical research on lesson plans. He concluded that the typical planning model makes teachers less sensitive to students' needs and more rigid in their teaching. He argues that once teachers identify lesson outcomes, their teaching is focused on achieving them and not on dealing with students' ideas. He proposes a model of lesson plans that includes specific teaching behaviors that would be sensitive to pupils' needs, would reflect on pupils' remarks and ideas, and would enable the teacher to decide when and in what order to use them.

The role of aims and objectives in lesson planning has become a point of investigation by several researchers, who have challenged the linear model of lesson planning (Clark and Peterson 1986). For instance, Sardo Brown (1990) suggests that a single format for lesson plans restricts teachers and discourages them from using nontraditional instructional models, such as cooperative learning, and the research conducted by Kagan and Tippins (1992) concludes that the traditional lesson plan format is counterproductive for both elementary and secondary teachers for different reasons. This linearity is attributed, according to Mallows (2002), to Newtonian, positivist, and mechanistic discourses that dominate our view of the world, the teaching profession, and consequently all educational practices. Mallows (7) argues that traditionally, "we approach lesson plan 'construction' through Newtonian eyes," by focusing on aims and sub-aims, deciding before the class what students should learn. At this point he agrees with Zahorik (1970) that careful planning does not leave any room for reaction to students' needs as they appear in the course of a lesson, because the lesson is driven by the teacher's linear expectations. Mallows also notices that, although teachers are trained in their preservice education to view aims and sub-aims as the building blocks of a lesson, there is always the risk of "hindering their ability to view the whole of the lesson" and of ultimately "producing teachers who are unaware of the complex patterns that are woven in the interaction between learners and the language to which they are exposed, and which they produce" (8). A similar consideration is raised by Tasker et al. (2010, 135), who draw a useful distinction between *being prepared* (i.e., knowing about the topic and deciding how to present it) and *being planned*, or having a rigid plan for how to teach something and following it regardless of students' reactions.

A number of models for lesson plans have been proposed based on research findings, and researchers often discuss what should be included in a lesson plan. For instance, combining the models proposed by Knop (1982) and James (1992), Rifkin (2003) provides guidelines for lesson planning in the foreign language classroom. He proposes a spiral *five-phase lesson plan,* which includes the *overview* phase, the *preparation* phase, the *drill and practice* phase, the *check* phase, and the *follow-up* phase.[1] Related research has also explored the planning practices of novice and experienced teachers (Carter et al. 1987; Kinchin and Alias 2005; Roskos 1996) and has concluded that they differ significantly. It is generally thought that novice teachers rely more on detailed, step-by-step lesson plans; do not anticipate students' reactions; and are not able to make adjustments when needed, because of their focus on implementing the lesson plan. Experienced teachers, it is said, tend to plan in more circular and learner-centered ways, paying less attention to what they are doing and focusing more on actual student learning (Tasker et al. 2010). According to Thornbury (1999, 4), this happens because experienced teachers have *experientially gathered lesson blueprints,* that is, internalized representations of lessons that act as examples for the lessons to be taught.

Lesson plans have been used for a variety of purposes, ranging from professional training to promotion of examples of good practice, and in many contexts,[2] but what is presented here under the heading of *traditional lesson plan* does not constitute a single, unified tradition of lesson planning. Quite the opposite. This brief review aims mainly to reveal how the notion of *lesson plan* has progressed in educational research and how the genre of lesson plans has taken its current form as a dominant professional tool. The term *traditional,* which some readers may not accept, has two main meanings in the context of this book. First, it refers to the dominant genre in the minds of most educators of what a lesson plan is and how it is structured. This linear, scripted lesson plan is in fact the most common form of planning. Second, the term *traditional* is used in contrast to the *reflective* lesson plan, (analyzed later in this chapter), which constitutes an alternative to the dominant genre.

The Genre of *NewsHour Extra* Lesson Plans

Like the linear, traditional lesson plan model, the lesson plans in *NewsHour Extra* follow a specific format quite strictly. They target different grade levels (mostly grades 7–12) and school subjects, such as English, mathematics, journalism, history, world history, and government. They are sophisticated documents, characterized by professionalism and advanced technicality. Table 4.2 presents the parts of the genre of lesson plan as it is realized in *NewsHour Extra*. Although minor variations may be found, most of the curriculum's lesson plans follow this template.

Table 4.2 The Lesson Plan Template in *NewsHour Extra*

Title of the lesson	Descriptive content title
Type of the lesson	e.g., critical analysis
Author and affiliation	e.g. Lisa Greeves, English and journalism teacher
Overview/ background	Includes introduction to the general theme and lesson objectives
Time	e.g., 30 minutes
Materials	A list of necessary materials (e.g., handouts, notebooks and pens, Internet connection) usually in bullet form
Procedure	A step-by-step analysis of classroom activities (numbered steps)
Extension ideas/ homework	Suggestions for additional activities
Correlation to national standards	Reference and links to national standards
Short author biographical note	Includes information concerning author's typical qualifications, affiliation, and teaching experience.
Contact information	To find out more about opportunities to contribute to this site, contact Leah Clapman at extra@NewsHour.org.

A thematic title in large, capital letters gives the reader an idea of the main topic to be discussed in the lesson plan, and a description of the type of lesson appears in the next line. In most cases, the lessons are characterized as *critical analysis,* as shown in the following examples.

MILITARY WOMEN
Critical Analysis

✳   ✳   ✳

CREATING A NEW MEDIA IN THE ARAB WORLD
Critical Analysis

In other cases, though, the description of the lesson becomes more specific, by referring to the type of suggested activities, as in the following example.

DEBATING IRAQ
Discussion Questions, Role Plays and Vocabulary Development

Combination of these two types is also common:

A CALL TO JIHAD
Critical Analysis and Role Play

*   *   *

RESPONDING TO QUOTES AND APHORISMS
Critical Analysis and Writing

The author of the lesson plan follows in the third line, together with his/her title and/or affiliation (e.g., English teacher; assistant editor with *Online NewsHour* and a former high school English and journalism teacher; a social studies teacher at Thomas Jefferson High School for Science and Technology in Alexandria, Virginia; or teacher and executive director of the Constitution Project in Portland, Oregon).

The main headings of the lesson plan are marked in bold letters, and they align left. They typically include sections on overview/background, objectives, materials, procedure, extension ideas/homework, and national standards. The section on national standards is a relatively recent addition to the lesson plan templates, and its inclusion is related to the prominence given to national standards in the United States education system since the 1990s. The fact that the same format is generally followed in all lesson plans leads us to the assumption that authors are given some general specifications on how to structure the overall lesson plan and each section separately. The lesson plans are quite detailed, usually ranging from three to five printed pages, and they adopt the formal language usually found in traditional lesson plans. Emphasis is placed on objectives and a detailed description of activities to be handled in class in a prespecified order.

The overview section (called "Background" in some lesson plans) is usually a paragraph long (although in some cases it extends to more paragraphs), and it provides useful background information concerning the topic to be dealt with in the specific lesson plan. The paragraph starts with some factual background information, presented in an impersonal tone that aims to introduce the reader to the topic. This is identified as Move 1[3] in Table 4.3. The present tense is extensively used here to indicate proximity in time, hence verifiability, factuality, and reality (Hodge and Kress 1988, 126). The next part of the overview (identified as Move

2) connects the general topic to the specific lesson and introduces the broad aim of the lesson. The most frequently used tense here is future, to indicate predictability (e.g., "This activity will guide teachers and students through analysis of initial war coverage," "This lesson plan asks students to consider ..."), although imperative may also be used (e.g., "Explore with your journalism students the pros and cons of ..."). Personalized language is used in most cases, because the texts address their intended readers (assumed to be teachers) directly (e.g., your students, your class). This is a feature of several media texts (McLoughlin 2000) that address a large, yet unspecified, body of readers (here, teachers who will read these lesson plans online). A third, optional part (Move 3) presents the suggested educational context for the lesson in a rather formulaic way (e.g., "*This lesson is especially relevant* in a government or civics class *but may be used in* any social studies class."). This is the most typical ordering of the information, although variations do exist that present the second part first (as in the second example in Table 4.3).

Table 4.3 Moves in the "Overview" Section of Two *NewsHour Extra* Lesson Plans

Overview:	MOVE 1 (S 1–2)
The coalition forces are introducing a new television station and newspaper to the Iraqi people in the hopes of bringing them messages about the new future of Iraq. In English, the new Arabic TV network will be called "Towards Freedom."	
Explore with your journalism students the pros and cons of introducing government-sponsored media into a war-torn country and whether the news conveyed will be considered to be information or propaganda. ("Creating a New Media in the Arab World")	MOVE 2 (S 3)
Overview:	MOVE 2 (S 1)
In this lesson, your students will examine U.S. embassies and the work they do in order to better understand why they are sometimes targets of terrorist attacks. As the U.S. returns sovereignty to Iraq and establishes a large embassy there, students will consider the role embassies play and how this role sometimes varies depending on the host country. This lesson is especially relevant in a government or civics class but may be used in any social studies class in which current events or international relations are discussed. ("The Role of American Embassies")	MOVE 1+2 (S 2)

Estimated time and grade level appropriate for the specific lesson plan may also be included in the overview section or follow separately in short sections.

The objectives section is typically presented in bullet form, through the use of strong modality realized with *will* or *should*. The objectives may be identified in terms of the content that will be developed in the lesson, as in the following example ("Who Should Rule the Interim Government in Iraq?").

Objectives:
- Students should look at the potential groups and individual leaders and decide who should have power in postwar Iraq.
- Students should consider the priorities of the new government.
- Students should understand who the potential leaders are and the issues they will confront.

They may also be recorded according to the language activities students will be involved in ("Reporting on War in the 21st Century").

Students will:
1. Review the components of a news article and lead.
2. Review interviewing strategies, sources, and ethical concerns involved with general reporting.
3. Identify the main elements of a news article in selected examples.
4. Discuss observations and comparisons.
5. Write a reaction to an extension reading.

The next section, "Time," is a short one that specifies the time required for the completion of the suggested lesson. This usually ranges from an individual activity, which may take twenty to thirty minutes, to a series of lessons. The materials section, which is organized in bullet form and which describes the resources that will be needed to complete the suggested lesson, comes next ("The Role of American Embassies").

Materials:
- Online *NewsHour Extra* Article: U.S. Opens First American Embassy in Baghdad in Over a Decade: http://www.pbs.org/newshour/extra/features/jan-june04/iraq_6-28.html (Printer-friendly PDF)
- HANDOUT (Printer-friendly PDF)
- TEACHER KEY (Printer-friendly PDF)

- Computers with Internet access or printed copies of articles from the Web sites given below.

In addition to *NewsHour Extra* articles and downloadable handouts (with activities, definitions of terms, quotes, transcripts with extracts from discussions, interviews, etc.), a wealth of electronic materials becomes available to the teachers through the portal, such as maps of Iraq, articles from other sources, and various public documents. Less frequently, teachers are invited to collect their own materials (e.g., copies of local, regional, and national newspaper articles). In addition, computers with Internet access, notebooks, and pens are noted among the materials needed.

The procedure section provides a detailed description of the steps to be followed to complete the activities in the classroom. It is the largest part of the lesson plan, usually extending from one to three printed pages, and it consists of numbered parts that address the order to be followed. There is a linear progression from one step to another. Information here is structured in the form of instructions grammatically realized through the use of imperatives, as in the next example (e.g., *begin, show, have, discuss*). It is this section of the lesson plan, more than the others, that can be seen as characteristic of classroom discourse. Teachers are specifically told what to do and how to do it in the classroom. In this sense, this section tells the story of the suggested lesson (with a beginning, development, and an end) from the perspective of the teacher, as the next example illustrates ("The Role of Exiles in Post-Saddam Iraq").

Procedure:
1. Begin by providing for the students two relevant definitions.
2. Then show students the *NewsHour* transcript with Iraqi-Americans, or provide transcript of it to read as a class. (Click here for streaming video).
3. Next, have the students carefully read the *Online NewsHour* article on the exiles in Iraq, either independently or in pairs.
4. Afterwards, have the students work in pairs or small groups to address the following question: *What could be some of the obstacles that exiles may encounter when working with the Iraqi civilian population?*
5. Discuss the responses as a class in relation to the excerpt on Afghan exiles from *The Christian Science Monitor.*

No doubt this will be a sophisticated and carefully organized lesson, but what is the role of students in this and other similar lessons? A reading of the procedure section from the students' perspective is quite revealing. Students' reactions may not be anticipated, but their behavior is to a great extent predicted, because the context within which they are invited to function is rather restricted. The next example focuses on only those parts of the procedure section that refer to students ("Reporting on War in the 21st Century").

Procedure:
1. Review with students the main components of a news article.
2. Provide students with copies of Handout #2 and Handout #3. Have students read these two handouts prior to step 3.
3. Have students read each article silently.
4. After students have finished reading, have students brainstorm silently for ten minutes the similarities and differences that they can see.
5. Share as a class the students' observations of similarities and differences in the news articles. For instance, students might point out that ... or....
6. Encourage students to discuss as a class each of the following:
7. Finally, ask students to determine if any of the information seems to have been derived from pool reporting or from a press conference.
8. For homework, provide students with a copy of Handout #4. Have students read it and write a response to it. Students should react in two ways to this article.

In almost all the cases in this lesson, student actions are a reaction to teachers' actions. When they are asked to do something on their own, as in the case of homework, the framework is given to them (Step 8) and it is very restricted (e.g., "react in two ways to this article"). It is obvious that student responses are to a great degree specified in advance and known to the teacher, and there is no space for student creativity. Similarly, there is no indication in these lessons of how to deal with students' feelings, views, or emotions. The element of control seems to be quite important. The type of professionalism permeating these lesson plans is closely related to controlling all aspects of the lesson and predicting them beforehand.

The next section, Extension Ideas, describes in detail additional activities (e.g., project work or writing tasks) to be used either in class or to be assigned for homework. Again here, students have to operate in a prespecified and rather rigid framework ("The Decision to Go to War").

Extension Ideas:
Ask students to select one of the following quotes and respond thought-fully and analytically in writing. This activity may be done in class or for homework. Responses should demonstrate students' understanding of the quote as well as reveal their thoughts and concerns regarding the possibility of war. You may also wish to use the quotes to spark further discussion or review vocabulary terms.

In this suggestion for activity, for instance, students choose one of the quotes given to them so they can respond to it in a specified way (in writing) in order to do specific things: demonstrate their understanding of the quote and reveal their thoughts and concerns regarding an issue also given to them.

The last section of the lesson plan is on national standards. Its length varies from a few lines to a page or two. Reference is made to the specific national standards the suggested lesson adheres to, and occasionally the content of each national standard is provided, as in the following example ("Reporting on War in the 21st Century").

National Standards:
National Council for the Social Studies
    Standard V: Individuals, Groups and Institutions
Social studies programs should include experiences that provide for the study of interactions among individuals, groups, and institutions.
    Standard VI. Power, Authority and Governance
Social studies programs should include experiences that provide for the study of how people create and change structures of power, authority, and governance.

Actually, national standards hold a prominent position in *NewsHour Extra* lesson plans. In addition to their placement at the end of each lesson plan, in some cases, there is a hyperlink entitled "Correlation to National Standards" (in bold letters), placed as a separate section after Materials and before Procedure, which leads directly to the last section of the lesson plan. Often the standards are briefly mentioned, and a link to the website shows where the teacher can find them in detail.

Overall, the language employed in *NewsHour Extra* lesson plans is formal and impersonal, appropriate to the "objectivity" that a technical document is endowed with. The detailed reference to national standards actually reinforces the technical aspect of the text, adding credibility to the professional style of the lesson plans.

The lesson plan concludes with a brief biographical note, usually three to five lines long, by the author. Although variations do exist, this is the basic format followed by the lesson plans on the *NewsHour Extra* website. In fact, the same template is being used for the lesson plans in other subjects and topics as well.

National Standards

To understand the significance of the extensive reference to national standards in the *NewsHour Extra* lesson plans and their absence, as we shall see in what follows, from the *Rethinking Schools* lesson plans, it is useful to look briefly at the history of the standards and some of the issues that have been raised during their implementation. National curricula and standardized testing were at the center of educational reform in various English-speaking and other countries during the 1990s (Tyler 1999). Discussion about national standards in the United States started in the early 1980s, when policy makers primarily called for national intervention in education (Kirst and Guthrie 1994, 159). In 1990, President Bush announced world-class content standards and a set of achievement tests in five core subjects, a position followed by the Clinton administration in the later years. *National standards* and *performance assessment* became the buzzwords of the 1990s in US education. Work on four national projects commissioned by the US Department of Education was succeeded by work at state and local levels. Educators, administrators, and policy makers were to decide whether and how they would incorporate national standards into their program of study, but more often than not, they disagreed about what quality standards are (Rhoads, Sieber, and Slayton 1996).

Educational theorists have voiced various opinions on the usefulness of national standards and the ways they have been implemented. Reflecting on experience from standards implementation, Hughes (2004) suggests that teachers now tend to focus more on what is being tested, by training students into skills-based and memorized linear knowledge, and they often neglect other significant areas of the curriculum that may not be measured. In effect, he argues that

> a reliance on standards as the solution to perceived ineffectiveness has disconnected education from the more complex set of needs that should be addressed. To meet standards, teachers must often ignore issues which may also need to be addressed, but for which they are not being evaluated. Additionally, teachers must allow someone else to

determine what is of value—even if that means ignoring the cognitive, cultural, and societal developmental needs of learners. (43)

The paradox here seems to be that whereas standards initially entered schools in order to combat student failure, their implementation has actually led to keeping children from succeeding in school because of the resulting narrow curriculum that does not engage them. For Apple (1993, 1996b), the problem with national standards is that they are not employed to investigate the real patterns of differential benefits American schools produce. Through a rhetoric of "declining achievement," they have merely managed to increase the power of state-centered testing, to disqualify poor students, to intensify teachers' jobs in one more way, and even to blame schools. According to Apple (1996a, 2001), national standards constitute part of the neoconservative agenda that aims to centralize control over "official knowledge" and of the neoliberal agenda, which aims to turn schools into places whose primary function is to meet the needs of the economy, viewing students merely as future employees. In an era where the citizen is replaced by the individual consumer, Apple cautiously suggests that through their centralizing and rationalizing impulses, national standards may serve as the first steps toward marketization and privatization: "Employers will rely on high school transcripts and there will be a closer connection between what schools focus on and the skills needed to 'succeed in the workplace'" (Apple 1996b). In addition, McLaren (1995, 31) suggests that "the application of rigorous standards is never innocent of social, economic, and institutional contexts," and he argues that the standards of achievement for all young Americans are "premised on the cultural capital of the Anglo middle class" (122). As a result, the gap will widen between those with the monetary capital to gain intellectual capital and those who will be prepared only for low-wage, routine work.

In addition, national curricula have been seen as a defensive and protective device of an "imagined national past" (Tyler 1999), which reaffirms national shared knowledge and values and produces subjects with a national identity (see Dendrinos 2001). Street (1995, 125) makes an interesting connection between educational discourses and discourses of nationalism, arguing that the signification of literacy needs

> to be decoded not simply in terms of a discourse around education—school quality, teacher performance, testing and evaluation, approaches to writing instruction, and the like—but in terms of discourses of nationalism: it is around the concept of nation and national identity that the social issues currently diverted into the literacy debate essentially focus.

He brings up the example of literacy "standards" in the United States, which he suggests make explicit and implicit reference to nationalism. Street specifically refers to Hirsch's (1988) concept of *cultural literacy*, arguing that it is based on the idea of a "shared national standard" (Street 1995, 126).

Drawing on this, it is not surprising that *NewsHour Extra* lesson plans, which voice the official view of the country on the topic of the Iraq War, also follow closely the official position of incorporating national standards in education. Therefore, through their content as well as their form (genre), these lesson plans support the official US program in every possible way, at both the political and educational levels. It would not, then, be unrealistic to suggest that the incorporation of the national standards section in the *NewsHour Extra* lesson plans and their total absence from the *Rethinking Schools* lesson plans is perhaps related to the position adopted by site editors on this complex issue in the history of US education. Eventually, as Street (1995, 125) argues, "The pedagogized literacy ... becomes an organizing concept around which ideas of social identity and value are defined; what kinds of collective identity we subscribe to, what kind of nation we want to belong to."

The Genre of the Reflective Lesson Plan

Whereas *NewsHour Extra* lesson plans are prepared along the lines of the traditional lesson plan, *Rethinking Schools* lesson plans follow an alternative format, which draws on what we will call the reflective lesson plan. In the context of reflective teaching, teachers are seen as reflective professionals who grow through experience and reflection (Posner 1985; Richards 1990). Shkedi (2000, 95) defines *reflection* as "meta-thinking (thinking about thinking) in which we consider the relationship between our thoughts and our actions in a particular context." Schön (1983, 1987) makes an interesting distinction between *reflection-in-action*, which refers to on-the-spot examination of classroom events (something teachers do, whether they are aware of it or not), and *reflection-on-action*, which refers to deliberate reflection conducted by teachers. In any case, one of the basic premises of reflective teaching is that teachers think metacognitively about their teaching practices, they become aware of their implementation of instructional strategies and classroom management techniques, and, consequently, they are in the position to respond actively to what is happening in their classroom. Farrell (2004) argues that reflecting on teaching practice may lead to improved classroom interaction, awareness of practice, awareness of the assumptions and values teachers bring to their classrooms, awareness of oneself as a learner, and collaboration with other teachers.

In language education, reflective accounts of lessons have primarily been explored either as a way to enhance teachers' professional development (Richards and Lockhart 1996) or as methods of data collection in classroom research (McDonough and McDonough 1997; Wallace 1998). Related literature describes a number of ways to record teacher experience and reflection systematically, such as the teaching journal or diary, the lesson report, and the reflective lesson plan. The teaching journal is a written account of teaching experiences, a teacher's written response to teaching events (Richards and Lockhart 1996, 7). Here teachers record daily events and their reactions to them, including instructional practices, student issues, classroom management, and other issues related to their day-to-day teaching. Although the teaching journal is not meant to be published, it is suggested to serve two main purposes: to record ideas for the purpose of later reflection and to help trigger insights about teaching. A teaching journal is mainly suggested to include personal reactions to things that happen in the classroom, observations about problems that occur in teaching, descriptions of significant aspects of lessons or school events, ideas for future analysis, or things to do in the future. In her research on teachers' reflective notes, Halbach (2002) found three main types of reflective journal entries: summarizing, exemplifying, and commenting.

Another way to systematically record teacher experience and reflection is the lesson report. It is suggested that both the teaching journal and the lesson report may be used to assess teaching practices as well as student learning (Gunn 2010, 211). Richards and Lockhart (1996, 9) describe a lesson report as a structured inventory or list that enables teachers to describe their recollections of the main features of a lesson. They distinguish between a lesson plan, which describes what a teacher intends to do during a lesson, and a lesson report, which describes what actually happened in the classroom from the teacher's point of view.

A lot of discussion has also taken place about the reflective lesson plan. Generally it has been seen to consist of two main parts: the typical lesson plan and diary or reflective notes. The reflective lesson plan often has the following format: On the left side of the paper, teachers record what is known as the typical lesson plan, in which they describe what they intend to do in a lesson by identifying duration, level, objectives, procedure, outcomes, and the like. On the right, they keep diary or reflective notes about what occurred at each point of the lesson. The reflective plan is prepared before and after a particular class. The idea is for the teacher to read the reflective notes and later make changes to the lesson plan, based on the feedback collected after its first implementation. Ho (1995, 66) suggests that this type of reflective plan can be used as "a useful means of reflection in order to build on experience and bring about improvement in teaching." She maintains that the use of reflective lesson plans brings insights into both levels of teacher education that Richards (1990) identifies: At the micro level, teachers may modify their lesson plans when they repeat the teaching of the same lesson, as a result of the reflection; at the macro level, teachers may reflect on the underlying principles of their teaching when they write their diaries. The ideas generated from reflection are put into practice in the next lesson and help improve teaching practices through a bottom-up approach.

Analysis of the reflective lesson plans in four English for Specific Purposes (ESP) classes has shown that as a result of this reflective practice, the teacher was able to make better decisions in subsequent lessons about her timing, visual presentation of material, design of activities, and how she dealt with students' problems (Ho 1995). Similarly, mastering the genre of the reflective lesson plan was the aim of a written assignment. Gunn (2010) asked her graduate students to prepare a typical lesson plan and then attempt to reflect on their plan before the actual class, not after, which is the usual practice. For this assignment, teacher trainees had to link each activity to their beliefs about teaching and learning and to describe in writing how the activities met the objectives of the lesson. They were also asked to participate in an online blog discussion on the assignment. Gunn found that the resistance to writing reflections was mostly because of teacher trainees' difficulty in discussing their negative thoughts and sharing personal information in a written document. The author concludes: "Once the factors were addressed and overcome, the students' reflections moved beyond description and showed the students trying to make sense of their new teaching identities as they confronted their beliefs about teaching and learning" (Gunn 2010, 221–222).

Doyle and Holm (1998) suggested another form for the reflective lesson plan to be used with their preservice teachers. They introduced the *story or narrative lesson plan* as an alternative form, which they considered more open-ended and cyclical, and closer to what experienced teachers use. As they say:

> We reframed the traditional lesson plan as a story hoping that stories would provide a means for our preservice teachers to interpret and reinterpret teaching events. We also hoped that in using a story format

to plan and reflect on teaching, students would create an image of instructional activities with children at the center of the "action" (p. 72).

In writing a story lesson plan, teachers have to consider the elements of *setting* (which includes a description of the "where"), *characters* (a description of the "who" in the story: for instance, who the students are, who will engage in the lesson and answer the questions), and *plot* (the "what" of the lesson: what is being taught, what the learning expectations are, and what will happen at the end of the story).

For the purposes of the specific course in which it was embedded, pre-service teachers first prepared their story lesson plan, then they conducted the class, using the predictive story as a framework. After the class they rewrote the lesson plan, describing what actually happened. Doyle and Holm performed a detailed analysis of the pre-teaching and post-teaching story lesson plans, to find how they differed from the traditional lesson plans. They found that the pre-teaching lesson plan included two main themes not typically found in traditional lesson plans: (1) descriptions of anticipated student interactions and reactions to the "story" and (2) teachers' feelings and thoughts about teaching the lesson. The most common theme found in the post-teaching story lesson plans was the focus on the students, with descriptions of what they said and did, how they reacted to the teaching, and how the teacher had to intervene so that students would experience success during the lesson. In some cases there were descriptions of how individual students responded to the "teaching episode." As the authors state, the focus on students in story lesson plans differs significantly from the focus on the mechanics of teaching found in traditional lesson plans (Doyle and Holm 1998, 76).

Similarly, an analysis of the teaching journals, in which preservice teachers recorded their experience with the story lesson plan, revealed that the teachers felt free to be creative when they did not have to think about all the parts of the traditional lesson plan. The format of the lesson plan helped them see students in a different way and put students at the center of their planning; it also helped them visualize more clearly how the lesson would flow.

The Genre of *Rethinking Schools* Lesson Plans

The genre of lesson plans in *Rethinking Schools* draws on the reflective lesson plan and the premises of reflective teaching, and it differs significantly from the typical traditional lesson plan. First, each lesson plan is written in the form of continuous text, with sections that vary depending on the issue discussed. Some of the lesson plans do not have any sections at all, whereas others are divided into thematic parts. Box 4.1 lists the sections of eight lesson plans. We notice that instead of the fixed categories that reflect distinct elements of a lesson (such as background/overview, time, materials, procedure, and extension), the categories here are related to the theme discussed in each lesson. Second, there are distinct differences in the language and the adopted perspective. Whereas the traditional lesson plans are predictive and future-oriented, the lesson plans in *Rethinking Schools* are retrospective narratives of lessons that have already been conducted. Therefore, both the format and the language used in *Rethinking Schools* lesson plans do not at all resemble the typical lesson plans teachers are generally trained to develop. One may wonder whether these are actually lesson plans, but in the portal they are recorded as *Lesson Plans and Teaching Ideas about the Iraq War.*

Box 4.1 Sections of *Rethinking Schools* Lesson Plans

Rethinking the Teaching of the Vietnam War
Roots of a War
Role-Playing an Historic Choice
Student Handout (French Business/ Government Leader)
Student Handout (Viet Minh Member)

The World Up Close
Writing and Poetry
Why Do They Hate Us?
Land Mines and Children
Global Inequalities
Sept. 11 and the War

Defeating Despair
Question of Alternatives
Views of Human Nature
Prosperity and Free Trade
Horror into Hope

Drawing on History to Challenge the War
Challenging War Rhetoric
Alternative Perspectives
Action Research to Educate

Entering History Through Poetry
100 Poems Against the War
A Verse to War
Tackling Big Questions
Entering History
Are There Children?

Whose "Terrorism"?
Lesson on Terrorism
Defining Terrorism
Economic Terrorism
Terrorism's Ghosts

Teaching Gulf War II
Creating the "Enemy"
Bush's Blank Check
Silent War of Sanctions
Why War?

Poetry in a Time of Crisis
Chaos and Justice

For someone familiar with the work conducted by *Rethinking Schools,* this alternative generic structure is far from surprising. This generic structure of the lesson plan seems to be consistent with their general philosophy about an alternative, critical pedagogy. Reflective teaching, action research, and alternative methods are part of the agenda in the suggested lessons, and the selection of an alternative lesson plan seems to be part of this agenda. We could say that the dominant structure of the lesson plan in *Rethinking Schools* is a combination of the story lesson plan and reflective notes or diary.

Perhaps the most prevailing characteristic of the *Rethinking Schools* lesson plans is their close connection to the classroom through the use of narrative accounts of lessons that have been already tried out, along with a detailed description of what happened in the classroom. Instead of the use of imperatives and high modality to describe steps to be followed, these lesson plans make extensive use of past tense to narrate classroom events ("Teaching Gulf War II").

> I **introduced** the cartoon by telling students that I **wanted** them to think about the images.... I **read** aloud a quote.... I **told** them.... I **wanted** them to think about aspects of the secret education children were exposed to. On the board I **wrote**.... After the video, students **wrote** ... before we **talked**.

The narrative line of what happened in the classroom, which is marked by the use of past tense, is often disrupted by explanatory entries (usually in present tense) ("Drawing on History to Challenge the War").

> As I **watched** the mainstream media minimize the tremendous opposition to the Bush administration's drive to attack Iraq, I **became** determined to encourage my students to think critically.... I **created** an effective unit using 1) a video on disinformation about the Gulf War; 2) a media project to explore alternative media perspectives on the Internet; and 3) an action project to educate others about Iraq....
>
> *Hidden Wars of Desert Storm* is a revealing documentary on the history.... To engage students' empathy, I **began** the unit with the last seventeen minutes of the sixty-four-minute video.... The second day, I **showed**.... The video opens with....

When the description of classroom practices goes beyond the particular lesson, as in the form of general reflective notes, this is also expressed in present tense ("Teaching with Protest Songs").

Public libraries **are** another decent source of finding CDs—especially with online searchable catalogs—although generally those **are** for the older CDs. **I prefer** ultimately to have a copy of the songs **I use** in a CD, either one that I've **purchased, downloaded,** or **copied.**

In the next extract, the narrative line is disrupted by a coteacher's question, followed by two student answers and the author's interpretation. All these different voices weave together within the same text ("Whose 'Terrorism'?").

> As we **wrapped up** in one class, Sandra **asked** a wonderful question: **"What difference do you think it would make if students all over the country were having the discussion that we're having today?"**
>
> There **were** two quick answers before the bell rang: **"I'd feel a lot better about the U.S.,"** and **"I think we'd lose a lot of people who'd want to go fight for the country."**
>
> **My interpretation**: The more students **understand** about the exercise of U.S. power in the world—both military and economic—the less likely they **are** to want to extend it.

A careful reading of these lesson plans reveals that they include most of the features found in the traditional lesson plan, such as background information, description of objectives, target group, and procedures. However, because these features are part of the narrative employed in the texts, they are differently realized. For instance, the target group of students to whom the suggested lesson is addressed is often identified in an introductory note, which, like an editorial comment, follows the title of the lesson.

> A bilingual elementary teacher helps students think about the images of war that they see—and don't see—in the U.S. media. ("Images of War")

> *   *   *

> High school educators call on the power of poetry to help students critique injustice and develop empathy. ("Poetry in a Time of Crisis")

> *   *   *

> An English teacher draws on student experiences with losing a loved one to help them cope with the Sept. 11 tragedy. ("Letters to the Universe")

> *   *   *

A fifth grade teacher helps his students explore issues of war and terrorism as they look at the war in Afghanistan. ("The World Up Close")

In some other cases, the target group is mentioned inside the text, as in the following examples.

Although I teach university students, this unit can be used with high school students. ("Drawing on History to Challenge the War")

*   *   *

It's amazing what my fifth graders will remember from a song, as compared to what they forget from my talking. ("Teaching with Protest Songs")

The general aims and specific objectives of the suggested lessons are also found in the lesson plans. They may not be neatly listed in infinitive forms but they are incorporated in the narrative of the text and they include the main purpose of the lesson.

I wanted to design a lesson that would get students to surface the definitions of terrorism that they carry around—albeit most likely unconsciously. And I wanted them to apply their definitions to a number of episodes, historical and contemporary, that involved some kind of violence or destruction. ("Whose 'Terrorism'?")

*   *   *

Students need to learn to distinguish explanations from descriptions, like "war broke out," or "chaos erupted." Thinking about social events as having concrete causes, constantly asking "Why?" and "In whose interests?" need to become critical habits of the mind for us and our students. It's only through developing the tools of deep questioning that students can attempt to make sense of today's global conflicts. ("Rethinking the Teaching of the Vietnam War")

Another part of the traditional lesson plan that is differently realized in the reflective lesson plans in *Rethinking Schools* is the procedure part, which describes the activities to be used in the course of the lesson. It should be noted that, whereas lesson plans in *Rethinking Schools* place particular emphasis on *what* is to be taught, the extent to which *how* is explicitly addressed varies. For instance, some lesson plans describe procedures in detail (e.g., "Drawing on History to Challenge the War," "Teaching

Gulf War II," "Rethinking the Teaching of the Vietnam War"), whereas others (e.g., "Entering History Through Poetry," "Teaching with Protest Songs," "The World Up Close," "Songs with a Global Conscience") have less explicit reference to the steps to follow in the classroom.

We notice that only one of the suggested lesson plans ("Predicting How the U.S. Government Will Respond to the Iraqi Government") follows the step-by-step description, using the language and format of the traditional lesson plan. Adopting a predictive perspective, this lesson plan uses present tenses and imperative forms extensively to describe in numbered lists the activities to be conducted in the lesson and a number of extension ideas. In all other lesson plans the procedure part is included in the narrative of the lesson account. Often, as in the next two examples, the step-by-step procedure may be described for individual activities only, not for a minute-by-minute account of how to proceed in the whole lesson ("Poetry in a Time of Crisis").

> After discussing the content of the poem, we pointed out how Wong creates a movie close-up of the moment. We see the father with his arms folded; we hear them talk; we watch the waitress ignore them.
>
> Then we asked students to create a poem detailing one of the acts of discrimination against Arab-Americans we read about earlier. We encouraged students to use details to help their readers see and hear the story in their poem.

The objective account of an authoritative voice found in traditional lesson plans is here replaced by the subjective tone of a teacher talking to other teachers, often in first-person singular ("Drawing on History to Challenge the War").

> I introduced the media project by saying that we could find news other than the "official story" because the Internet makes it possible for us to seek out different perspectives from non-corporate alternative media, and from media of other nations.
>
> For the assignment I asked students to collect examples of how both the mainstream media and the alternative press were covering the war buildup.

What would be expressed with imperatives in the traditional lesson plan language, as instructions to follow (e.g., "Introduce the media project by saying that ..." "for the assignment ask students to collect ...") is here presented as a personalized account of what a teacher did in her classroom. The personal tone is also kept in cases when the teacher describes some of her usual teaching practices ("Songs with a Global Conscience").

When I introduce a song, I use our classroom map to go over the geographical connections. I also explain any difficult words. Finally, and most importantly, I give the social context. Depending on whether I use the song at the beginning of a unit of study or in the middle, the amount of "context setting" varies.

The subjective tone is met not only in procedural matters, such as the previous three extracts, it is also found elsewhere in the text, where teachers describe their personal experience from teaching the lesson. In addition to the features found in the traditional lesson plan, the reflective lesson plans in *Rethinking Schools* also include in their narrative account some other features rooted in the philosophy of reflective teaching. These features can be divided into two broad categories: those describing the teachers' reflections on the lesson and those giving voice to students and their reactions to the lesson.

In fact, teachers' reflections in *Rethinking Schools* lesson plans are of different types. They may refer to teachers' practices in the classroom or to students' reactions to these practices. For instance, the teachers' reflections of the lesson often include the following.

Evaluative comments about aspects of the lesson:

A fuller explanation will need to engage students in exploring the central role that Iraq's oil … plays in this conflict. ("Teaching Gulf War II")

✻   ✻   ✻

Watching students attempt to apply their definitions of terrorism, I was impressed by their eagerness to be consistent…. Most groups wanted more information on the motives of various actors. ("Whose 'Terrorism'?")

✻   ✻   ✻

In the weeks to come, I know I will need to build on our initial discussion. ("Images of War")

Suggestions for future improvements:

The next time I teach this unit, I'd like to increase the focus on international media. I feel strongly that we need to find ways to bring international news into our schools and make it a part of our lives. ("Drawing on History to Challenge the War")

Corrective practices, adjusting their teaching to students' needs:

> My students find the video a bit dry, so in order for students not to feel overwhelmed by information, I stop it often to talk about key incidents and issues. ("Rethinking the Teaching of the Vietnam War")

Description of unsuccessful teaching:

> Frankly, when I've tried to design lessons to get students to imagine overarching social alternatives, these have not been compelling. ("Defeating Despair")

* * *

> The student panel of readers read right up until the bell. Surely, not all students were as engaged as I had hoped. I had envisioned each of them reading a letter out loud instead of a uniform panel of readers. I had hoped that more students would feel comfortable saying about a letter, "That's mine!" ("Letters to the Universe")

Discussion of teachers' hesitations and uncertainties:

> I didn't know for certain, but my hunch was that as students applied definitions consistently they might be able to call into question the "We're good/They're bad" dichotomies that have become even more pronounced on the political landscape." ("Whose 'Terrorism'?")

Personal accounts by the author:

> And there I am, feeling my way along, trying to piece together a curriculum that urges students to think critically about the antecedents to the coming war. ("Teaching Gulf War II")

Personal information:

> As I'm on leave this year, my colleague invited me into her classroom to teach this lesson to her 11th grade Global Studies students. ("Whose 'Terrorism'?")

* * *

During the Vietnam War, I was in high school in Eureka, Calif. In history, I studied World War II. In English, we dutifully read from a dull anthology until the afternoon Mike Brazee liberated us by throwing the whole lot of them out the second floor window. ("Entering History Through Poetry")

✳ ✳ ✳

I began my activism as a teenager protesting the war in Vietnam. The more I read, the more horrified I became at the atrocities committed by the U.S. government, and by the government's consistent lying about Vietnam, going back to the end of World War II. I first felt bitterness and anger—emotions that found expression in Bob Dylan's unforgiving song, "Masters of War," which I listened to over and over. ("Defeating Despair")

Teachers often discuss their own teaching and become reflective of their practices. In the following example, for instance, the teacher is careful not to impose her viewpoint on the students ("Entering History Through Poetry").

As I taught these poems in Kathy Anderson's sophomore English class at Roosevelt High School, I became aware that I didn't leave much room for students who support the war. Two students did write and share poems that could be interpreted as endorsing Bush's push to war. I mention this because I don't like to strong-arm students into adopting my point of view. Students should feel comfortable entering a classroom conversation; otherwise, we're not wrestling with issues; we're pinning them down and force-feeding them.

A characteristic feature of this personal account of the lesson is the employment of informal language that one would not normally expect to find in a professional document. We often find expressions such as the following: "To get students started, I ran through one example," "These papers were fun to read" ("Drawing on History to Challenge the War"), "I mention this, because I don't like" ("Entering History Through Poetry"), "As I sat down recently to figure out how I was going to teach," "And there I am feeling my way along" ("Teaching Gulf War II"), "I want my students to be comfortable" ("The World Up Close"), "If we are to give peace a chance, then we must think honestly about the roots of war" ("Rethinking the Teaching of the Vietnam War").

Another important category of features in *Rethinking Schools* lesson plans refers to students' actions and their interaction with teachers. Students are not a voiceless cohort (Linne 2001), but subjects with their voices heard. Their reactions to the lesson are recorded at different parts of the lesson account.

> "I was so proud to know how to argue with my dad. I told him 'I'm telling you realities. You think what they want you to think.'" "My mom actually checked out the Zmag website herself!" Students were also discouraged at how little people knew. "My friend thinks he knows everything and won't listen to reason." ("Drawing on History to Challenge the War")

*   *   *

Michael, another student in Anderson's class, clearly understood the connection between our actions and war when he wrote, "Where were we when wars were engaging in other parts of the world? Maybe we were pumping gas into our cars or sleeping with no worries." ("Entering History Through Poetry")

*   *   *

I talked with students about why poetry should be used in history. Mira said, "Poetry made history come to life. When we wrote after *Hearts and Minds,* I was there. I was a soldier. I identified with what was going on. I felt their feelings. I got more involved. This wasn't just history. This was life. Poetry helped me examine why the war happened because I got inside the people who witnessed it." ("Entering History Through Poetry")

Of particular interest here is the way students are represented in the lesson plans. What they say is not reported through the teachers' words. The transfer of students' exact words, through the use of direct speech, and the reference to their names (Michael, Mira) gives them a prominent position in the text and allows their voices to be heard. They are not anonymous students who might have said something reported by their teacher. They are given a space to voice their perspective and to express their enthusiasm, their worries, their views, their questions, their agreements, and their disagreements, as in the following two examples.

> One student said he heard that the United States was dropping yellow mines on Afghanistan. Another responded that the yellow things were food, not bombs. I explained that unfortunately both students were right and we were dropping both food and bombs.

"That doesn't make sense!" one student said. "If we want to help them, why do that?" ("The World Up Close")

✳ ✳ ✳

One student wrote: "To me, this cartoon is saying that we (the U.S., portrayed by Popeye) can do whatever we want to other people in other cultures, because we're always right. Violence is alright and gives you power and control." ("Teaching Gulf War II")

Holly (1984) discusses teacher diaries as a narrative genre that includes three main themes: an account of what the teacher did in the classroom, a description of what students did and how they responded, and an account of interactions. In the context of reflective teaching, these three themes have actually entered the professional genre of the lesson plan, transforming both its generic structure and its lexicogrammar. As a result, the objective account of the traditional lesson plan has been replaced by an alternative generic form, which is sensitive to students' and teachers' needs and which leads to a more participatory, student-centered pedagogy.

Professional Identities and the Genre of Lesson Plans

In this chapter, we conceptualized the genre of lesson plan as a sociohistorical and cultural practice, suggesting that it is differently realized in different pedagogical paradigms. After a brief literature review, we proceeded to an analysis of two different generic realizations, the traditional and the reflective lesson plans, and identified the main features of each type. Specifically, it was found that the lesson plans in *NewsHour Extra* draw on the traditional lesson plan, which is descriptive and procedural, follows a set structure, and uses a technical "objective" language. *Rethinking Schools* lesson plans, on the other hand, draw on the reflective lesson plan. They have been written after a particular class has been conducted, and in this sense they are retrospective. Instead of the formal language adopted in *NewsHour Extra,* in *Rethinking Schools* lesson plans teachers present materials directed to other teachers for use in the classroom, and they discuss their personal experience, including personal evaluations, uncertainties, and failures as well as successes. It is suggested that the differences between the two generic realizations are attributed to the different pedagogical paradigms to which they adhere: critical thinking and critical pedagogy.

In examining the implications of these differences for the discursive construction of identities, we need to take into account two important issues. First, the lesson plan is a professional genre, through which teachers communicate their practices, and as a result, it contributes to the discursive construction of professional identities. At the same time, it is a text that stands for something else, the suggested lesson, and it is thus indicative of the dominant classroom discourse (Linne 2001) in an imagined classroom, the one described in the suggested lesson plan. What is the role of the teacher in these educational contexts? What reading positions and professional identities are discursively constructed through these texts for the producers and the consumers of these texts, the teachers? Based on my analysis of the genre of lesson plans, and taking into account that "the planning options a teacher employs reflect the teacher's beliefs about teaching and learning" (Richards and Lockhart 1996, 82), we may come to some conclusions concerning the professional identities that are discursively constructed in the two portals.

The teacher in *NewsHour Extra* lesson plans is a sophisticated professional who composes and consumes technical documents. The author identity is that of a professional who gives accounts of lessons and instructions to other professionals. She addresses her audience using the technical language of the teaching profession. She is aligned with the official educational policy, which directs her to apply standards in her lessons, and she connects her plan to the official national standards, which she knows well.

The lesson plans also offer reading positions for the intended readership, that is, teachers who are interested in incorporating related lessons in their curriculum. Specifically, the *NewsHour Extra* lesson plans position the reader as a professional who is given all teaching resources and detailed instruction on how to use them in the classroom. No initiative for selection of materials is left up to the individual teacher, therefore she is someone who is expected to function within a specified framework. Her personal history and views are not to intervene in the teaching process, and the lesson plan provides detailed steps to follow during the class. In the particular lesson plans, the teacher is also assumed to support the government's decision to go to war. Her role, as repeatedly stated, is to inform her students about the necessity of this decision and to prepare them to become knowledgeable citizens who rationally analyze the advantages and disadvantages of each situation they encounter in their lives. This, in fact, seems to be the overall aim of the portal.

In contrast, the teacher in *Rethinking Schools* lesson plans is conceived of as a transformative intellectual, who is expected to take a lot of initiative in the classroom, rather than simply follow a predefined plan. She selects her teaching materials from a variety of available resources and engages in an ongoing dialogue with her colleagues, sharing experience and reflecting on her teaching practices. She reads suggested lesson plans and other teaching materials to get some ideas from how her colleagues have conducted lessons and their reflections on the lessons. She is assumed to take a critical stance toward the war and is expected to develop students' empathy and critical awareness of the war. Her personal history and views are considered important parts of her subjectivity as a teacher and an educator. Positioning herself in the context of critical pedagogy, she is an active participant in the educational process. She is sensitive to students' needs and adjusts her teaching accordingly. Moreover, she understands that her goal as an educator is to prepare her students to become active participants in society, citizens who will challenge the official view and will be critical readers of the media.

Chapter 5

Hypermodality

A New Form of Textuality

> A new medium is never an addition to an old one, nor does
> it leave the old one in peace. It never ceases to oppress the
> older media until it finds new shapes and positions for them.
> *Marshall McLuhan, 1964*

CHAPTER 4 FOCUSED ON THE GENRE OF THE LESSON PLAN AND ITS
different realizations in the educational materials of the *NewsHour Extra*
and *Rethinking Schools* portals. In the genre analysis attempted in the
previous chapter, the lesson plans were mainly treated as print texts, and,
in fact, most of the analysis was conducted with printouts of the online
materials. Although this analysis served the purpose of identifying the
generic features of the lesson plans, it inevitably left out some unique
features of the online genres. Recognizing that if we simply analyze printouts of online genres and treat them as static products, we neglect the
characteristics of the medium that significantly influence and contribute
to the way genres look and are used (Askehave and Nielsen 2005, 121), this
chapter attempts a complementary analysis. It explores the differences
that arise when the print lesson plan moves online, the ways in which
the two portals exploit the affordances of the Internet medium, and the
extent to which these differences relate to the employed pedagogies. In
other words, this chapter deals with the ideology of the Internet medium
and the ways it affects the construction of the specific online genre.

This type of analysis is important if we consider that the interaction of different semiotic resources (visual, verbal, audio, and kinetic) in websites gives rise to new forms of textuality and calls for new theoretical and methodological accounts that will deal adequately with processes of text composition. Therefore, there is also a need to explore the new forms of textuality emerging in these online educational materials, in terms of both informational and design complexity and to develop an understanding of the processes of text composition. Analysis of these processes involves understanding the semiotic characteristics of the various modes brought together and of their more general semiotic properties, which allow them to be related to other semiotic modes (Kress 2000; Kress and van Leeuwen 2001, 2006; van Leeuwen 2005; Zammit and Callow 1999).

This chapter draws on discourse analysis and hypermedia design theories, in order to identify the features of the online genre of lesson plans and to explore the ways in which the online genre is realized in the two portals. The first part of the chapter discusses some basic similarities and differences between the print lesson plan and the hypermodal lesson plan. In terms of meaning-making, this comparison enables us to identify some differences in meaning that may arise from the employment of a different medium. The chapter continues with a presentation of website hierarchy and content organization in the two websites. Drawing on studies of signaling in online environments, the chapter next presents an analysis of the types of hyperlinks found in the lesson plans of the two portals and their interconnection with content organization and webpage and navigation design. It is suggested that in order to understand the complex ways in which hypertextuality operates (its functions and types) in an online genre, it is not enough to merely analyze the different types of hyperlinks found in a specific online genre. It is also necessary to consider the immediate context of the website in which the online genre appears as well as the broader context in which the website is included (e.g., a media broadcast portal) and to place discussion of hypertextuality at all of these levels.

The Genre of the Print Lesson Plan

One difference between print texts and online texts has often been conceived in terms of the principle of linearity, with the former being considered as linear and the latter as nonlinear texts. However, scholars who deal with multimodality have often stressed that print texts are not truly linear texts, at least not in the way that spoken monologues are.

Lemke (2002, 300) argues that written texts use the visual medium in different ways. Among the various sources of visual salience that he identifies on a page are titles, headers and footers, sections, sidebars, paragraphs, typeface (italic, bold, small caps, fonts), and illustrations (figures, tables, graphs). To illustrate that readers do not read linearly, he describes what he calls a "traversal" of the print medium:

> We do not always start a printed text at the title page, or the first paragraph of the main text. We may leaf through a book, glancing at this page or that; we may turn to an index, we may follow the page numbers in a table of contents, we may look from a line to a footnote, to a bibliography of references, to an author index, and back to another page. This is a traversal in the print medium, using the technology of the book, both materially (turning pages) and by means of its genre elements (page numbers, index, etc.). (301)

Similarly, we could say that the print lesson plan exploits the visual medium in many ways. It is a highly codified text with clearly identified headings and distinct typeface, such as bold and italics. Information is often given in bulleted lists. Because of its strict codification, the headings are quite predictable, at least in the basic form of the genre, and, thus, are easily recognizable. As we have seen, they usually include some of the following: introduction/overview, objectives, students' level, time, materials, procedure, evaluation, and extension ideas.

Information is arranged in distinct sections and in a sequence that is to a great extent predictable. For instance, the "Aims and Objectives" section of the lesson plan is placed toward the beginning of the text; it describes what the lesson aspires to do and what the student is expected to know by the end of the lesson. The aims and objectives are presented in predictive statements, such as: "By the end of the lesson students should be able to," or, "The aims/objectives of this lesson are." The sections of "Required Time" and "Grade Level," usually placed below "Aims and Objectives," do not usually exceed one line, but provide useful information for the teacher. In the "Materials" section that follows, readers expect to find all the resources necessary for the suggested lesson, ranging from pen and paper to the specific reading texts students are invited to read. The "Procedure" section, which often includes numbered statements of all the steps that should be followed during the lesson, comes next. The expected sequence of different sections is not only predictable, it also holds the different elements together in a unifying narrative. Genre variations keep the same basic narrative form and play with the addition of some other categories that come to enrich, and, thus, reaffirm, the basic generic structure.

The reading of the lesson plan is sequential, yet far from linear. In an attempt to locate important information, the readers' eyes may wander over the different sections of the lesson plan, which are usually preceded by distinct headings in bold letters. A suggestion for a whole lesson is stretched out in front of the readers' eyes by means of clear categories. Skimming through them, readers get an overview of the lesson in a matter of seconds. They may move from grade and topic to procedures and materials and back to required time and overview or they may move down to the extension ideas. This may be seen as a traversal of a print lesson plan by means of its genre elements.

The Genre of the Hypermodal Lesson Plan

Lemke (1998) reminds us that what look like the same genre on paper and on screen (for instance, the print and the online lesson plan) are not functionally the same, because they follow different meaning conventions and require different skills for their successful use. He claims that it is important to clarify in what ways hypertextuality differs from textuality, and he explains that "typical meaning differences arise because people exploit the affordances of one medium differently from those of another" (Lemke 2002, 300). In the move from page to screen, Jewitt (2002) and Snyder (1998) argue, a range of representational modes, such as voice, image, and moving picture, become available as meaning-making resources. In the case of Internet genres, the medium adds unique properties to the online genre in terms of production, distribution, and reception, which cannot be ignored in the genre characterization, according to Askehave and Nielsen (2005, 125).

Different theories have developed concerning the hypertext medium and the reading process. Finnemann (1999, 25) considers hypertext as a text system that activates at least two modal shifts in the reading process: the *reading mode*, which involves reading as we know it (similar to the reading of a printed text, whether it is linear or not), and the *navigation mode*, which allows the reader to navigate the site (and perhaps other sites as well) and to construct her own reading path. He further argues that reading in both modes is sequential, because, even in the navigation mode, the reader makes one choice at a time. Drawing on his work, Askehave and Nielsen (2005, 128) developed a model according to which Internet users shift all the time between acting as readers (by zooming in on the text and by using the online text as a print text) and acting as navigators (by zooming out of the text and using the online text as a medium, exploiting its navigation possibilities). The authors argue that with the

Internet, the medium itself constitutes an integral part of the genre that should be taken into account in descriptions of generic structures. They draw on Swales's (1990) functional theory of genre to suggest a generic structure of the homepage. For Landow (1997) and Bolter (2001), the emphasis is not on how hypertexts are structured and produced but on how the reader assesses them. They argue that on the Internet there is no clear distinction between text production and reception, because readers may choose where to begin their reading and where to end it. They create their own reading path and their own "text" in the hypertext system, becoming a kind of author. This type of hyperreading has resulted from the constraints imposed on the reading pattern by the hypertext system, according to Sosnoski (1999, 135).

In his exploration of the interactions and the multiple interconnections of image, text, and sound in hypermedia, Lemke (2002, 300) introduces the notion of *hypermodality* to refer to the meaning-making potential of the interaction between the two defining features of hypermedia genres: their *hypertextuality* and their *multimodality* (i.e., the interplay of different modes, which, in the case of websites, goes beyond the conventions of traditional multimodal genres). As he states, "Hypermodality is more than multimodality in just the way that hypertext is more than plain text." The difference lies, he argues, in the way that

> the web of connectivity of a hypertext activates our expectations that there will be links out from any present text unit and that there will be no single default reading sequence of a main text to return to, or against which we should be reading the content of an excursus. In hypertext there is only excursus—trajectories and loops on different scales without a single unifying narrative or sequential development of a thesis.

In fact, he argues that there is a need to reexamine the notion of the "whole text" in the hypertext medium, because in hypermedia, there are more interconnections (possible trajectories, or traversals) than are found in print genres.

When considering the genre of the online lesson plan, we would, in many respects, agree with Lemke's (1998) comment that when a document moves online, its "old practices migrate en masse" (287) too, recreating what is already familiar. At first glance, an online lesson plan greatly resembles the print lesson plan in terms of generic structure. There are, however, distinct differences as well. In a study that examined two hundred unique sources of available Web-published lesson plans on the teaching of the English language, Koszalka, Breman, and Moore (1999, 146–147) found that the most frequently used components of

Web-based lesson plans include procedures, description of the lesson subject, objectives, and materials. Compared with print teacher-generated lesson plans, which were found to include more logistical references (such as time frame for the lesson and evaluation methods), the study found that Web-published lesson plans include more descriptive information, which allows teachers to search efficiently for specific types of lesson plans that best fit their needs. They also found that databases maintained by universities and various educational organizations included hundreds of lesson plans published in identical formats.

In terms of meaning-making, one main difference from the print lesson plan refers to the web of connectivity of a hypertext, which activates the readers' expectations that there will be links in the main text. These links constitute the essence of *hypertextuality* and extend beyond the conventions of traditional multimodal genres. In the case of lesson plans, they usually connect the main text to other text units (e.g., readings, activities) and visual elements (e.g., diagrams, maps, videos), and create a spiral effect that allows the reader to move back and forth between them. Still, however, these links do not seem to seriously disrupt the overall generic structure, because they constitute local links that connect specific points of a text to a hypertext and back to the main text. Contrary to other online genres, in which there is no single default reading sequence of a main text to return to, the online lesson plan has a dominant narrative that holds the different parts together. This dominant narrative is also stressed by the use of structural cues (e.g., through headings in bold letters), which remain from the print version of the genre. The various links, on the other hand, provide ready-to-use handouts for students, evaluation criteria for teachers, readings to be downloaded for students, and suggestions for related websites to be explored for the topic under analysis.

The similarity of formats that was identified by Koszalka, Breman, and Moore (1999) is attributed to the existence of several similar online lesson plan tools that are available on the Internet today for generating lesson plans. These include ready templates with predefined areas to be filled in, some of which are more detailed than others. Several are free tools that teachers can use on their own or in collaboration with other teachers, and others constitute parts of specialized software on classroom management. Adopting a business model, this type of specialized software attempts to transfer the management model to what is known as class management, and it includes tools to be used by both administrators and teachers. Among the software programs addressing teachers are flowcharts, mind maps, worksheets, annotation tools, customized testing suites, and templates for automated lesson plans. Embedded within a "help" discourse, these software tools are presented as the solution to "problems" teachers face in organizing their work (Mitsikopoulou 1999). The online tools for Web-generated lesson plans and specialized software, together with the publication of several thousand lesson plans on a variety of subjects, construe the hypermodal genre as a highly codified text type with strict prespecified format and content.

Website Hierarchy and Content Organization

At first sight, it would seem that the online lesson plan is a rather homogeneous genre, with predictable categories and organization of content. But how is this genre related to the rest of the website, and what types of interconnections are employed in the portal? What is the role of hypertextuality in the construal of pedagogical meanings? To what extent are the different hypermodal realizations consistent with the overall pedagogic identities and ideologies permeating the two portals? How do the two portals use the available hypermodal features in the websites with online educational materials about the Iraq War?

Drawing on studies of signaling in online environments and navigational links, we turn to exploring the types of hyperlinks and their interaction with the main text, specifically their interconnections with content organization, webpage, and navigation design. First, though, it is important to place the online genre of the lesson plan within its broader context, and that includes the context of the website where it is published (here, the website about educational materials on the Iraq War) and the context of the portal that hosts the educational website. As we shall see, hypertextuality can only be fully captured when discussion takes into account both of these contexts.

To explore the online genre of lesson plan in its broader context, we need to employ the notion of *website hierarchy*. Djonov (2007, 148) argues that this notion derives from the understanding that "not all webpages and navigation options within a website enjoy the same status." She refers to two dominant perspectives on website hierarchy: the *segmental,* which focuses on individual webpages instead of groups of webpages, and the *holistic,* in which the highest level (the homepage) is followed by subsections, their sub-subsections, and so on. She claims that the latter is more popular in website architecture, because it places greater emphasis on the "meaningful grouping of webpages" (150) and because it conceives of a webpage not just as an HTML document with hyperlinks, but as part of a larger group of webpages. She further claims that "for studies of hypermodality, another advantage of the holistic perspective is that it acknowledges the role of webpage areas and items, and thus webpage design, in the construction of website sections (and their subdivisions) and of the website as a whole" (ibid.).

In fact, both the *NewsHour Extra* and *Rethinking Schools* portals have been built on the *holistic* perspective of website hierarchy, with several lesson plans on the same topic being grouped together under a main page. As shown in Boxes 5.1 and 5.2, the lesson plans on the Iraq War are grouped together under main pages. In the case of the first portal (Box 5.1), we notice that the group section on the Iraq War lesson plans is placed below the "Teacher Resources" section of *NewsHour Extra,* which in turn is placed as a section of the main PBS website. In *Rethinking Schools,* the individual lesson plans are placed below the section of "Lesson Plans and Teaching Ideas," which in turn is placed under a main page that includes other resources on the Iraq War (Box 5.2).

A point worth mentioning here concerns the *visibility* of the subsection on the Iraq War in relation to the other sections and subsections in the website. Whereas in the early days of the Iraq War, the sections on the war

---

Box 5.1 The Iraq War Lesson Plans in the Website Hierarchy of *NewsHour Extra*

Pbs.org
   NewsHour
      NewsHour Extra
         Teacher Resources
            Iraq War lesson plans
               Lesson plan 1
               Lesson plan 2
               Lesson plan 3
                  etc.

Box 5.2 The Iraq War Lesson Plans in the Website Hierarchy of *Rethinking Schools*

RethinkingSchools.org
   Iraq War main page (War index)
      Lesson Plans and Teaching Ideas
         Lesson plan 1
         Lesson plan 2
         Lesson plan 3
           etc.

in both portals held a prominent position in the main pages of the two portals, a few years later the relevant sections are no longer visible in the homepages of the two portals. In the years since their first publication on the website, hundreds of other lesson plans have been added to the two educational websites, and, as a result, the more recent ones have received greater attention. Furthermore, in *NewsHour Extra,* the graphics and the visual representation of the recent lesson plan template has changed to a more sophisticated and elaborate Web design.

This backgrounding of the lesson plans on the Iraq War in the two portals is quite revealing of the function of educational materials in the media, particularly in cases where the suggested lesson plans relate to current events and draw their readings from feature articles of the respective media portal. When the topic becomes less salient in the news, the respective lesson plans become less salient in the portal as well. The same has happened with other current events, such as the lesson plans on Hurricane Katrina. There is, therefore, a temporal issue in these educational materials that is related to the aim of the portals to bring current events into the classroom (see, for instance, the *NewsHour Extra* mission statement at www.pbs.org/newshour/extra/mission.html). Related to the *visibility* issue in the portal is the *accessibility* of the online educational materials. Whereas in the early days of the Iraq War, the announcement of the special sections on the war was placed higher in the website order, specifically on the homepages of the educational websites, these materials today can mainly be found through a search in the portal.

The Main Pages of *NewsHour Extra* and *Rethinking Schools* on the Iraq War

Exploring the context in which the hypermodal lesson plans appear, we will now analyze the main pages of *NewsHour Extra* and *Rethinking Schools* websites on the Iraq War, which, as we shall see, share similar characteristics with a homepage. Askehave and Nielsen (2005, 124) present the homepage as a new genre that shares features with existing genres from print media (such as the newspaper front page) but that also conveys unique properties: It only exists online, it has no direct parallel outside the Internet, and its form has quickly become conventionalized. For instance, the homepage has a different design from all other pages of a website and it communicates information about the purpose of the website (e.g., it includes a summary sentence of what the website does; it indicates website hierarchy and its highest-priority tasks). It also includes information about the owners of the website (through distinct categories such as "About Us," "Contact Us," "Policy"), and it allows users to search the website (e.g., through input boxes, which allow queries on the website). The homepage genre also has distinct features in terms of language (simple, self-explanatory words and labels; imperative forms), typography (consistent capitalization of first words and style standards; avoidance of emphatic punctuation such as exclamation marks), content (focus on important information only; no redundant or ambiguous content), structure of information (grouped in clear categories or bulleted lists), and various multimodal features (graphics, photos, animation, etc.) (Nielsen and Tahir 2001).

We notice that the two main pages of *NewsHour Extra* and *Rethinking Schools* on the Iraq War (Figures 5.1 and 5.2, respectively) include most of these characteristics of the homepage. At the same time, because both websites are parts of larger organizations, they relate to the organizations in several different ways. In the case of *NewsHour Extra* (see Figure 5.1), at the top of the main page is a horizontal menu of the PBS portal, which includes the categories of "Programs A-Z," "TV schedules," "Watch Video," "Support PBS," and "Shop PBS." Below the horizontal menu on the left, we find the logo of the *NewsHour Extra* website, and centered in the middle, the heading "Teaching the Iraq War." There is a left menu below the website logo that leads the visitor to the main categories of the *NewsHour Extra* website. These include "Home," "Resources for Students," "Teachers & Educators," subdivided thematically into "Arts/English," "Science," "Math/Economics," "World," "US History/Gov't," and "Heath/ Fitness." This general menu is not related to the main page of the Iraq War section. A list of materials on the Iraq War is presented in the main part of the page and organized into "Lesson Plans," "Iraq Themes," "NewsHour Resources," and "PBS Partners" sections. A preview of the contents is given, with a title serving as a hyperlink: a one-sentence summary of what each resource includes, followed by publication date. The main page also includes a short introductory paragraph about the purpose of the website.

> As coalition forces in Iraq shift focus to rebuilding the war-devastated country, *NewsHour Extra* is shifting to two lesson plans a week. Our goal is to continue covering the developments in the region and help students follow the aftermath of the war.
>
> Please send any comments or suggestions to extra@NewsHour.org.

Through this paragraph the main page attempts to recruit[1] readers (Kress 1989) in the website. A corporate professional identity is constructed to this text, through the use of the exclusive *our* in "our goal" to refer to the editors and the people in charge of the website. Moreover,

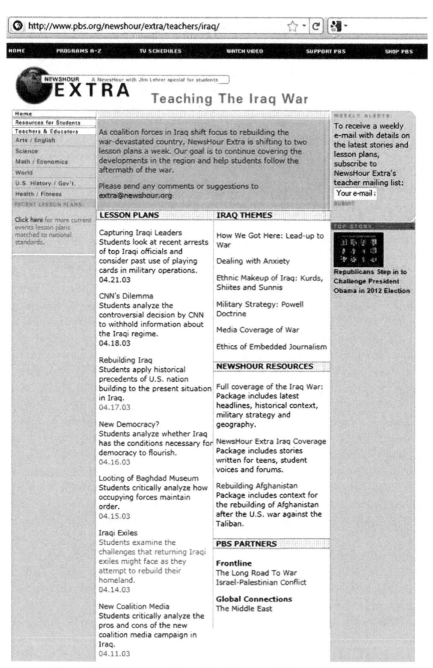

Figure 5.1 Homepage of *NewsHour Extra* website on the Iraq War.

RS | http://www.rethinkingschools.org/war/ideas/index.shtml

Rethinking Schools

| HOME | ABOUT | MAGAZINE | BOOKS | SUBSCRIBE | RS NEWS | ARCHIVE | SUPPORT US |

This collection includes lesson plans and teaching ideas created by the editors of Rethinking Schools, as well as teaching materials created by other teachers around the country who are trying to come to grips with the issues raised by the war. If you would like to contribute a lesson plan or teaching idea to this collection please email Bob Peterson at repmilw@aol.com.

Drawing on History to Challenge the War | pdf
By Polly Kellogg
Using the video *Hidden Wars of Desert Storm* **in the classroom.**

- **Alternative Media Websites** | pdf

Entering History Through Poetry | pdf
By Linda Christensen
Poetry can help students examine the consequences of war.

Teaching Gulf War II | pdf
By Bill Bigelow
Lessons can encourage students to question the official story on Iraq.

- **More Student-friendly Articles** | pdf

Teaching with Protest Songs | pdf
By Bob Peterson
Songs can be used to motivate and educate.

- **War Statistics** | pdf

"A World Up Close," | pdf
By Bob Peterson

SUBSCRIBE
ONLINE & SAVE
Current issue pdf just
$4.95. Subscribe
Print Share

TEACHING ABOUT THE
WAR

Lesson Plans and
Teaching Ideas

Suggested Readings
for Teachers and
Students

Background
Documents and
Related Materials

Maps and Geography
Activities

Resources for
Teachers

Links About the War

Teacher Groups
Against the War

Teacher Resolutions
Against the War

Figure 5.2 Homepage of *Rethinking Schools* **website on the Iraq War.**

a critical thinking discourse is echoed in the description of the aims of these educational materials to "continue covering the developments of war" and to "help students follow the aftermath of the war." As discussed in Chapter 1, the consistent employment of this discourse construes teachers as well-informed professionals, who teach their students about current events, and students as subjects, who strive to understand the world around them. Teachers are invited to subscribe to the teacher's mailing list in order to receive "a weekly email with details on the latest stories and lesson plans." There is no indication that these or other materials from the website are available for purchase.

Similarly, the *Rethinking Schools* website on the Iraq War (Figure 5.2) also includes an introductory paragraph.

> This collection includes lesson plans and teaching ideas created by the editors of Rethinking Schools, as well as teaching materials created by other teachers around the country who are trying to come to grips with the issues raised by the war. If you would like to contribute a lesson plan or teaching idea to this collection please email Bob Peterson at repmilw@aol.com.

This short text in the main page attempts to recruit readers into the website through an activist, participatory discourse. To this aim, it invites all interested teachers to actively participate in the website content and to send a lesson plan or a teaching idea to be published in the website. This is part of their more general agenda to engage more and more teachers in their cause for more democratic schooling. The voice of the website editors joins the voices of "teachers around the world" who "are trying to come to grips with the issues raised by the war." Thus, an inclusive professional identity is construed here for teachers who are not represented as simply trying to understand the external world around them but as subjects who "struggle" ("come to grips") in their attempt to deal with this matter of public concern ("issue").

The main page of the *Rethinking Schools* website includes a horizontal menu that includes the categories of "Home," "About," "Magazine," "Books," "Subscribe," "RS News," "Archive," and "Support Us." The visitor is directed to the various publications through the main categories of "Magazine," "Books," and "Archive" in the horizontal main menu of the website. The dropdown menu of the "Magazine" category includes a submenu consisting of hyperlinks leading to "Current issue," "Archives," "Special issues," and "Topical collections." The "Books" category includes a dropdown submenu with three main hyperlinks: "RS publications," "Special magazine issues," and "Download a catalog now." The "Archive" category does not have a dropdown menu but leads the visitor to the collection of all magazine issues organized chronologically, starting from the most recent one. In all these categories, the visitor is given access to the table of contents, some background information concerning the publication, and the price. The possibility of buying these resources online is given to the visitor through an "Add to cart" button, which also gives information about the price of each issue.

Consequently, the main principle of organizing the various teacher resources in this portal is the medium of publication[2] (magazine, special issue, book); the visitor may arrive at the same publication through different pathways. For instance, the visitor may locate a specific magazine issue by visiting any of the three main categories in the menu, because they all include options for the magazine issues. This can be seen as an indirect form of commercial promotion of the *Rethinking Schools* magazine[3] through the website. Visitors are also encouraged to become subscribers of *Rethinking Schools,* in order to receive access to its full contents.

Individual articles, teaching ideas, and lesson plans may be included in more than one publication or mode. For instance, in "How Many Must Die?", a teacher resource available at www.RethinkingSchools.org/special_reports/sept11/16_02/many162.shtml, we read that "a longer version of this article originally appeared in *Rethinking Schools,* Volume 13, No. 3, Spring 1999. The full text is available at www.RethinkingSchools.org/archive/13_03/iraq.shtml." The first link is available to all visitors, whereas the second one can only be accessed by subscribers. We notice, therefore, that the same resource is available in three formats: as a stand-alone resource that may be accessed online; as part of a magazine issue available in print and PDF form; and in an extended form, as an online resource available through subscription.

Overall, as we have seen, the two main pages seem to serve the two main functions of the homepage, as identified by Askehave and Nielsen (2005, 124): to introduce the reader to the general content of the website, by presenting information about its content and to enable the reader to access and navigate the website through navigational tools. By adopting a *holistic* perspective, the two educational websites bring together a number of teacher resources on the Iraq War in different subsections grouped in clear categories. In fact, it is this grouping of the materials in the specific portals, their common generic form, and their consistent ideological positioning (for the Iraq War in the case of *NewsHour Extra* and against the war in the case of *Rethinking Schools*) that has led us to consider these resources as special kinds of informal curricula. Moreover, we notice that both websites attempt to involve teachers. For instance, both aspire to construct an online community of teachers, who, in the case of *NewsHour Extra,* receive new lesson plans every week, with the ultimate purpose of using them in the classroom. With *Rethinking Schools,* teachers are asked to be more actively involved both by contributing their work for publication and by joining the *Rethinking Schools* critical teaching Listserv in order to "participate in this project of peace and justice curriculum development" ("Teaching Gulf War II").

Finally, we notice that, despite the fact that *Rethinking Schools* is an activist, nonprofit organization, it draws on marketing techniques in order to promote its materials. Publications can be found in several parts of the website, together with an "Add to cart" button, and the current issue of the magazine is placed under a "Subscribe online & save" button located on the top right of the website's main page, under the main horizontal menu. This promotion of publications may be related to the fact that *Rethinking Schools* also advertises itself as an "independent publisher," which needs to raise money to maintain its publications and website. In contrast, as part of PBS, a public broadcast organization, *NewsHour Extra* offers its educational materials for free.

Investigating Traversals of the Hypermodal Lesson Plans

For the analysis of hyperlinks used in the two websites on the Iraq War, I have developed an analytic tool that draws on the work of Djonov (2007) and Spyridakis et al. (2007) in order to explore different dimensions of how hypertextuality functions in the two websites (Box 5.3). The first dimension refers to whether hyperlinks are website-internal or website-external. Website-internal links connect webpages that belong to the same website. For instance, they may connect different sections or subsections. Drawing on systemic functional linguistics and hypermedia theory, Djonov (2007) suggests that the connection of website-internal links may be along a scale of *temporal subordination,* in which some webpages may not be visited before some others (as, for instance, in some educational websites, in which required steps must be followed to ensure readers' progress), or along a scale of *containment,* in which higher levels contain lower ones (as, for instance, where information is packaged in unified wholes, such as paragraphs, chapters, or website sections). On the other hand, website-external links transcend the website's structure and connect one website to another. The connections to other websites are highly ideological selections, revealing what is considered as worthwhile information and legitimate knowledge. In terms of website hierarchy, Djonov (2007, 146) argues that website-internal links may obscure the website structure, whereas website-external links do not have the potential to reveal the website structure and may blur the boundaries of a website.

The second dimension in the analytic tool refers to whether hyperlinks are embedded in a text or are listed outside a text. Spyridakis et al. (2007)

Box 5.3 A Tool for the Analysis of Hyperlinks

Djonov (2007)	**Website-internal links** They connect webpages belonging to the same website.	**Website-external links** They transcend a website's structure and connect webpages belonging to different websites.
Spyridakis et al. (2007)	**Embedded links** They are embedded in the narrative of a text.	**Links in lists outside a text** They list hyperlinks to subordinate pages.

---

report on studies that give mixed results about the effectiveness of embedded hyperlinks. For instance, some studies have suggested that embedded links increase comprehension and website exploration, provide context for links, and make searching fast and effective (Bernard, Hull, and Chaparro 2005). Especially in previews of websites, embedded hyperlinks have been found to increase inferential comprehension. On the other hand, some other studies have suggested that embedded links may disrupt the narrative flow of text, requiring readers to make inferences about information relationships (Burbules 1998; Dalal, Quible, and Wyatt 2000), and eventually they distract the reader from searching (Spool et al. 1997). In any case, it seems that the wording of embedded links plays a decisive role in their effectiveness (Wei et al. 2005). Hyperlinks in lists outside a text have been found to enhance search speed, particularly in cases where the information associated with the hyperlinks is already known (Bernard et al. 2005). Lists outside the text that are not accompanied by website previews have been found to lead to greater website exploration than subordinate lists that are placed below a preview (Spyridakis et al. 2007).

The analytic tool was applied to the lesson plans in the data, and the results of the application are presented next. The purpose of this analysis is to reveal the type of hyperlinks used in the lesson plans of the two portals and to identify emerging patterns of use.

Hypertextuality in *NewsHour Extra*

A factor that seems to play an important role in the selection of specific types of hyperlinks in the hypermodal lesson plan is related to the status of the lesson plans in the website and refers to whether the website is self-contained or a collaborative design project (e.g., part of a larger organization or corporate website, such as a university or some sort of broadcast). Self-contained websites include independent educational institutions, whose main aim is to publish online resources for teachers and students. Many broadcast portals today also host educational websites with teacher resources, such as lesson plans, which draw their materials extensively from the articles and reports published in the portal. In fact, educational websites in these portals seem to have been built on the idea of exploiting available media texts (e.g., articles, reports, interviews, videos, and other types of multimodal texts) from the broadcast. It is, therefore, not surprising in these cases to find plenty of website-internal hyperlinks in their lesson plans.

At least this seems to be the case with *NewsHour Extra*, which is hosted in the PBS portal. As we have seen, the main page of the website includes a section of lesson plans and several shorter sections on other teacher resources under the headings of "Iraq Themes," "NewsHour Resources," and "PBS Partners." All these shorter sections include hyperlinks from materials drawn from the PBS portal. In addition, the lesson plans rely mainly on website-internal sources that are embedded in the lessons. There are no sources in outside lists. The conducted analysis of the lesson plans has revealed that 81 percent of the total number of links are website-internal and only 19 percent are website-external (see summary of analysis in Appendix II). The website-internal hyperlinks are mainly of two types: Most of them are *content* hyperlinks, whereas the rest serve a *functional* role (e.g., connecting different parts of the text). Overall, the website-internal hyperlinks include the following:

- *NewsHour Extra* news articles and feature stories, especially written for students at the tenth grade reading level
- interview transcripts from *Online NewsHour,* an hour-long daily news broadcast that covers (among other subjects) international reports and analysis, the global economy, health issues, science and technology, politics, and the arts
- interview transcripts from PBS *Frontline,* a companion website that includes extended interviews, video, and teacher resources
- other lesson plans from a companion website, PBS *Teachers* (www.pbs.org/teachers)
- specially designed handouts by the teachers who have prepared the lesson plans; these may include reading and discussion questions, vocabulary practice, or questions for listening activities

- links to different parts of the same document (e.g., to lesson procedures or to national standards listed at the end of the lesson plan).

A distinction should be drawn at this point between website-internal and portal-internal hyperlinks.[4] Being part of a much broader corporate portal, *NewsHour Extra* includes a lot of website-internal as well as portal-internal hyperlinks. For instance, both PBS *Frontline* and PBS *Teachers* constitute two websites that are not parts of the *NewsHour Extra* website, but they are all hosted in the PBS portal. In fact, it seems that there is a strong web of connectivity among these companion websites, with one drawing materials from the other. Interestingly, one educational website draws materials from another educational website at the same portal.

Boxes 5.4 and 5.5 list the hyperlinks used in two lesson plans. The first consists only of website-internal hyperlinks. It includes a link to a feature article published in the website; two student handouts, with facts about casualties in the first Gulf War, and a detailed presentation of new US weapons to be used in Iraq; a link to resources, mainly transcripts from radio interviews, from *Online NewsHour*; a hyperlink on national standards

---

Box 5.4 Hyperlinks in the Lesson Plan "War Expectations"

Website-internal hyperlinks

NewsHour Extra article
www.pbs.org/newshour/extra/features/jan-june03/market_3-26.html

Correlation to national standards

Handout 1: Estimates of Casualties of 1991 Gulf War
www.pbs.org/newshour/extra/features/jan-june03/expectations_3-26_
handout1.html

Handout 2: New U.S. Weaponry
www.pbs.org/newshour/extra/features/jan-june03/expectations_3-26_
handout2.html

Online NewsHour: Press conferences and briefings
www.pbs.org/newshour/bb/middle_east/iraq/war/campaign.html

More Social Studies lesson plans from PBS *Teachers*
www.pbs.org/teachers

Box 5.5 Hyperlinks in the Lesson Plan "Democracy in the Middle East"

Website-internal hyperlinks

Link to an online evaluation form of the lesson plan
www.pbs.org/newshour/extra/forms/form_lessonplan.php

Correlation to national standards

Student Handout: Opening Activity: Spreading Freedom throughout the
World
www.pbs.org/newshour/extra/teachers/lessonplans/world/me_open.pdf

Student Handout: Where Is Democracy in the Middle East?
www.pbs.org/newshour/extra/teachers/lessonplans/world/me_where.pdf

Student Handout: Is Democracy Possible in the Middle East?
www.pbs.org/newshour/extra/teachers/lessonplans/world/me_possible.pdf

President Bush's second-term inaugural speech
www.pbs.org/newshour/inauguration2005/index.html

Link to "Lesson Procedures" (pdf)
www.pbs.org/newshour/extra/teachers/lessonplans/world/me_procedures
.pdf

Website-external hyperlinks

Opinion article: Democracy Is Not a Devil for Islamic Parties
http://islamicsydney.com/ story.php?id=2192

Policy article: The Democratic Ideal
   (From American Enterprise Institute for Public Policy Research)
www.aei.org/publications/ filter.all,pubID.21929/ pub_detail.asp

Policy article: The Trouble with Democracy in the Middle East
   (From Cato Institute)
www.cato.org/dailys/11-30-03.html

Video clip on White House website
www.whitehouse.gov/news/ releases/2005/01/20050120-1.html

CIA World Factbook
www.cia.gov/cia/publications/factbook

NPR (National Public Radio) Special Series on the Middle East
www.npr.org/news/specials/mideast/the_west

NewsHour Background Reports on the Middle East
www.pbs.org/newshour/bb/middle_east/middle_east.html

More social studies lesson plans from PBS *Teachers*
www.pbs.org/teachers

that leads to the last part of the lesson plan, where the specific standards this lesson adheres to are presented; and a link to the main page of PBS *Teachers,* for many other lesson plans.

On the other hand, only a few of the lesson plans use both website-internal and website-external hyperlinks. In the lesson plan "Democracy in the Middle East," for instance, there are nine website-internal and six website-external hyperlinks. A variety of website-internal links are included in this lesson plan. The *content* links include three student handouts, a transcript from *Online NewsHour,* and a link to a main page with many resources on the Middle East. In addition to *content, functional* hyperlinks are being used. One of them leads to an online evaluation form of the specific lesson plan. The questionnaire addresses teachers and includes questions about the type of subject teachers teach, the frequency with which they visit the *NewsHour Extra* teacher pages, the extent to which they use news stories or whole lesson plans, and so forth. Another *functional* link leads to an integral part of the lesson plan, "Procedures," which is not included here in the main lesson plan.

The website-external hyperlinks include one opinion article from an Australian newspaper and two policy articles from the American Enterprise Institute for Public Research and the Cato Institute, two right-wing think tanks. They also include a video clip from the White House website on President Bush's second-term inaugural speech. Another link directs students and teachers to the CIA's *World Factbook* website, which includes information on world history, geography, economy, government, transportation, military, and communications issues. Students in groups are assigned a specific country of the Middle East and are asked to locate information on its government, constitution, political parties, and legal system, among other things. There is also a link to the Special Series in the Middle East, a main page of the National Public Radio (NPR, PBS's partner in public broadcasting) website. This page includes a timeline called *The Middle East and the West (1098–2004): A Troubled History* and previews of stories, maps, and biographies covering the period from the Crusades up to the September 11 attacks.

Therefore, we notice that *NewsHour Extra* mainly draws its materials for the suggested lessons on the Iraq War from the sources available in the portal, and the majority of the links found in the lesson plans are internal links. The external links, on the other hand, are usually links to conservative, right-wing sources. Consequently, the pro-war position adopted in the lesson plans is further supported, with the selection of links from right-wing sources that support the decision to go to war.

Hypertextuality in *Rethinking Schools*

Whereas *NewsHour Extra* resources are part of a larger broadcast website, *Rethinking School* resources are part of an activist, nonprofit, educational publishing organization. Its publications include, as we have seen, special reports, such as the Special Report on "War, Terrorism and Our Classrooms"; books, which include teacher articles and lesson plans; and a magazine with teaching ideas, teacher resources, and analysis articles. The website on the Iraq War groups its resources through hyperlinks in a vertical list, appearing on the right of the webpage. This list is found in the main page and in all subsequent pages when a lesson plan or a reading is retrieved; it is placed under a specially designed logo that reads "Teaching about the War" on a black background. The list includes the following:

- lesson plans and teaching ideas, developed by the editors of *Rethinking Schools* and by other teachers
- suggested readings for teachers and students, from the *Rethinking Schools* archives and other sources
- background documents and related materials, such as the complete text of relevant United Nations resolutions
- maps and geography activities, such as maps in PDF for classroom use, and an online drag-and-drop map game, in which students are asked to put the right name on every country in the Middle East
- resources for teachers, such as books, videos, and other external sources
- links about the war, including an annotated list of website-external hyperlinks on topics such as Islam, Islamophobia, and antiwar groups
- teacher groups against the war: a listing of teacher groups that have been formed with contact details
- teacher resolutions against the war, which includes the texts from teacher organizations around the world who have taken a stand against the war.

From these categories, it becomes clear that the availability of these resources does not simply aim to provide a few ready activities to be used in the classroom about the war; its purpose extends to offering visitors background knowledge on the topic of the Iraq War and to maintaining a community of teachers who actively participate in the enrichment of these resources with new content. In most of these webpages, teachers are invited to contribute to the teacher resources on the Iraq War, by sending their own lesson accounts and teaching ideas. Overall, the suggested teacher resources in this list mostly consist of website-external hyperlinks that share one common feature: They are against the war.

Turning now to the hyperlinks included in the lesson plans and teaching ideas, we notice that very few embedded hyperlinks are found in the *Rethinking Schools* data. Of them, 28 percent are website-internal, and 68 percent are website-external hyperlinks (see summary of analysis in Appendix II). So despite the limited use of embedded links, we notice here, too, that there is a clear tendency in *Rethinking Schools* teacher resources to draw their materials from external sources. These include articles from well-known newspapers (e.g., *The Guardian* and the *New York Times*), extracts from various texts by prominent individuals (e.g., a speech by Martin Luther King), writings by laypeople (e.g., a letter from parents who have lost their son, a speech by a schoolgirl in an antiwar rally), literary texts (e.g., from an Indian novelist and a Palestinian poet), and texts from activist organizations.

Most of the lesson plans and the teaching ideas in the data include one or two website-internal or website-external hyperlinks (Box 5.6) and only four out of thirty-four include more links. For instance, in "Teaching Gulf War II" (Box 5.7), there are several website-external hyperlinks. Among them is an article from Common Dreams website, a nonprofit, activist organization, and an article from *Yes!* magazine, which, according to its mission statement, is "a non-profit publication that supports people's active engagement in solving today's social, political, and environmental challenges."[5] The resources are supplemented by multimodal materials. The first is a well-known video from Teaching for Change, an organization that aims "to transform schools into centers of justice where students learn to read, write and change the world."[6] The second is a video from the Media Education Foundation, which "produces and distributes documentary films and other educational resources to inspire critical reflection on the social, political, and cultural impact of American mass media."[7] The website-external links also contain the editors' email addresses, which are often included at the end of the article.

Therefore, in *Rethinking Schools,* hypertextuality extends beyond the links embedded in the genre of the lesson plan, to include the web of connectivity, which relates embedded links to links organized in lists.

Box 5.6 Hyperlinks in the Lesson Plan
"Poetry in a Time of Crisis"

Website-internal hyperlinks

Link to the poem
www.RethinkingSchools.org/special_reports/index.shtml

Attacks on Muslims and Arab Americans: An article from "War, Terrorism and Our Classrooms"
www.RethinkingSchools.org/special_reports/sept11/16_02/atta162 .shtml

Wong's poem in *Rethinking Our Classrooms*, Vol. 2 and also at "Waiting at the Railroad Café"

Website-external hyperlinks

Janet Wong's website with poetry
www.janetwong.com

Linda Christensen's email (editor of the article)

Box 5.7 Hyperlinks in the Lesson Plan
"Teaching Gulf War II"

Website-external hyperlinks

The Tonkin Bay Resolution, 1964
www.fordham.edu/halsall/mod/1964Tonkinbay.html

Resolution of the Bush administration
www.msnbc.com/news/810152.asp?cp1=1

Article: Iraqi Sanctions: Without Medicines and Supplies, the Children Die
www.commondreams.org/views/102300-103.htm

Article: What Happens to Your Heart (*Yes!* magazine, spring 2002)
www.futurenet.org/21American/morse.htm

Bill Bigelow's email address (*Rethinking Schools* editor)

Hidden Wars of Desert Storm
www.teachingforchange.org

Toxic Sludge Is Good for You
www.mediaed.org

Especially in the case of hyperlinks listed outside the lesson plan, there is not a default reading of the materials, and the website looks more like a depository of resources on the Iraq War, from which teachers may select their teaching materials. However, we notice here, too, that the context is clearly given and it is one-sided: All materials are against the war, and they aim to develop an antiwar awareness. Moreover, the fact that *Rethinking Schools* mostly relies on external links is understandable, if we take into account that it is not part of a broader media outlet, from which it can draw instructional materials. In addition, the website on the Iraq War also relies heavily on contributions from its members and readers. Several readings for both students and teachers are texts written by educators who are associated with *Rethinking Schools,* all of which adopt a position against the war.

Toward a Critical Hypermodal Literacy of the Media

This chapter attempts to reveal some of the ways in which the Internet medium and its affordances affect the social contexts of production, distribution, and circulation of the online lesson plan genre. It particularly focuses on the notion of hypertextuality, which is viewed as an aspect of hypermodality, and on revealing some of the different ways hypertextuality was employed in two websites with different orientations. Of course, the concept of *hypertextuality* is much more complex than is presented here, and a growing body of research in information design focuses on various other aspects, such as explicitness of local navigation links, informative phrasing of hyperlinks, text previews, and navigation menus, to name just a few (Spyridakis et al. 2007).

What this chapter does point out, though, is that in order to understand how hypertextuality operates in a specific online genre, it is not enough to focus only on the hyperlinks in the online genre; it also requires investigating the web of connectivity that relates the online genre to its immediate context (the website in which it is published) and its broader context (the portal hosting the website). This contextual perspective is necessary to reveal the discursive effects that result from the connection of previously unrelated texts through the use of hyperlinks. On the one hand, the lesson plans in the *NewsHour Extra* website have been found to systematically connect to different parts of the PBS portal. They select their instructional texts (written, audio, visual) from the respective media portal, thereby transforming their nature from media to educational texts, thus extending both their function and circulation in another context.

This practice of selecting portal-inside media texts for instructional purposes holds in itself important ideological and political implications, as we saw in Chapter 3. The orientation of these lesson plans to teach a current events topic is closely related to the fact that they constitute part of a media broadcast organization. Consequently, they use their own media texts in order to teach the war. The lesson plans in *Rethinking Schools,* on the other hand, have a very different orientation. Being part of an activist organization that openly adopts an antiwar position, the website with teacher resources on the Iraq War draws systematically on external links that all have the same aim: to develop students' antiwar awareness.

In fact, it is perhaps the first time in the history of literacy that educational materials have become freely available worldwide to such an extent, owing to the affordances of the Internet medium, something with unprecedented effects in terms of text distribution and circulation. Although the educational impact of these materials remains to be seen, their very existence points to the direction of developing new methodological and theoretical constructs to account for the new types of educational resources that all teachers of the world are exposed to. These resources, which may be viewed as different forms of informal curricula, have their own agenda (with commerce being just one of them) and shape teachers' practices to a certain extent.

For this reason it is of utmost importance to equip teachers with critical hypermodal literacy, which will enable them to analyze these resources critically. An inherent difficulty here is that, through their initial training, teachers have been exposed to a logocentric literacy, and this is how they have been trained to approach their work. Yet "the skills and experiences we have acquired from centuries of reading print documents must be adapted to a new environment," according to Spyridakis et al. (2007, 242). Practically, this means that, on the one hand, teachers need to develop some kind of hypermodal literacy; on the other hand, they will also need to be equipped with the tools to critically analyze hypermodal environments and new genre forms. Taking into account, after Gee (1996), that there are as many literacies as there are multimedia genres, and that a literacy is always a literacy of some genre that must be defined with respect to the employed sign systems, this chapter has contributed to an understanding of online discursive practices of one online genre and can thus be seen as a contribution toward the development of this media literacy.

Chapter 6

Conclusion

THE RESOURCES ON THE IRAQ WAR ANALYZED IN THIS BOOK CONSTITUTE instances of educational and political discourse at the same time. As instances of educational discourse, they are revealing of embedded pedagogies, identities, and systems of knowledge and beliefs. As instances of political discourse, they are imbued with notions of citizenship and political ideologies. In all parts of the book, the political is intermingled with the educational, revealing how struggles over different political interests and goals play out in the design of educational materials. The aim of this book has not been to question the pedagogies used[1] or to claim that one is better than the other, but rather to foreground their deeper political nature and to illustrate some constitutive elements of the pedagogies. However, this position should not be seen as a claim to neutrality and impartiality. Far from it. The critical methodology employed in the book is based on the premise that any approach adopted by an analyst is filtered by her subjectivity, and that is also true of this book. It also considers all ways of understanding as historically and culturally relative, and knowledge as a product not of an objective observation of the world, but of the social processes and interactions through which people constantly engage each other.

By comparing educational resources in two websites with different political ideologies and positions about the Iraq War, this book attempts to show that the discursive construction is consistent and is realized at different levels: at the level of pedagogy (critical thinking vs. critical literacy in Chapters 1 and 2), at the level of the types of suggested activities (enhancing competitiveness vs. raising empathy for the other), at the level of reading texts for students (the foregrounding vs. backgrounding of war as injury and war as contest in Chapter 3), at the level of the genre addressing teachers (traditional vs. reflective lesson plans in Chapter 4), and at the level of hypertextuality employed in the two websites (Chapter 5). Tables 6.1, 6.2, and 6.3 summarize the most important findings of the conducted analysis in terms of each pedagogy's main features (Table 6.1), of the discursive identities for teachers and students (Table 6.2), and of the lesson plan genre as it is realized in the two websites (Table 6.3).

Table 6.1 The "How" of War Pedagogy

	NewsHour Extra	*Rethinking Schools*
Website Ideology	Pro-war position: not openly stated (inferred by overview section).	Antiwar position: explicitly stated (e.g., in titles of lesson plans, introductory paragraphs, through pictures).
Lesson Aims	To follow current events and to inform students about them.	To develop antiwar consciousness and a critical awareness.
Topicality	Emphasis on "current events"; focus on topicality. Discussion around "everyday events" and the Iraq War as episodes (no reference to the broader context).	No emphasis on the current war; connection with previous wars and with the broader context (causes leading to the war, political interests in the Middle East area).
Text Analysis	"Critical analysis" of texts in the tradition of critical thinking (development of good argumentative skills).	Development of "critical habits" in the tradition of critical pedagogy (developing the tools of deep questioning through which students can attempt to make sense of today's global conflicts).
Lesson Focus	Students read a text and respond to reading comprehension questions (e.g., they identify a text's main idea and supporting arguments) in order to understand it better.	Students read multimodal texts (including pictures, videos, films, songs) and use obtained knowledge to challenge a text's ideology.
Language Analysis	No emphasis on language analysis; few activities, for instance, focus on an analysis of war vocabulary.	Emphasis on language analysis, mainly lexical analysis, as a tool to reveal ideological positioning.

(continues)

The differences between the two websites that are identified at almost all levels of analysis are not incidental. From the beginning of the analysis, it is clear that the two websites do not merely present two different views on the war but constitute realizations of two broad approaches to education, the dominant and the critical, which aim at the construction of different pedagogic subjects. Most importantly, political positions have been found to conflate with educational practices. The conservative government's decision to go to war finds its realization through a

Table 6.1 The "How" of War Pedagogy (continued)

	NewsHour Extra	*Rethinking Schools*
Materials	Types of materials: mainly media texts (from hosting portal, such as news reports, feature articles, and transcripts from interviews); governmental documents and right-wing policy texts; and prepared, ready-to-use handouts. Limited use of technology.	Variety of resources: Internet websites (mainly activist sources); war statistics; maps; antiwar literature, songs, videos, articles, books, etc. Some of these are given through hyperlinks; for some others, information is offered as to how to locate them (e.g., electronic address, publisher). Extensive use of technology.
Activity Types	Types of activities: pair work, group work, presentations, project work. Students respond to comprehension questions, participate in oral debates and role-plays, write argumentative essays, analyze the pros and cons of a situation, etc.	Types of activities: pair work, group work, simulations, role-playing, project work, presentations. Students write their own poems; prepare bulletin boards with photos, maps, and student writing; prepare a poster on land mines with pictures of victims, maps, essays, facts, etc.
Activity Aims	To obtain knowledge on a topic through the development of argumentative skills (suggested sources: library or Internet search on a particular subject).	To focus on students' feelings and emotions, to encourage empathy, and to sensitize students to an alternative view of the war.
National Standards	Close connection to national standards. Systematic attempt to justify the appropriateness of the lesson plans to national standards. Skills developed in each lesson are clearly specified.	No reference to national standards. Skills developed in each lesson not always considered. Focus on raising students' awareness against the war.

Table 6.2 Identities and Social Relationships

	NewsHour Extra	*Rethinking Schools*
Teacher Identity		
	As someone who is given all material and detailed instructions as to how to use it. Limited initiative is left up to the teacher for decisions.	As someone who selects teaching materials from a variety of available resources. Exchanging ideas with colleagues is valued. Cooperative spirit.
	As someone who functions within the specified framework.	As someone who selects appropriate materials and decides how these will be used in the classroom.
	As someone who is assumed to support the government's decisions.	As someone who takes a critical stance toward the war and sees it as his/her purpose to develop students' critical awareness.
	As someone whose personal history and views are not to "intervene" in the teaching process (objectives or steps to be followed by all teachers).	As someone whose personal history, views, evaluation are considered important. In line with Freire's view that teachers should attempt to "live part of their dreams within their educational space."
	As an instructor.	As an active participant in the teaching process.
Student Identity		
	Subjects to be "taught" about the war. Emphasis on informing them. Representation of students as subjects who are told what to do and who are expected to respond accordingly.	Subjects prepared to become active participants in society. Emphasis on students' emotions and feelings and on the development of critical skills.
Author's Voice		
	A professional giving "objective" accounts of lessons and instructions.	A colleague writing to other colleagues sharing experience.
Writer-Reader Relationship		
	A professional talking to other professionals.	A colleague sharing experience with other colleagues.

Table 6.3 The Genre of Lesson Plans in *NewsHour Extra* and *Rethinking Schools*

	NewsHour Extra	*Rethinking Schools*
Generic Structure	Typical format in all lesson plans: Overview, Materials, Aims and Objectives, Procedure, Extension Ideas/Homework, National Standards. Each section is organized according to specifications.	Reflective lesson plan (not typical format). Written in the form of continuous text, a narrative with a beginning, middle, and end, with thematic sections that vary from one lesson plan to another.
Content	Emphasis on *what* and *how* it is to be taught. Detailed description of activities (in the Procedure section) to be handled in class in a prespecified order. Particular attention as to the *how*. All materials are given to teachers, ready to be used in the classroom.	Emphasis on what is to be taught. The extent to which *how* is explicitly stated varies. Some lesson plans just report on different material to be used (e.g., different antiwar songs) with no reference as to how to teach them.
Orientation	Prescriptive: A typical description of what is to be done. *How* is described in terms of future activities, with the use of future tense and imperatives. Training of students in transferable skills (e.g., learning how to analyze something in groups and report back to class).	Retrospective: Description of lessons that have already been tried out. Narrative of what has happened in the classroom; use of past tenses.
Discourse Formality	A technical document written in objective language (third person, no direct reference to the audience, full verb forms). A teacher-only perspective is adopted (emphasis on what the teacher should do in the class). No student responses to activities are included.	A subjective account of a lesson. Frequent personal accounts by the author and informal language (first person, direct reference to the audience, short verb forms). Both teacher and student perspectives are used (e.g., teachers talk about their uncertainties, their own evaluation of the class, future improvements, and failures; students' responses to activities are frequently reported).

161

pedagogy that assumes knowledge to be objective and neutral (following the tradition of positivism) and that focuses on delivering predefined knowledge and critical thinking skills to students. The voicing of an alternative perspective against the war is realized through a critical pedagogy that raises questions of the type "whose knowledge?" and "whose benefit?" and moves beyond the construction of polarizing positions of the type "us versus them." The political agenda in both websites is clear, and it is consistently supported by compatible pedagogies, ideologies, and identities.

In terms of pedagogy, *NewsHour Extra* has developed a critical thinking pedagogy that takes a pro-war position and aims to inform young Americans about the official US position and help them understand "the decision to go to war." The website's educational materials are part of the overall agenda of teaching current events in the classroom. *NewsHour Extra* clearly attempts to manage pedagogic discourse along the lines of the official US politics concerning the war. This could be seen as an articulation of "compulsory patriotism" (Apple 2002, 305) recontextualized in lesson plans, and perhaps the main reason why the opposite side is not voiced. The critical thinking approach teaches students argumentative skills and exposes them to activities that enable them to argue and to analyze a text by responding to comprehension questions. Giroux calls it a "pedagogy of understanding," because it equips students with the resources that will enable them to understand the world around them. He argues, however, that argumentation skills, although important, should only be seen as a first step of a much richer educational experience that prepares future citizens to act upon their environment, not merely to understand it.

Interestingly, the suggested lessons in *NewsHour Extra* attempt to restrict the possibility of the creation of what Bernstein called a "potential discursive gap." They do so through meanings that "create and unite two worlds," in this case, the students' and teachers' world, with the world of the official US administration. The meanings that create and unite the two worlds always imply, according to Bernstein, some kind of relation with a specific material base: a specific social division of labor and a specific set of social relationships within that division of labor (1996, 44). In the case of *NewsHour Extra*, educational practices, discursive identities, and implied ideologies all contribute to the conservative agenda of supporting the decision to go to war.

Moreover, these meanings also create specific subject positions that position social subjects exactly in discourse. In the context of *NewsHour*

Extra, teachers are discursively constructed as sophisticated professionals who produce and consume technical documents. They are willing
to promote national standards and, at moments of crisis, such as this
one, they help their students "follow the aftermath of war." Their task is
restricted, however, to the implementation of specified steps: All information and materials needed to complete the lesson are provided as well as
detailed instructions on how to use them. Limited initiative is left to the
teacher. Professionalism is based on objective accounts of the teaching
situation, and there is no reference to the effects of teaching. Similarly,
students are discursively constructed as social subjects who respond to
the suggested activities according to the specified lesson plan objectives
and who develop skills in attaining national standards. They are trained
to explore a situation's advantages and disadvantages, assuming that in
this way they are exposed to all opposing views before they "choose" one
position. Moreover, they are good patriots, and they are proud of their
country's glorious past and present.

On the other hand, the suggested lessons of *Rethinking Schools,* an activist organization, openly adopt a position against the war and attempt to
give students an alternative view of the war in the context of critical pedagogy. The website's educational materials are part of the overall agenda
of an alternative vision of education, one that promotes social justice. In
Giroux's account, this is a "pedagogy of intervention," because it equips
students with the resources that will enable them to act upon the world
around them. At a first level, critical pedagogy focuses on the primacy
of dialogue, understanding, and critique and aims at the development
of critical readers who speak back to authority. It particularly "seeks to
enable students to recognize that things may not be what they seem and
that a different world is possible, one in which society never reaches
the limits of social justice or its democratic vistas" (Giroux 2004, 124).
At a second level, critical pedagogy prepares students for democratic
citizenship, by getting them to act on what they know, thus encouraging
active participation, engagement with important social problems, and
public responsibility. For Giroux, "this approach connects a pedagogy
of understanding with practices that are empowering and oppositional,
practices that offer students the knowledge and skills needed to believe
that a substantive democracy is both possible and worth taking responsibility for and struggling over" (ibid.).

In Bernstein's terms, the critical pedagogic discourse found in *Rethinking Schools* educational materials enhances the creation of a "potential
discursive gap," in an attempt to shape students who think differently.

This discourse develops a critical stance toward the official US politics concerning the war and suggests an alternative pedagogy, urging students toward the "yet to be thought" (Bernstein 1996, 44). Bernstein calls it the meeting point of order and disorder, of coherence and incoherence, and he suggests that the creation of this space may become a site for alternative possibilities, for alternative realizations that change the relation between the material and the immaterial.

In this realm, teachers are discursively constructed as active participants in the pedagogical practice who are invited to select their own teaching materials from a variety of available resources. They negotiate meanings together with their students, and they teach a curriculum of "tolerance" that deals with the destructive effects of the war. Emphasis is on dealing with students' emotions and feelings. Coming from an activist publishing organization, the informal curriculum on the Iraq War aims to turn students into activists who are well informed and who can argue and persuade their audience against the mainstream view. However, it should be noted that here, too, the opposite side often exists only to be refuted, and the context is given as well: Both students and teachers are assumed to adopt an antiwar position and to become activists who restore truth and reverse misplaced views, thereby developing students' critical awareness. Generally, students seem to be easily convinced to adopt the suggested alternative explanation of events, and there is little account of their reservations or resistance.

Further differences between the two websites concern the way they adopt a global and local perspective (Apple 2002) and the way they manage to connect the private with the public. In the case of *NewsHour Extra,* despite frequent references to "coalition forces," the war is seen from a local point of view, as a war between the United States and Iraq. There is no reference to the rest of the world or any attempt to discuss cultural, religious, or other aspects. In *Rethinking Schools,* there is a systematic attempt to connect the local with the global, the current situation with past situations, and the Iraq War with broader US foreign affairs and interests.

Both pedagogies have opened up a space in which the personal is used as a way to discuss public issues and concerns, and both engage students in some kind of text analysis. However, in this book, we see that the pedagogical task involves much more than the actual translation and analysis of texts. Subject positions and embedded ideologies in the reading texts, in the language tasks addressing students, even in the genre addressing teachers all affect the terms through which engagement will take place in the continuous translation between the personal and the public.

Politics Again: What Kind of Citizens?

It is clear that the educational materials in the two websites assume different conceptions of citizenship with different curricular implications. Considering the political nature of these materials, we eventually come to ask the questions: *What is the conception of citizenship in each set of educational materials, and what kind of citizens are they trying to shape? What political interests are embedded in the conception of citizenship assumed by the two informal curricula, and what kind of values are promoted by each one of them?* Research reveals that educational researchers and policy makers have developed curricular programs that align with different conceptions of citizenship. Conservative educators, for instance, have been found to promote curricula that emphasize individual character and societal problems as caused by personal deficits (Bennett 1998), whereas curricula promoted by left-oriented educators focus on social critique and structural change (Freire 2005; Shor 1992).

In their award-winning article "What Kind of Citizen? The Politics of Educating for Democracy," Westheimer and Kahne (2004a) identify three different conceptions of citizenship in current educational programs and curricula: the *personally responsible* citizens, the *participatory* citizens, and the *justice oriented* citizens. Although the authors are clear from the beginning that each category reflects a distinctive set of theoretical and curricular goals, they accept the fact that it would be possible for a given curriculum to prepare students for more than one kind of citizenship. In what follows I engage in a rereading of my research findings along the lines of these three conceptions of citizenship, in order to identify the kinds of citizens developed in each set of educational materials.

According to Westheimer and Kahne (2004a, 2004b, 2006), a curriculum that aims at developing *personally responsible* citizens prepares students to act responsibly in their community by obeying laws, helping those in need, engaging in volunteer work, dealing with social problems, being committed to core democratic values (such as freedom of speech and liberty), being well informed about how government works, and building virtuous behavior with traits such as honesty, integrity, and self-discipline. The authors acknowledge the importance of these traits, yet they stress that too much emphasis on individual character may distract attention from analysis of the causes of social problems and from identification of systemic solutions. They also argue that the vision of obedience and patriotism that is found in this conception of citizenship may be at odds with the democratic aims they promote in the first place. The authors also warn about the conservative political agenda that these educational programs and curricula entail. However, the development of the *personally responsible* citizens seems to be quite popular in American schools, because research on students' perceptions of citizenship has indicated that most students define citizenship through character traits such as obeying the laws and helping others (Chiodo and Martin 2005; Hickey 2002; Martin and Chiodo 2007).

The curriculum that aims at developing *participatory* citizens prepares students to be active participants in the civic affairs and the social life of their community; engage in collective efforts; be knowledgeable about how government and various community organizations work; be informed about the importance of planning and participating in organized efforts; be sensitive to those in need; and understand the importance of developing relationships, common understandings, trust, and collective commitments. Westheimer and Kahne argue that these programs support civic participation, but they do not necessarily develop students' abilities to analyze and critique root causes of social problems.

Finally, a curriculum that aims at developing *justice oriented* citizens prepares them to engage in informed analysis and discussion concerning social, political, and economic structures; address root causes of social problems; use rhetoric that calls attention to matters of social injustice; focus on collective work and community-related issues; deal with structural critique; and consider collective strategies for social change. Acknowledging that this conception of citizenship is the least pursued in curricula, the authors point to the common ground it shares with *participatory* citizenship for community-related issues and to those features that distinguish it from the previous conceptions of citizenship (critical analysis of social issues, actions taken to restore social injustice and bring social change).

Returning to our data in this book, and attempting to relate the two informal curricula with these three conceptions of citizenship, we could claim that the conception of citizenship employed in *NewsHour Extra* is closer to the *personally responsible* notion of citizenship, while, at the same time, it also partly draws on the *participatory* notion of citizenship. The *NewsHour Extra* informal curriculum takes for granted students' (and teachers') loyalty and patriotism, unquestionably accepts government decisions, and prepares well-informed citizens who analyze the various aspects of an issue in order to come up with reasonable argumentation in support of the position they hold. By employing a "pedagogy of understanding" it puts at rest any possibility of critiquing government decisions and promotes loyalty, obedience, and patriotism. The focus on visions of patriotism noted in *NewsHour Extra* materials is not only characteristic of that specific website. In fact, there has been a renewed interest in several high school civics, social science, and history educational programs to promote visions of patriotism after 9/11. As Westheimer (2003, 17) put it, "The attacks on the World Trade Center and the accompanying dialogues on domestic security and foreign policy have further spurred educators to reexamine the role of schools in educating students to be thoughtful and engaged citizens." The focus of these programs, along similar lines as *NewsHour Extra,* is to convey knowledge of important historical facts and a sense of national pride. The role of this type of curriculum is to advance "some unified notion of truth that supports—without dissent—officially accepted positions" (Westheimer 2004, 232). Politics is here conceived as the opposite of patriotism, and "being political" is considered as something that devalues the public good and should therefore be "reserved for exploring views that are unpopular" (ibid.).

Furthermore, although the *NewsHour Extra* curriculum builds young Americans' characters and prepares them to become good patriots equipped with adequate knowledge on current events and affairs, at the same time, it encourages them to be active supporters of their country's decision to go to war. In other words, it seems that the concept of citizenship promoted here is not just limited to building character; it also extends to include a particular type of *participatory* conception of citizenship. The students who are taught this curriculum are expected to be both knowledgeable about current political issues and affairs and active members of their community, by participating in some kind of collective work. They have been trained for this through a number of group activities, role-plays, and simulations that they have practiced in the classroom (see Chapter 1). At the same time, the building of character together with the extensive political knowledge they have received prepares them to take up leadership positions within established systems and community structures, which is another characteristic of the *participatory* citizenship perspective.

On the other hand, analysis of suggested readings (Chapter 3) and classroom activities (Chapter 2) in *Rethinking Schools* curriculum suggests that it promotes a *justice oriented* notion of citizenship. The core assumption in this conception of citizenship is, according to Westheimer and Kahne (2004b, 242), that in order for today's students and future citizens to solve social problems and improve society, "they must question and change established systems and structures when they reproduce patterns of injustice over time." An activist organization that promotes critical pedagogy and a strong supporter of public education, *Rethinking Schools* develops a curriculum that asks the "why" and "whose interest" questions and stays away from dichotomies of the type "political or patriotic." Here, being political is a good thing and necessary in the process of becoming a *justice oriented* citizen. Consequently, whereas educators in *NewsHour Extra* focus on a narrow view of patriotism, *Rethinking Schools* educators prioritize a different kind of teaching for democratic citizenship: They recognize ambiguity and conflict, accept human conditions and aspirations as complex and contested, and embrace debate and deliberation "as a cornerstone of democratic societies" (Westheimer 2004, 231). This curriculum insists on the importance of developing literate citizens, who are able to participate in democratic affairs of the community and change the world around them by restoring social injustice. The notion of *participatory citizenship* is also claimed here, yet in a different way from the one we find in the *NewsHour Extra* curriculum. Participation here does not involve activities like charity and volunteerism, but rather activities like protests, community drives, and grassroots campaigns that are directed at restoring social injustice and effecting social change. Students in the *Rethinking Schools* curriculum are seen as agents of change.

Looking closely at the two informal curricula, we notice that both sets of analyzed data draw upon the notion of *participatory citizenship,* but they seem to understand it differently. In fact, the situation seems to be more complex than the one defined in the three categories of citizens described previously. Although each one of the suggested types of citizens has distinct characteristics, this study indicates that there is not necessarily a neat progression from one kind of citizenship to another. Both curricula analyzed in this book claim a *participatory* ground. In the first case, it is from the perspective of the *personally responsible* citizens, who are supporters of their country's decision to go to war, well informed about the reasons that have led to war, and willing to participate actively in their community for that cause. In the second case, the curriculum that adopts the perspective of the *justice oriented* citizenship prepares students who are approaching the war and its causes within a broader sociohistorical context, relating the present war to wider geopolitical and economic interests, challenging the necessity to go to war in the first place, and organizing action against it. Student participation here takes several different forms and may involve discussing with other members of the family, trying to convince them, writing up letters of protest, and preparing posters for their schools and their communities, among other things.

In fact, it seems that in the case of the two curricula under discussion, there is a defining concept of citizenship (that of the *personally responsible* for the first one and the *justice oriented* for the second), which also regulates the conception of *participatory citizenship* and, in effect, the nature of student participation in community activities in each case: Obedient citizens who unquestionably accept governmental decisions in the context of a narrow vision of patriotism are expected to be involved in community activities that are different from the activities of students who challenge governmental decisions and are willing to take action in order to restore social and political injustice. This defining concept of citizenship principle is not irrelevant to the employed pedagogy: The conception of the *personally responsible* citizenship in *NewsHour Extra* is realized through the pedagogy of critical thinking, operating in the context of a broader "pedagogy of understanding," whereas the conception of the *justice oriented* citizenship in *Rethinking Schools* is realized through critical pedagogy in the context of a "pedagogy on intervention" (cf. Hyslop-Margison and Thayer 2009). We notice, therefore, that although both curricula are quite sophisticated, each has its own political agenda, approaches the notion of democracy and its teaching differently, and ultimately employs a different notion of citizenship. After all, we would agree with Westheimer (2004, 233) that curricular choices are not arbitrary, but political choices with political consequences.

Developing a Critical Media Literacy

The need for a critical media literacy may have been a recent addition to the educational agenda, but its importance increases significantly as media extend to new forms of interaction, giving rise to new types of genres and discourses, blended and hybrid forms of identity and representation, and new spatial and temporal relations. Today media culture strongly influences our daily lives in multiple and complex ways, whose effects on public and private life we have only begun to research. Gounari (2009, 148), for instance, proposes that we view new information and communication technologies as sites of public pedagogy where particular forms of knowledge and literacies are produced and reproduced. Defining public pedagogy as "a process that constitutes a broader category beyond classroom practices and the confines of official curricula and educational canons" (167), she suggests that critical media literacy extends beyond "interpretive understanding" of the new genres and discourses to a "paideia of autonomy," in which people have the capacity to challenge and transform themselves (172). To develop critical media literacy, both students and educators must have the tools to critically analyze online multimodal texts and to recognize how online texts construct and position viewers and readers. They must approach media texts as socially constructed, affected by and affecting social and cultural change.

In concluding this book, I think it is useful to list some critical questions educators may ask in their analysis of online educational materials and their development of critical media literacy with their students. These questions result from the analysis conducted in this book. They serve as a starting point for approaching online educational materials, and, thus, they contribute to the development of a methodology that critically analyzes online educational resources. Teachers may consider this series of critical questions when they are called on to make selections from available online resources.

Questions concerning language tasks and the employed pedagogy:

> What types of activities are students engaged in?
> What discourses are drawn on in the verbalizing of language activities?
> What role are the students invited to occupy in these activities?
> What subject positions are students invited to adopt during the activities?
> Are there any ideologically valued presuppositions and implicatures in the activities' instructional discourse that lead students to adopt a particular point of view?
> Are there any assumptions that set up the framework for expected answers?

Critical questions concerning the ideology of the instructional texts:

> What kinds of texts are used for reading?
> Where were the instructional texts originally published?
> What is the ideological position of the sources?
> Who wrote them, and for what purpose?
> How are they structured?
> What position do they adopt?
> Is this position consistent throughout?
> What kinds of representations of the world and of the main protagonists do they imply?
> How naturalized are these representations? What kind of reading positions do the texts construe for the reader?
> How are the media and other discourses transformed into pedagogic discourses?
> How do the main recontextualized principles operate in the instructional texts?

Are there any other kinds of instructional materials used, such as
   photos, letters, or songs?
Are students involved in the "reading" of multimodal texts?

Critical questions concerning online resources for teachers:

How are the materials for teachers organized?
Are they made available in the form of lesson plans for teachers to
   follow in their classroom?
How are the lesson plans organized?
What kinds of lesson plans are used?
Are teachers' personal accounts included in lesson plans?
Are any "success stories" included in lesson plans? Are any failure
   stories included in addition to success stories?
Is there any reference to national standards?
Is there any reference to any types of standards or other forms of
   evaluation criteria?

Critical questions concerning hypermodality:

How is meaning construed in the websites that address teachers?
What degree of importance is assigned to different modes and their
   combinations?
What is the hypermodal composition (content organization and navi-
   gation design) of these websites?
How is the website with teacher resources organized?
Is it a self-contained website or part of a larger organization?
What is the broader context of the teacher website?
What kinds of hyperlinks are used? How are hyperlinks organized?
Are hyperlinks embedded or in lists? To what extent?
Do hyperlinks lead to website-internal or website-external sources?

A Concluding Note

In closing, I would like to account for yet another reading of this book's
findings. It seems that in the late-modern period of fragmentation
(Chouliaraki and Fairclough 1999), the grand narratives of nation,
national identity, and citizenship, on the one hand, and (international)
justice, on the other hand, are coming back and, surprisingly, by different

pedagogies. The symbolic power of September 11 and the Iraq War, as well as their deployment as symbolic resources, are difficult to specify, because they have the potential to be used to mobilize, criticize, or legitimate a number of competing positions.

> For progressive educators, it has come to symbolize the need for greater international and intercultural understanding. For more conservative or repressive forces, it has come to symbolize the need to check or oppose the influence of Islam, and to "protect" certain dominant cultural traditions. For others, it serves to represent the tensions between these perspectives. (Centre for Public Policy Research 2002, 315)

National identity, as a complex of common beliefs, opinions, emotional attitudes, and behavioral dispositions (such as the willingness to take sides with a nation and to protect it when threatened), is shaped by state, political, institutional, educational, media, and everyday social practices (Wodak et al. 1999). The construction of a common political past (around myths of origin, mythical figures, political successes, times of crisis, and prosperity) and of a common political present and future (around citizenship, political achievements, crises and dangers, current and future political problems, future political objectives, and political virtues) is based on the formation of sameness and difference. This book addresses how these competing positions and the notions of sameness and difference have permeated teacher resources available online and have formed different war pedagogies. It is recognized, though, that an analysis that attempts to understand the "urge to have schools participate in a complicated set of patriotic discourses and practices that swept over the United States" in the wake of September 11 and the Iraq War should look at the broader context and examine how the global is dynamically linked to the local and how dominant public discourses have become common sense (Apple 2002, 299). However, despite much theoretical discussion on the matter, any attempt to pedagogize issues related to nation and justice seems to raise more questions than it answers.

Appendix I

NewsHour Extra Data

Lesson Plans

A Call to Jihad, by Lara Maupin, social studies teacher at Thomas Jefferson High School for Science and Technology in Alexandria, VA
www.pbs.org/newshour/extra/teachers/lessonplans/iraq/saddam_4-1.html

Analyzing U.S. Policy in Iraq, by Lisa Iverson, social studies educator at Cascade High School in Turner, Oregon
www.pbs.org/newshour/extra/teachers/lessonplans/world/iraq_strategy2_01-07.html

Choices in War: What Would You Save First?, by Lisa Greeves, English and journalism teacher
www.pbs.org/newshour/extra/teachers/lessonplans/iraq/choices_4-14.html

Creating a New Media in the Arab World, by Lisa Greeves, English and journalism teacher
www.pbs.org/newshour/extra/teachers/lessonplans/iraq/newmedia_4-10.html

Debating Iraq, by Laura Greenwald, The Paul H. Nitze School of Advanced International Studies (SAIS) of Johns Hopkins University in Washington, DC, August 8, 2010
www.pbs.org/newshour/extra/teachers/lessonplans/middle_east/iraq.html

Democracy in the Middle East, by Greg Timmons, teacher and executive
director of The Constitution Project in Portland, Oregon
www.pbs.org/newshour/extra/teachers/lessonplans/world/mideast
_democracy.html

Getting to Democracy, by Annie Schleicher, associate editor of *NewsHour
Extra,* former high school teacher
www.pbs.org/newshour/extra/teachers/lessonplans/iraq/democracy_4-15
.html

Humanitarian Aid in Iraq, by Joanne Dufour, classroom teacher, teacher
trainer, and curriculum developer in the New York and Seattle areas
www.pbs.org/newshour/extra/teachers/lessonplans/iraq/aid_3-24.html

Iraq's Latest Strategy: Suicide Attacks, by Doug DuBrin, English and history
teacher, editor, and writer
www.pbs.org/newshour/extra/teachers/lessonplans/iraq/suicide_short_3
-30.html

Military Women, by Lara Maupin, social studies teacher at Thomas Jefferson
High School for Science and Technology in Alexandria, VA
www.pbs.org/newshour/extra/teachers/lessonplans/iraq/women_4-2.html

Najaf—A Holy City Caught in the Crossfire, by Lara Maupin, social studies
teacher at Thomas Jefferson High School for Science and Technology in
Alexandria, VA
www.pbs.org/newshour/extra/teachers/lessonplans/iraq/najaf_3-31.html

Reconstruction of Iraq: A Lesson of Historical Precedents, by Alexa D. Pot-
ter, historian
www.pbs.org/newshour/extra/teachers/lessonplans/iraq/rebuild_4-16
.html

Reporting on War in the 21st Century, by Lisa Greeves, English and journalism teacher
www.pbs.org/newshour/extra/teachers/lessonplans/iraq/war_21century
.html

Responding to Quotes and Aphorisms, by Raven Tyler, assistant editor with
Online NewsHour and former high school English and journalism teacher
www.pbs.org/newshour/extra/teachers/lessonplans/iraq/quotes.html

The Cost of War, by Sally Fredriksen, retired Fairfax County teacher
www.pbs.org/newshour/extra/teachers/lessonplans/iraq/budget_3-25
.html

The Decision to Go to War, by Lara Maupin, social studies teacher at Thomas Jefferson High School for Science and Technology in Alexandria, VA
www.pbs.org/newshour/extra/teachers/lessonplans/iraq/war.html

The Ethics of Embedded Journalists, by Lisa Greeves, English and journalism teacher
www.pbs.org/newshour/extra/teachers/lessonplans/iraq/embedded_3-2.html

The Powell Doctrine, by Doug DuBrin, English and history teacher, editor, and writer
www.pbs.org/newshour/extra/teachers/lessonplans/iraq/powelldoctrine.html

The Rights of Detainees at Guantanamo Bay, by Lara Maupin, formerly a social studies teacher and student government adviser at Thomas Jefferson High School for Science and Technology in Alexandria, VA
www.pbs.org/newshour/extra/teachers/lessonplans/world/guantanamo.html

The Role of American Embassies, by Lara Maupin, formerly a social studies teacher and student government adviser at Thomas Jefferson High School for Science and Technology in Alexandria, VA
www.pbs.org/newshour/extra/teachers/lessonplans/world/embassies_6-28.html

The Role of Exiles in Post-Saddam Iraq, by Doug DuBrin, English and history teacher, editor, and writer
www.pbs.org/newshour/extra/teachers/lessonplans/iraq/exile_4-13.html

The Role of the Kurds, Sunni and Shiitesi n Iraq, by Sally Fredriksen, retired Fairfax County teacher
www.pbs.org/newshour/extra/teachers/lessonplans/iraq/ethnic.html

The Role of the United Nations in Postwar Iraq, by Doug DuBrin, English and history teacher, editor, and writer
www.pbs.org/newshour/extra/teachers/lessonplans/iraq/unrole_4-6.html

The Rules of Engagement: The Geneva Convention, by Doug DuBrin, English and history teacher, editor, and writer
www.pbs.org/newshour/extra/teachers/lessonplans/iraq/prisoners_3-23.html

To Report or Not to Report?, by Lisa Greeves, English and journalism teacher
www.pbs.org/newshour/extra/teachers/lessonplans/iraq/jorda_4-17.html

War Expectations, by Lara Maupin, social studies teacher at Thomas Jefferson High School for Science and Technology in Alexandria, VA
www.pbs.org/newshour/extra/teachers/lessonplans/iraq/expectations_3-26.html

Weapons of Mass Destruction in Iraq, by Lara Maupin, social studies teacher at Thomas Jefferson High School for Science and Technology in Alexandria, VA
www.pbs.org/newshour/extra/teachers/lessonplans/iraq/wmd_4-7.html

What Are the Conditions for Victory in Iraq?, by Lara Maupin, social studies teacher at Thomas Jefferson High School for Science and Technology in Alexandria, VA
www.pbs.org/newshour/extra/teachers/lessonplans/iraq/baghdad_4-9.html

Who Should Rule the Interim Government in Iraq? What Should Be Their Priorities?, by Sally Fredriksen, retired Fairfax County teacher
www.pbs.org/newshour/extra/teachers/lessonplans/iraq/postwar_4-8.html

World Media: Comparison of Iraq War Accounts, by Lisa Greeves, English and journalism teacher
www.pbs.org/newshour/extra/teachers/lessonplans/iraq/arabmedia_4-3.html

Rethinking Schools Data

Lesson Plans

Defeating Despair, by Bill Bigelow, classroom editor of *Rethinking Schools*
www.RethinkingSchools.org/war/ideas/Desp163.shtml

Drawing on History to Challenge the War, by Polly Kellogg, instructor at St. Cloud State University in Minnesota
www.RethinkingSchools.org/war/ideas/draw173.shtml

Entering History Through Poetry, by Linda Christensen, high school language arts coordinator for Portland, OR, Public Schools, and an editor of *Rethinking Schools*
www.RethinkingSchools.org/war/ideas/ente173.shtml

Images of War, by Kelley Dawson, primary school teacher at La Escuela Fratney in Milwaukee, WI, and editorial associate of *Rethinking Schools*
www.RethinkingSchools.org/special_reports/sept11/16_02/imag162.shtml

Letters to the Universe, by Tracy Wagner, teacher of English at Madison East High School, in Madison, WI
www.RethinkingSchools.org/special_reports/sept11/16_02/lett162.shtml

Poetry in a Time of Crisis, by Linda Christensen, high school language arts coordinator for Portland, OR, Public Schools, and an editor of *Rethinking Schools*
www.RethinkingSchools.org/special_reports/sept11/16_02/poet162.shtml

Predicting How the U.S. Government Will Respond to the Iraqi Government, by the editors of *Rethinking Schools*
www.RethinkingSchools.org/war/ideas/lessiraq.shtml

Rethinking the Teaching of the Vietnam War, by Bill Bigelow, classroom editor of *Rethinking Schools*
www.RethinkingSchools.org/war/ideas/viet173.shtml

Songs for Global Conscience, by Bob Peterson, teacher at La Escuela Fratney and editor of *Rethinking Schools*
www.RethinkingSchools.org/war/ideas/Song152.shtml

"Stand Up! It's the Law!", by Kate Lyman, teacher of a combined second and third grade classroom in Madison, WI
www.RethinkingSchools.org/special_reports/sept11/16_02/stan162.shtml

Teaching Gulf War II, by Bill Bigelow, classroom editor of *Rethinking Schools*
www.RethinkingSchools.org/war/ideas/gulf173.shtml

Teaching with Protest Songs, by Bob Peterson, teacher at La Escuela Fratney and editor of *Rethinking Schools*
www.RethinkingSchools.org/war/ideas/song173.shtml

The World Up Close, by Bob Peterson, teacher at La Escuela Fratney and editor of *Rethinking Schools*
www.RethinkingSchools.org/special_reports/sept11/16_02/clos162.shtml

Whose "Terrorism"?, by Bill Bigelow, classroom editor of *Rethinking Schools*
www.RethinkingSchools.org/war/ideas/whos162.shtml

Readings and Teaching Ideas
From the Special Report "War, Terrorism and Our Classrooms"

Afghanistan: The Route to Riches, by Andy Rowell, reporter for *The Guardian*
www.RethinkingSchools.org/special_reports/sept11/16_02/rich162.shtml

A Time of Gifts, by Stephen Gould, professor of zoology at Harvard, author of *Questioning the Millennium*
www.RethinkingSchools.org/special_reports/sept11/16_02/gift162.shtml

An Alternative to War, by Michael Ratner, former director of the Center for Constitutional Rights in New York City, and Jules Lobel, professor of law at the University of Pittsburgh School of Law
www.RethinkingSchools.org/special_reports/sept11/16_02/alt162.shtml

Backyard Terrorism, by George Monbiot, weekly columnist for *The Guardian* and author of *Captive State: The Corporate Takeover of Britain*
www.RethinkingSchools.org/special_reports/sept11/16_02/yard162.shtml

Bush Signs Anti-Terrorism Law, by the American Civil Liberties Union
www.RethinkingSchools.org/special_reports/sept11/16_02/law162.shtml

Dear Parents, by Ann Pelo, teacher at Hilltop Children's Center for ten years, coauthor, with Fran Davidson, of *That's Not Fair: A Teacher's Guide to Activism with Young Children* (Redleaf Press, 2000)
www.RethinkingSchools.org/special_reports/sept11/16_02/dear162.shtml

Facts about Arabs, by Marvin Wingfield, director of education and outreach at the American-Arab Anti-Discrimination Committee (ADC)
www.RethinkingSchools.org/special_reports/sept11/16_02/fact162.shtml

"First Writing Since," by Suheir Hammad, author of a book of poems, *Born Palestinian, Born Black,* and the memoir *Drops of This Story*
www.RethinkingSchools.org/special_reports/sept11/16_02/firs162.shtml

Free Speech: Concept Versus Reality, by Charlotte Aldebron, a twelve-year-old who attends Cunningham Middle School in Presque Isle, ME
www.RethinkingSchools.org/war/readings/speech.shtml

House "Stimulus" Money Grab, by Citizens for Tax Justice
www.RethinkingSchools.org/special_reports/sept11/16_02/hous162.shtml

How Many Must Die?, by George Capaccio, writer from Arlington, MA
www.RethinkingSchools.org/special_reports/sept11/16_02/many162.shtml

New World Disorder, by Arundhati Roy, author of *The God of Small Things,* for which she received the Booker Prize, and *The Cost of Living*
www.RethinkingSchools.org/special_reports/sept11/16_02/neww162.shtml

Not in Our Son's Name, by Phyllis and Orlando Rodriguez, parents of one of the World Trade Center victims
www.RethinkingSchools.org/special_reports/sept11/16_02/name162.shtml

Sept. 11 and Our Classrooms, by the editors of *Rethinking Schools*
www.RethinkingSchools.org/special_reports/sept11/16_02/sept162.shtml

Talking to Children, by Educators for Social Responsibility
www.RethinkingSchools.org/special_reports/sept11/16_02/talk162.shtml

Teaching About Sept. 11, by Alfie Kohn, author of eight books on education and human behavior
www.RethinkingSchools.org/special_reports/sept11/16_02/kohn162.shtml

The Geopolitics of War, by Michael Klare, a professor at Hampshire College in Massachusetts, with the Five College Program in Peace and World Security Studies
www.RethinkingSchools.org/special_reports/sept11/16_02/geop162.shtml

The Palestinian Uprising: A Primer, by the Middle East Research and Information Project
www.RethinkingSchools.org/special_reports/sept11/16_02/pale162.shtml

What About the Iraqi Children?, by Charlotte Aldebron, a twelve-year-old who attends Cunningham Middle School in Presque Isle, ME
www.RethinkingSchools.org/war/readings/children.shtml

What Is Islam?, by Semya Hakim, teacher at St. Cloud State University in St. Cloud, MN
www.RethinkingSchools.org/special_reports/sept11/16_02/what162.shtml

"When Silence Is Betrayal," by Martin Luther King Jr.
www.RethinkingSchools.org/special_reports/sept11/16_02/sile162.shtml

Where Does the Violence Come From?, by Rabbi Michael Lerner
www.RethinkingSchools.org/special_reports/sept11/16_02/viol162.shtml

Appendix II

NewsHour Extra Data Analysis on Website
Internal/External Links

	Internal Links	External Links
A Call to Jihad	6	0
Analyzing U.S. Policy in Iraq	10	3
Choices in War: What Would You Save First?	8	2
Creating a New Media in the Arab World	6	0
Debating Iraq	10	1
Democracy in the Middle East	9	6
Getting to Democracy	5	4
Humanitarian Aid in Iraq	4	6
Iraq's Latest Strategy: Suicide Attacks	5	2
Military Women	5	1
Najaf—A Holy City Caught in the Crossfire	4	0
Responding to Quotes and Aphorisms	6	1
Reconstruction of Iraq: a Lesson of Historical Precedents	7	3
Reporting on War in the 21st Century	7	0
The Cost of War	5	0
The Decision to Go to War	6	0
The Ethics of Embedded Journalists	7	3
The Powell Doctrine	5	1
The Rights of Detainees at Guantanamo Bay	10	3
The Role of American Embassies	8	7
The Role of Exiles in Post-Saddam Iraq	5	1
The Role of the Kurds, Sunni and Shiites in Iraq	5	0
The Role of the United Nations in Postwar Iraq	3	1
The Rules of Engagement: the Geneva Convention	4	3
To Report Or Not to Report?	5	2
War Expectations	6	0
Weapons of Mass Destruction in Iraq	9	0
What Are the Conditions for Victory in Iraq?	4	2
Who Should Rule the Interim Government in Iraq?	5	0
World Media: Comparion of Iraq War Accounts	9	0
TOTAL (N=233)	**188**	**45**

Rethinking Schools Data Analysis on Website
Internal/External Links

	Internal Links	External Links
Defeating Despair	1	1
Drawing on History to Challenge the War	0	3
Entering History Through Poetry	1	2
Images of War	0	0
Letters to the Universe	0	0
Poetry in a Time of Crisis	3	2
Predicting How the U.S. Government Will Respond to the Iraqi Government	0	14
Rethinking the Teaching of the Vietnam War	0	0
Songs for Global Conscience	0	2
"Stand Up! It's the Law!"	0	0
Teaching Gulf War II	0	7
Teaching with Protest Songs	1	10
The World Up Close	1	3
Whose "Terrorism"?	2	1
Afghanistan: The Route to Riches	1	1
A Time of Gifts	1	0
An Alternative to War	1	1
Backyard Terrorism	1	1
Bush Signs Anti-Terrorism Law	1	1
Dear Parents	0	0
Facts About Arabs	1	1
"First Writing Since"	1	0
Free Speech: Concept Versus Reality	1	0
House "Stimulus" Money Crab	1	1
How Many Must Die?	2	1
New World Disorder	1	1
Not in Our Son's Name	1	0
Sept. 11 and Our Classrooms	0	0
Talking to Children	0	1
Teaching About Sept. 11	0	2
The Geopolitics of War	1	1
The Palestinian Uprising: a Primer	0	1
What About the Iraqi Children?	1	1
What Is Islam?	1	7
"When Silence Is Betrayal"	1	1
Where Does the Violence Come From?	1	1
TOTAL (N=95)	**27**	**68**

Notes

Introduction

1. Discourses are here understood as representing aspects of the world. Consequently, "different discourses are different perspectives on the world, and they are associated with the different relations people have to the world, which in turn depends on their positions in the world, their social and personal identities, and the social relationships in which they stand to other people" (Fairclough 2003, 124).

2. The notion of subject position (Foucault 1972) implies that every text offers a number of subject positions from which the reading of the text seems natural and unproblematic. The construction of subject positions in discourse is important, because it positions writers and readers in the text, instructing them what role to assume and what stance to take, while it constructs them as certain kinds of linguistic and social beings (Kress 1989, 39).

3. An example of how this "selective tradition" operates in practice can be found in Balourdi's (2012) research. In her analysis of world representations in reading comprehension texts of three language certification systems, Balourdi identifies distinct differences. The reading texts of the American test mainly deal with US history and culture, scientific research and development, advertising, and consumerism. The texts of the British test deal mainly with personal development and achievement, promotion of life experiences, fame, and success as central values. The reading texts of the Greek certification system deal with ecological, health, and sociopolitical issues, stressing its nature as a local system with a global perspective.

Chapter 1

1. A point worth mentioning here is related to terminology. The word *passage* is commonly used in the curriculum of *NewsHour Extra,* especially in the instructions, to refer to texts that students are invited to read in critical thinking activities. The selection of the specific term is quite interesting. According to Webster's, a passage is a "brief portion of a written work or speech that is relevant to a point under discussion or noteworthy for content or style." In the context of English language

teaching (ELT), the term *passage* was used for texts, usually not authentic ones, especially written for a textbook. The term was abandoned when the use of authentic texts was introduced in the teaching of English with the communicative approach to language teaching in the 1970s, and later with the use of different text types in genre-based approaches.

2. For example, Ennis (1987) refers to critical thinking abilities and skills; Siegel (1988, 41) to "a wide variety of reasoning skills"; Lipman (1991, 40) to cognitive skills, such as inquiry skills, reasoning skills, information-organizing skills, and translation skills; and McPeck (1990, 12) to a set of "thinking skills."

3. Ennis (1987, 10) provides the most widely used definition of skills-plus-disposition approach to critical thinking as "reasonable thinking focused on deciding what to believe or do." He also suggests a taxonomy of "goals for critical thinking," which is a detailed list of skills, abilities, and dispositions that critical thinkers must have.

4. Arguing in favor of a skills-plus-dispositions approach, Siegel characterizes the critical thinker as one who is "appropriately moved by reasons" (1988, 23). He suggests that critical thinking "must seek to foster a host of attitudes, emotions, dispositions, habits and character traits as well as a wide variety of reasoning skills" (1988, 41). Moreover, for Siegel, one of the main aspects of critical thinking is the reason assessment component, that is, the ability to assess reasons properly and the ability to warrant beliefs, claims, and actions.

5. This point is attributed to Dimitris Koutsogiannis, who had in mind patriotic films and TV serials of the 1960s and early 1970s, whose stories aimed at promoting national ideals and celebrating the uniqueness and significance of Greek culture. Several of these films were promoted in Greek primary and secondary schools during the dictatorship years, 1967–1974.

Chapter 2

1. In fact, Peterson (2003, 365) states that, although one would expect such marked differences between the traditional and the critical pedagogies, one would not probably expect so many differences between the critical and the progressive pedagogies, which are organized in student-centered and holistic ways. Similarly, Benesch (2001, 135) warns that progressive and critical pedagogies should not be conflated, nor should all student-centered teaching be misconstrued as critical.

2. For instance, feminist approaches to critical pedagogy (Gore 1992; Luke 1992; Weiler 1994) have drawn attention to issues of gender, race, and ethnicity. Calling for a critical study of racism, a number of studies have developed antiracist perspectives (Allen 2004; Darder and Torres 2004; Elenes 2003; Leonardo 2002, 2004; Lynn 2004; McLaren 1997) and have pointed to the need to consider race as a central structuring principle of school processes.

3. Available at www.RethinkingSchools.org/archive/18_01/roc181.shtml.

4. Stated in "Rethinking Our Classrooms," an article in *Rethinking Schools Journal* (fall 2003), available at www.RethinkingSchools.org/archive/18_01/roc181.shtml.

Chapter 3

1. A large department store–like shop operating on US military installations worldwide.

2. Found in *Rethinking Schools* (2001), "War, Terrorism and Our Classrooms: Teaching in the Aftermath of the September 11th Tragedy. Special Report," p. 11. Available in *Rethinking Schools* website, www.RethinkingSchools.org/sept11.

3. The article was originally published in *The Progressive Magazine* (Oct. 2002) and reprinted with permission by *Rethinking Schools Online*.

4. For the complete poem, see www.RethinkingSchools.org/war/readings/we162 .shtml.

5. Information about submissions to *Speak Out* can be found at www.pbs.org /newshour/extra/students/submissions.html..

Chapter 4

1. Various other formats have been suggested for a variety of teaching contexts. For instance, Friend and Cook (2007); Keefe, Moore, and Duff (2004); and Ploessl et al. (2010) have proposed the use of lesson plan templates for coteaching. Sophisticated lesson templates were developed for a variety of purposes and audiences. After examining a great number of lesson plans, Perry and Lewis (2009) developed a lesson plan template to be used for multiple purposes.

2. Today the notion of lesson planning pervades all subject areas: English (Ballman 1996; Gunn 2010; Mallows 2002; Morton and Gray 2010), mathematics and science (Borko and Livingston 1989; Eick et al. 2003; Martin 1994), history (Kagan and Tippins 1992), music (Standerfer and Hunter 2010), and all levels of education, from elementary and secondary to tertiary (Kagan and Tippins 1992; Pridmore 2007; Sardo Brown 1988; Spear-Swerling 2009). It has also been an important component of professional development in preservice teacher training (Boikhutso 2010; Davis and Krajcik 2005; Eick et al. 2003; Fernandez 2002; Kinchin and Alias 2005; Morton and Gray 2010; Santagata and Angelici 2010).

3. The notion of moves used here is adopted from Swales (1990) to define the different parts in a genre. *S* is also used to refer to different sentences.

Chapter 5

1. According to Kress, one function of a text is to attempt to recruit new readers to "a certain 'reading position' from where the text seems unproblematic and 'natural.'" As he argues, a text "attempts to coerce the reader, by its 'obviousness' and 'naturalness,' to become its ideal reader, to step into the reading position constructed for the reader in the text" (1989, 39).

2. This contrasts with the organization found in several educational portals in which materials are thematically organized (e.g., in terms of school subjects). An

exception here is the main page with teacher resources on the Iraq War, which is thematically organized.

3. See more at www.RethinkingSchools.org/ProdDetails.asp?ID=RTSSUB.

4. For analytic purposes, website-internal and portal-internal hyperlinks have been calculated together here.

5. According to its mission statement at www.commondreams.org/about-us.

6. According to its mission statement at www.teachingforchange.org.

7. According to its mission statement at www.mediaed.org/wp/about-mef.

Chapter 6

1. This has already been covered extensively. See, for instance, Apple (1993, 2002), Koutsogiannis (2004), Lankshear (1997), Muspratt et al. (1997), Pennycook (2001).

References

Introduction

Apple, Michael W. 2000a. *Official knowledge: Democratic education in a conservative age* (2nd ed.). New York: Routledge.

———. 2000b. The shock of the real: Critical pedagogies and rightist reconstructions. In Peter P. Trifonas (Ed.), *Revolutionary pedagogies: Cultural politics, instituting education, and the discourse of theory* (pp. 225–250). New York: RoutledgeFalmer.

———. 2002. Pedagogy, patriotism, and democracy: On the educational meanings of 11 September 2001. *Discourse: Studies in the Cultural Politics of Education* 23 (3): 299–308.

Avery, Patricia G., and Annette M. Simmons. 2000/2001 (Fall/Winter). Civic life as conveyed in U.S. civics and history books. *International Journal of Social Education* 15: 105–130.

Balourdi, Amalia. 2012. *World representations in English language certification exams: A discourse analysis.* (Unpublished PhD thesis). University of Athens, Athens, Greece.

Bayley, Paul, (Ed.). 2004. *Cross-cultural perspectives on parliamentary discourse.* Amsterdam: John Benjamins.

Bernstein, Basil. 1990. *Class, codes and control (Vol. 4): The structuring of pedagogic discourse.* London: Routledge.

———. 1996. *Pedagogy, symbolic control and identity: Theory, research, critique.* London: Taylor & Francis.

Biser, Jennie Marie. 2008. Current events and the classroom: An investigation into teachers' integration of current events in the secondary social studies classroom. In Leah P. McCoy (Ed.), *Studies in teaching: 2008 Research Digest* (pp. 19–24). Winston-Salem, NC: Wake Forest University, Department of Education.

Brecher, Bob, Mark Devenney, and Aaron Winter, (Eds.). 2010. *Discourses and practices of terrorism: Interrogating terror.* London: Routledge.

Chilton, Paul. 2004. *Analysing political discourse: Theory and practice.* London: Routledge.

Chouliaraki, Lilie (Ed.). 2007. *The soft power of war.* Amsterdam: John Benjamins.

Clarke, Margaret A., and Victor Zelinski. 1992. *Focus on current affairs: A monograph for secondary social studies teachers.* Edmonton: Alberta Department of Education, Edmonton. Curriculum Branch. (ERIC Document Reproduction Service No. ED363541).

Collins, John, and Ross Glover, (Eds.). 2002. *Collateral language: A user's guide to America's new war.* New York: New York University Press.

Cortes, Carlos E. 1981. The societal curriculum: Implications for multiethnic educations. In James A. Banks (Ed.), *Educations in the 80's: Multiethnic education* (pp. 24–32). Washington, DC: National Education Association.

Dedaić, Mirjana N. 2006. Political speeches and persuasive argumentation. In Keith Brown (Ed.), *The encyclopedia of language and linguistics* (Vol. 9) (pp. 700–707). Oxford: Elsevier.

Dedaić, Mirjana N., and Daniel N. Nelson, (Eds.). 2003. *At war with words.* New York: Mouton de Gruyter.

Dendrinos, Bessie. 1992. *The EFL textbook and ideology.* Athens: Grivas Publications.

Duranti, Alessandro. 2006. The struggle for coherence: Rhetorical strategies and existential dilemmas in a campaign for the US Congress. *Language in Society* 35 (4): 467–497.

Eaton, Jana Sackman. 2004. Teaching about election 2004 through the international media. *Social Education* 68 (6): 395–400.

Fairclough, Norman. 1992. *Discourse and social change.* Cambridge: Polity Press.

———. 2000. *New Labour, new language?* London: Routledge.

———. 2003. *Analysing Discourse.* London: Sage.

———. 2006. *Language and globalization.* London: Routledge.

Foucault, Michel. 1972. *The archaeology of knowledge.* London: Tavistock Publications.

Gee, James P. 1996. *Social linguistics and literacies.* London: Taylor & Francis.

Giroux, Henry A. 1988. Literacy and the pedagogy of voice and political empowerment. *Educational Theory* 38 (1): 61–75.

———. 2006. Public pedagogy and the politics of neoliberalism. In Arif Dirlik (Ed.), *Pedagogies of the global* (pp. 59–75). Boulder, CO: Paradigm.

Haas, Mary E., and Margaret A. Laughlin. 2000. Teaching current events: Its status in social studies today. Paper presented at the Annual Meeting of the American Educational Research Association, New Orleans (ERIC Document Reproduction Service No. ED440899).

Hahn, Carole L. 1998. *Becoming political. Comparative perspectives on citizenship education.* Albany: State University of New York Press.

Hall, Stuart (Ed.) 1997. *Representation: Cultural representations and signifying practices.* London: Sage.

Halliday, Michael A. K. 1978. *Language as social semiotic.* London: Edward Arnold.

Hess, Diana, and Julie Posselt. 2002. How high school students experience and learn from the discussion of controversial public issues. *Journal of Curriculum and Supervision* 17 (4): 283–314.

Hodges, Adam. 2011. *The war on terror narrative: Discourse and intertextuality in the construction and contestation of sociopolitical reality.* Oxford: Oxford University Press.

Hodges, Adam, and Nilep Chad (Eds.). 2007. *Discourse, war and terrorism.* Amsterdam: John Benjamins.

Hunt, Maurice P., and Lawrence E. Metcalf. 1955. *Teaching high school social studies: Problems in reflective thinking and social understanding.* New York: Harper and Brothers Publishers.

Illie, Cornelia. 2006. Parliamentary discourses. In Keith Brown (Ed.), *The encyclopedia of language and linguistics* (Vol. 9) (pp. 188–196). Oxford: Elsevier.

Jackson, Richard. 2005. *Writing the war on terrorism: Language, politics, and counterterrorism.* Manchester, UK: Manchester University Press.

Jarvis, Lee. 2009. *Times of terror: Discourse, temporality and the war on terror.* New York: Palgrave Macmillan.

Journell, Wayne. 2009. *Teaching politics: A study of high-school government courses and the 2008 presidential election.* (Unpublished PhD thesis). University of Illinois, Urbana: ProQuest LLC.

———. 2010. The influence of high-stakes testing on high school teachers' willingness to incorporate current political events into the curriculum. *The High School Journal* 93 (3): 111–125.

Journell, Wayne, Laura A. May, Vera L. Stenhouse, Laura E. Meyers, and Teri Holbrok. 2012. Scaffolding classroom discourse in an election year: Keeping a cool mood in a heated season. *Social Studies and the Young Learner* 25 (1): 6–9.

Kahne, Joseph, Bernadette Chi, and Ellen Middaugh. 2006. Building social capital for civic and political engagement: The potential of high-school civics courses. *Canadian Journal of Education* 29 (2): 387–409.

Kahne, Joseph, and Ellen Middaugh. 2008. High quality civic education: What is it and who gets it? *Social Education* 72 (1): 34–39.

Kaplan, Laura Duhan. 1994. Teaching intellectual autonomy: The failure of the critical thinking movement. In Kerry S. Walters (Ed.), *Re-thinking reason: New perspectives in critical thinking* (pp. 205–220). Albany: State University of New York Press.

Kincheloe, Joe L., and Shirley R. Steinberg. 2004. *The miseducation of the West: How schools and the media distort our understanding of the Islamic world.* Greenwich, CT: Praeger Press.

Koutsogiannis, Dimitris, and Bessie Mitsikopoulou. 2004. The Internet as a global discourse environment. *Language Learning & Technology* 8 (3): 83–89.

Kress, Gunther. 1989. *Linguistic processes in sociocultural practice.* Oxford: Oxford University Press.

————. 1996. Representational resources and the production of subjectivity: Questions for the theoretical development of critical discourse analysis in a multicultural society. In Carmen Rosa Caldas-Coulthard and Malcolm Coulthard (Eds.), *Texts and Practices* (pp. 15–31). London: Routledge.

Kress, Gunther, and Theo van Leeuwen. 2001. *Multimodal discourse: The modes and media of contemporary communication.* London: Arnold.

Kyrala, Cadmus. 2010. Systemic linguistic analysis of samples from economic speeches by Barack Obama and John McCain. *Journal of Language and Politics* 9 (1): 74–95.

Lemke, Jay. 2002. Travels in hypermodality. *Visual Communication* 1 (3): 299–325.

Luke, Allan. 1996. Genres of power? Literacy education and the production of capital. In Ruqaiya Hasan and Geoff Williams (Eds.), *Literacy in society* (pp. 308–338). London: Longman.

McLaren, Peter. 1994. Foreword: Critical thinking as a political project. In Kerry S. Walters (Ed.), *Re-thinking reason: New perspectives in critical thinking* (pp. ix–xvii). Albany: SUNY Press.

Mitsikopoulou, Bessie. 2008a. The branding of political entities as discursive practice. *Journal of Language and Linguistics* 7 (3): 353–371.

————. 2008b. Representations of pain in "war against terrorism" pedagogies. In Chryssoula Lascaratou, Anna Despotopoulou, and Elly Ifantidou (Eds.), *Reconstructing pain and joy: Linguistic, literary, and cultural perspectives* (pp. 313–335). Newcastle, UK: Cambridge Scholars Publishing.

Mitsikopoulou, Bessie, and Dimitris Koutsogiannis. 2005. The Iraq War as curricular knowledge: From the political to the pedagogic divide. *Journal of Language and Politics* 4 (1): 93–117. Reprinted in Lilie Chouliaraki (Ed.). 2007. *The soft power of war* (pp. 85–107). London: John Benjamins.

Musolff, Andreas. 2004. *Metaphor and political discourse: Analogical reasoning in debates about Europe.* Basingstoke: Palgrave Macmillan.

Newman, Bruce I. 2001. Commentary—Image-manufacturing in the USA: Recent US presidential elections and beyond. *European Journal of Marketing* 35 (9–10): 966–970.

Niemi, Richard G., and Jane Junn. 1998. *Civic education: What makes students learn.* New Haven, CT: Yale University Press.

Niemi, Richard G., and Julia Smith. 2001. Enrollments in high school government classes: Are we short-changing both citizenship and political science training? *Political Science & Politics* 34 (2): 281–287.

O'Brien, Joseph, Aaron Grill, Stacia Schwarz, and Jennifer Schlicht. 2006. Tracking current events: Using the Internet to explore unfolding stories. *Social Education* 70 (3): 160–164.

Oliva, Peter. 1997. *The curriculum: Theoretical dimensions.* New York: Longman.

Oulton, Christopher, Vanessa Day, Justin Dillon, and Marcus Grace. 2004. Controversial issues—teachers' attitudes and practices in the context of citizenship education. *Oxford Review of Education* 30 (4): 489–507.

Patrick, John J. 2006. Content and process in education for democracy. *International Journal of Social Education* 20(2): 1–12.

Pennycook, Alastair. 2001. *Critical applied linguistics: A critical introduction.* New York: Lawrence Erlbaum.

Pescatore, Christine. 2007. Current events as empowering literacy: For English and social studies teachers. *Journal of Adolescent & Adult Literacy* 51 (4): 326–339.

Reisigl, Martin. 2008. Rhetoric of political speeches. In Ruth Wodak and Veronica Koller (Eds.), *Communication in the public sphere: Handbook of applied linguistics* (Vol. 4) (pp. 243–269). Berlin: De Gruyter.

Risinger, Frederick C. 2007. How to teach about "aligning elections" using the Internet. *Social Education* 71 (6): 292–294.

Rollins, Peter C., and John E. O'Connor (Eds.). 2003. The West Wing: *the American presidency as television drama.* Syracuse, NY: Syracuse University Press.

Seale, Alison, and Bob Carter. 2004. *Applied linguistics as social science.* London: Continuum.

Sperry, Chris. 2006. Seeking truth in the social studies classroom: Media literacy, critical thinking and teaching about the Middle East. *Social Education* 70 (1): 37–43.

Stanley, William B. 1992. *Curriculum for utopia: Social reconstructionism and critical pedagogy in the postmodern era.* Albany: SUNY Press.

Steinberg, Shirley R. 2007. Hollywood's curriculum of Arabs and Muslims in two acts. In Donaldo Macedo and Shirley R. Steinberg (Eds.), *Media literacy: A reader* (pp. 299–315). New York: Peter Lang.

Street, Brian. 2000. New literacies in theory and practice: What are the implications for language in education? *Linguistics and Education* 10 (1): 1–24.

Turner, Thomas N. 1995. Riding the rapids of current events. *Social Studies* 86 (3): 117–121.

Van Dijk, Teun. 1997. What is political discourse analysis? *Belgian Journal of Linguistics* 11: 11–52.

———. 2002. Knowledge in parliamentary debates. *Journal of Language and Politics* 2 (1): 93–129.

Van Ham, Peter. 2001. The rise of the brand state. *Foreign Affairs.* Available at www.foreignaffairs.org (accessed January 12, 2008).

Verba, Sidney, Kay Lehman Schlozman, Henry Brady, and Norman H. Nie. 1993. Citizen activity: Who participates: What do they say? *American Political Science Review* 87(2): 303–318.

Volosinov, Valentin Nikolaevich. 1986. *Marxism and the philosophy of language.* Trans. Ladislav Matejka and I. R.Titunik. Cambridge, MA: Harvard University Press.

Westheimer, Joel. 2004. The politics of civic education. *PS: Political Science & Politics* 38 (2): 231–235.

Williams, Raymond. 1977. *Marxism and literature.* Oxford: Oxford University Press.

Wodak, Ruth. 2009. *The discourse of politics in action: Politics as usual.* Basingstoke, UK: Palgrave Macmillan.

Wodak, Ruth, and Teun van Dijk (Eds.). 2000. *Racism at the top: Parliamentary discourse on ethnic issues in six European states.* Klagenfurt: Drava Verlag.

Zernike, Kate. 2002 (August 31). Lesson plans for Sept. 11 offer a study in discord. *New York Times.* www.nytimes.com/2002/08/31/us/lesson-plans-for-sept-11-offer-a-study-in-discord.html (accessed January 13, 2011).

Chapter 1

Allen, Matthew. 2004. *Smart thinking: Skills for critical understanding and writing.* Oxford: Oxford University Press.

Anderson, Terry, and Randy D. Garrison. 1995. Critical thinking in distance education: Developing critical communities in an audio teleconference context. *Higher Education* 29 (2): 183–199.

Annis, Linda F., and David B. Annis. 1979. The impact of philosophy on students' critical thinking ability. *Contemporary Educational Psychology* 4 (3): 219–226.

Atkinson, Dwight. 1997. A critical approach to critical thinking in TESOL. *TESOL Quarterly* 31 (1): 71–94.

Bailin, Sharon, Roland Case, Jerrold R. Coombs, and Leroi B. Daniels. 1999. Conceptualizing critical thinking. *Journal of Curriculum Studies* 31 (3): 285–302.

Barnett, Ron. 1997. *Higher education: A critical business.* Milton Keynes, UK: Open University Press/SRHE.

Bernstein, Basil. 1990. *Class, codes and control* (Vol. 4): *The structuring of pedagogic discourse.* London: Routledge.

———. 1996. *Pedagogy, symbolic control and identity: Theory, research, critique.* London: Taylor & Francis.

Billig, Michael. 1987. *Arguing and thinking: A rhetorical approach to social psychology.* Cambridge: Cambridge University Press.

Bowell, Tracy, and Gary Kemp. 2002. *Critical thinking: A concise guide.* London: Routledge.

Browne, Neil M., and Kari Freeman. 2000. Distinguishing features of critical thinking classrooms. *Teaching in Higher Education* 5 (3): 301–309.

Browne, Neil M., and Stuart M. Keeley. 2007. *Asking the right questions: A guide to critical thinking* (8th ed.). Upper Saddle River, NJ: Pearson Prentice Hall.

Buffington, Melanie. 2004. *Using the Internet to develop students' critical thinking skills and build online communities of teachers: A review of research with implications for museum education.* (PhD thesis). Ohio State University.

Bullen, Mark. 1998. Participation and critical thinking in online university distance education. *Journal of Distance Education* 13 (2): 1–32.

Burbules, Nicholas C., and Rupert Berk. 1999. Critical thinking and critical pedagogy: Relations, differences and limits. In Thomas S. Popkewitz and

Lynn Fendler (Eds.), *Critical theories in education: Changing terrains of knowledge and politics* (pp.45–65).New York: Routledge.

Carr, Kathryn S. 1988. How can we teach critical thinking? *Childhood Education* 65 (2): 69–73.

Chilton, Paul. 2002. Do something! Conceptualising responses to the attacks of 11 September 2001. *Journal of Language and Politics* 1 (1): 181–195.

Cottrell, Stella. 2005. *Critical thinking skills: Developing effective analysis and argument.* New York: Palgrave Macmillan.

Ellis, Dave. 1997. *Becoming a master student.* Boston: Houghton Mifflin.

Ennis, Robert H. 1962. A concept of critical thinking. *Harvard Educational Review* 32 (1): 81–111.

———. A taxonomy of critical thinking dispositions and abilities. In Joan Boykoff Brown and Robert J. Sternberg (Eds.), *Teaching thinking skills: Theory and practice* (pp. 9–26). New York: W. H. Freeman.

———. 2006. An annotated list of critical thinking tests. www.criticalthinking .net/TestList.html (accessed February 20, 2009).

Epstein, Richard L., and Carolyn Kernberger. 2004. *The guide to critical thinking in economics.* Boston: South-Western College Publishing.

Epstein, Richard L. (with Carolyn Kernberger). 2006. *Critical thinking* (3rd ed.). Toronto: Thompson Educational Publishing.

Facione, Peter A. 1998. *Critical thinking: What it is and why it counts.* Millbrae: California Academic Press.

———. 2000. The disposition toward critical thinking: Its character, measurement, and relationship to critical thinking skill. *Informal Logic* 20 (1): 61–84.

Fisher, Alec. 2001. *Critical thinking. An introduction.* Cambridge: Cambridge University Press.

Fung, Irene Y. Y. 2005. Critical thinking as an educational goal: A fulfilled or unfulfilled promise? Paper presented at the annual meeting of the Philosophy of Education Society of Australasia, November 24–27, in Hong Kong.

Garrison, Randy D. 1991. Critical thinking and adult education: A conceptual model for developing critical thinking in adult learners. *International Journal of Lifelong Education* 10 (4): 287–303.

Garrison, Randy D., Terry Anderson, and Walter Archer. 2001. Critical thinking, cognitive presence, and computer conferencing in distance education. *American Journal of Distance Education* 15 (1): 7–23.

Giroux, Henry A. 1994. Toward a pedagogy of critical thinking. In Kerry S. Walters (Ed.), *Re-thinking reason: New perspectives in critical thinking* (pp. 199–204). Albany: State University of New York Press.

———. 2005. Cultural studies in dark times: Public pedagogy and the challenge of neoliberalism. *Fast Capitalism* 1 (2). www.fastcapitalism.com/ (accessed January 23, 2011).

Gokhale, Anuradha A. 1995. Collaborative learning enhances critical thinking. *Journal of Technology Education* 7 (1): 22–30.

Gold, Jeff, David Holman, and Richard Thorpe. 2002. The role of argument analysis and story telling in facilitating critical thinking. *Management Learning* 3 (3): 371–388.

Graham, Leah, and Takis P. Metaxas. 2003. "Of course it's true; I saw it on the Internet": Critical thinking in the Internet era. *Communications of the ACM* 46 (5): 70–75.

Greenlaw, Steven A., and Stephen B. DeLoach. 2003. Teaching critical thinking with electronic discussion. *Journal of Economic Education* 34 (1): 36–52.

Halliday, Michael A. K. 1994. *An introduction to functional grammar.* London: Edward Arnold.

Halpern, Diane F. 2002. *Thought and knowledge: An introduction to critical thinking.* Hillsdale, NJ: Lawrence Erlbaum.

Harris, Theodore L., and Richard E. Hodges. 1981. *A dictionary of reading and related terms.* Newark, NJ: International Reading Association.

Jeong, Allan C. 2003. The sequential analysis of group interaction and critical thinking in online threaded discussions. *American Journal of Distance Education* 17 (1): 25–43.

Jonassen, David H., Chad Carr, and Hsiu-Ping Yueh. 1998. Computers as mindtools for engaging learners in critical thinking. *TechTrends* 43 (2): 24–32.

Kaasboll, Jens J. 1998. Teaching critical thinking and problem defining skills. *Education and Information Technologies* 3 (2): 101–117.

Kanar, Carol. 1998. *The confident writer.* Boston: Houghton Mifflin.

Kaplan, Laura Duhan.1994. Teaching intellectual autonomy: The failure of the critical thinking movement. In Kerry S. Walters (Ed.), *Re-thinking reason: New perspectives in critical thinking* (pp. 205–220). Albany: State University of New York Press.

King, Alison. 1995. Designing the instructional process to enhance critical thinking across the curriculum. *Teaching of Psychology* 22 (1): 13–17.

Kress, Gunther. 1996. Representational resources and the production of subjectivity: Questions for the theoretical development of Critical Discourse Analysis in a multicultural society. In Carmen Rosa Caldas-Coulthard and Malcolm Coulthard (Eds.), *Texts and Practices* (pp. 15–31). London: Routledge.

Kuhn, Deanna. 1991. *The skills of argument.* New York: Cambridge University Press.

———. 1999. A developmental model of critical thinking. *Educational Researcher* 28 (2): 16–26.

Kurland, Daniel J. 1995. *I know what it says ... What does it mean? Critical skills for critical reading.* Belmont, CA: Wadsworth Publishing.

Lipman, Matthew. 1991. *Thinking in education.* Cambridge: Cambridge University Press.

MacKnight, Carol B. 2000. Teaching critical thinking through online discussions. *Educause Quarterly* 23 (4): 38–41.

Martin, Jim R. 1992. Critical thinking for a humane world. In Stephen P. Norris (Ed.), *The generalizability of critical thinking. Multiple perspectives on an educational ideal* (pp. 163–180). New York: Teachers College Press.

Maudsley, Gillian, and Janet Striven. 2000. Promoting professional knowledge, experiential learning and critical thinking for medical students. *Medical Education* 34 (7): 535–544.

McPeck, John E. 1981. *Critical thinking and education.* New York: St. Martin's Press.

———. 1990. Critical thinking and subject specificity: A reply to Ennis. *Educational Researcher* 19 (4): 10–12.

Mejía, Andrés D. 2009. In just what sense should I be critical? An exploration into the notion of "assumption" and some implications for assessment. *Studies in Philosophy and Education* 28 (4): 351–367.

Moon, Jennifer. 2008. Critical *thinking: An exploration of theory and practice.* New York: Routledge.

Norris, Stephen P. 1985. Synthesis of research on critical thinking. *Educational Leadership* 42 (8): 40–45.

Norris, Stephen, P., and Robert H. Ennis. 1989. *Evaluating critical thinking.* Pacific Grove, CA: Midwest.

Oberman, Cerise. 1991. Avoiding the cereal syndrome, or critical thinking in the electronic environment. *Library Trends* 39 (3): 189–202.

Papastephanou, Marianna, and Charoula Angeli. 2007. Critical thinking beyond skill. *Educational Philosophy and Theory* 39 (6): 604–621.

Paul, Richard. 1990. *Critical thinking: What every person needs to survive in a rapidly changing world.* Rohnert Park, CA: Center for Critical Thinking and Moral Critique.

Paul, Richard, and Linda Elder. 2007. White paper. Consequential validity using assessment to drive instruction. Foundation for Critical Thinking. www.criticalthinking.org (accessed November 30, 2010).

Phillips, Virginia, and Carol Bond. 2004. Undergraduates' experiences of critical thinking. *Higher Education Research and Development* 23 (3): 277–294.

Siegel, Harvey. 1988. *Educating reason: Rationality, critical thinking and education.* New York: Routledge.

Siller, Thomas. 2001. Sustainability and critical thinking in civil engineering curriculum. *Journal of Professional Issues in Engineering Education and Practice* 127 (3): 104–108.

Sloffer, Susan, Bill Dueber, and Thomas M. Duffy. January 5–8, 1999. Using asynchronous conferencing to promote critical thinking: Two implementations in higher education. Proceedings of the 32nd Hawaii International Conference on System Sciences.

Twardy, Charles R. 2004. Argument maps improve critical thinking. *Teaching Philosophy* 27 (2): 95–116.

Walters, Kerry S. 1994. Critical thinking, rationality, and the vulcanization of students. In Kerry S. Walters (Ed.), *Re-thinking reason: New perspectives in critical thinking* (pp. 61–80). Albany: State University of New York Press.

Watson, Goodwin, and Edward M. Glaser. 1980. *Watson-Glaser critical thinking appraisal, Forms A and B manual.* San Antonio: The Psychological Corporation.

Weiler, Angela. 2004. Information-seeking behavior in Generation Y students: Motivation, critical thinking, and learning theory. *Journal of Academic Librarianship* 31 (1): 46–53.

Yeh, Stuart S. 2001. Tests worth teaching to: Constructing state-mandated tests that emphasize critical thinking. *Educational Researcher* 30 (9): 12–17.

Chapter 2

Allen, Ricky Lee. 2004. Whiteness and critical pedagogy. *Educational Philosophy and Theory* 36 (2): 121–136.

Apple, Michael. 2000a. *Official knowledge. Democratic education in a conservative age* (2nd ed.). New York: Routledge.

———. 2000b. Can critical pedagogies interrupt rightist policies? *Educational Theory* 50 (2): 229–254.

———. 2001. *Educating the "right" way: markets, standards, god, and inequality.* New York: RoutledgeFalmer.

———. 2004. *Ideology and curriculum* (3rd ed.). New York: Routledge.

———. 2005. Making critical pedagogy strategic: On doing critical educational work in conservative times. In Ilan Gur Ze'ev (Ed.), *Critical theory and critical pedagogy today* (pp. 95–113). Haifa, Israel: Faculty of Education, University of Haifa.

Aronowitz, Stanley, and Henry A. Giroux. 1991. *Postmodern education: Politics, culture, and social criticism.* Minneapolis: University of Minnesota Press.

Auerbach, Elsa R. 1995. The politics of the ESL classroom: Issues of power in pedagogical choices. In James W. Tollefson (Ed.), *Power and inequality in language education* (pp. 9–33). New York: Cambridge University Press.

Auerbach, Elsa, and Loren McGrail. 1991. Rosa's challenge: Connecting classroom and community contexts. In Sarah Benesch (Ed.), *ESL in America: Myths and possibilities* (pp. 96–111). Portsmouth, NH: Boynton/Cook Heinemann.

Bartolomé, Lilia I. 2003. Beyond the fetish method: Toward a humanizing pedagogy. In Antonia Darder, Marta P. Baltodano, and Rodolfo D. Torres (Eds.), *The critical pedagogy reader* (pp. 408–429). New York: RoutledgeFalmer.

Benesch, Sarah. 1993. Critical thinking: A learning process for democracy. *TESOL Quarterly* 27 (3): 545–548.

———. 1999. Thinking critically, thinking dialogically. *TESOL Quarterly* 33 (3): 573–580.

———. 2001. *Critical English for academic purposes: Theory, politics, and practice.* Mahwah, NJ: Lawrence Erlbaum.

Bernstein, Basil. 1990. *Class, codes and control* (Vol. 4): *The structuring of pedagogic discourse.* London: Routledge.

———. 1996. *Pedagogy, symbolic control and identity: Theory, research, critique.* London: Taylor & Francis.

Biesta, Gert J. J. 1998. Say you want a revolution ... Suggestions for the impossible future of critical pedagogy. *Educational Theory* 48 (4): 499–510.

Brady, Jeanne. 1994. Critical literacy, feminism, and a politics of representation. In Peter McLaren and Colin Lankshear (Eds.), *Politics of liberation: Paths from Freire* (pp. 142–153). London: Routledge.

Burbules, Nicholas C., and Rupert Berk. 1999. Critical thinking and critical pedagogy: Relations, differences and limits. In Thomas S. Popkewitz and Lynn Fendler (Eds.), *Critical theories in education: Changing terrains of knowledge and politics* (pp. 45–65). New York: Routledge.

Cho, Seehwa. 2010. Politics of critical pedagogy and new social movements. *Educational Philosophy and Theory* 42 (3): 310–325.

Cope, Bill, and Mary Kalantzis. 1993. The power of literacy and the literacy of power. In Bill Cope and Mary Kalantzis (Eds.), *The powers of literacy: A genre approach to teaching writing* (pp. 63–89). London: Falmer Press.

Darder, Antonia, Marta P. Baltodano, and Rodolfo D. Torres. 2003. Critical pedagogy: An introduction. In Antonia Darder, Marta P. Baltodano, and Rodolfo D. Torres (Eds.), *The critical pedagogy reader* (pp. 1–21). New York: RoutledgeFalmer.

Darder, Antonia, and Rodolfo D. Torres. 2004. *After race: Racism after multiculturalism*. New York: New York University Press.

Elenes, Alejandra C. 2003. Reclaiming the borderlands: Chicana/o identity, difference, and critical pedagogy. In Antonia Darder, Marta P. Baltodano, and Rodolfo D. Torres (Eds.), *The critical pedagogy reader* (pp. 191–210). New York: RoutledgeFalmer.

Ellsworth, Elizabeth. 1989. Why doesn't this feel empowering? Working through the repressive myths of critical pedagogy. *Harvard Educational Review* 59: 297–324.

Freire, Paulo. 1974. *Education for critical consciousness*. London: Continuum.

———. 1985. *The politics of education: Culture, power, and liberation*. New York: Bergin & Garvey.

———. 2005. *Pedagogy of the oppressed* (30th anniversary edition). New York: Continuum.

———. 2006. Foreword. In Donaldo Macedo, *Literacies of power* (pp. ix–x). Cambridge, MA: Westview Press.

Freire, Paulo, and Donaldo Macedo. 1987. *Literacy: Reading the word and the world*. South Hadley, MA: Bergin & Garvey.

Giroux, Henry A. 1983a. Critical theory and schooling: Implications for the development of a radical pedagogy. *Discourse: Studies in the Cultural Politics of Education* 3 (2): 1–21.

———.1983b. *Theory and resistance in education: A pedagogy for the opposition*. South Hadley, MA: Bergin & Garvey.

———. 1988a. Literacy and the pedagogy of voice and political empowerment. *Educational Theory* 38 (1): 61–75.

————. 1988b. *Schooling and the struggle for public life: Critical pedagogy in the modern era.* Minneapolis: University of Minnesota Press.

————. 1988c. *Teachers as intellectuals: Toward a critical pedagogy of learning.* South Hadley, MA: Bergin & Garvey.

————. 1997. *Pedagogy and the politics of hope: Theory, culture, and schooling.* Boulder, CO: Westview Press.

Giroux, Henry A., and Peter McLaren. 1989. Schooling as a form of cultural politics: Toward a pedagogy of and for difference. In Henry A. Giroux and Peter McLaren (Eds.), *Critical pedagogy, the state, and cultural struggle* (pp. xi–xxxv). Albany: SUNY Press.

Gore, Jennifer. 1992. What we can do for you! What can "we" we do for "you"? Struggling over empowerment in critical and feminist pedagogy. In Carmen Luke and Jennifer Gore (Eds.), *Feminisms and critical pedagogy* (pp. 54–73). New York: Routledge.

————. 1993. *The struggle for pedagogies: Critical and feminist discourses as regimes of truth.* New York: Routledge.

Johnston, Bill. 1999. Putting critical pedagogy in its place: A personal account. *TESOL Quarterly* 33 (3): 557–565.

Kanpol, Barry. 1999. *Critical pedagogy: An introduction* (2nd ed.). Westport, CT: Bergin & Garvey.

Kaplan, Laura Duhan. 1994. Teaching intellectual autonomy: The failure of the critical thinking movement. In Kerry S. Walters (Ed.), *Re-thinking reason: New perspectives in critical thinking* (pp. 205–220). Albany: State University of New York Press.

Kenworthy, Roger C. 2005. Review of *Critical pedagogies and language learning,* Bonny Norton and Kelleen Toohey (Eds.). 2004. Cambridge: Cambridge University Press. *System* 33: 637–639.

Lankshear, Colin. 1997. *Changing literacies.* Buckingham, UK: Open University Press.

Lather, Patti. 1992. Postmodernism in the human sciences. In Steinar Kvale (Ed.), *Psychology and postmodernism* (pp. 88–109). London: Sage.

Leonardo, Zeus. 2002. The souls of white folk: Critical pedagogy, whiteness studies, and globalization discourse. *Race Ethnicity and Education* 5 (1): 29–50.

————. 2004. The color of supremacy: Beyond the discourse of "white privilege." *Educational Philosophy and Theory* 36 (2): 137–152.

Lin, Angel M. Y. 2004. Introducing a critical pedagogical curriculum: A feminist reflective account. In Bonny Norton and Kelleen Toohey (Eds.), *Critical pedagogies and language learning* (pp. 271–290). Cambridge: Cambridge University Press.

Luke, Allan. 1996. Genres of power? Literacy education and the production of capital. In Ruqaiya Hasan and Geoffrey Williams (Eds.), *Literacy in society* (pp. 308–338). London: Longman.

————. 1997. Critical approaches to literacy. In Viv Edwards and David Corson (Eds.), *Encyclopedia of language and education, vol. 2 Literacy* (143–151). Dordrecht, Netherlands: Kluwer Academic Publishers.

Luke, Carmen. 1992. Feminist politics in radical pedagogy. In Carmen Luke and Jennifer Gore (Eds), *Feminisms and critical pedagogy* (pp. 25–53). New York: Routledge.

Lynn, Marvin. 2004. Inserting the "race" into critical pedagogy: An analysis of "race-based epistemologies." *Educational Philosophy and Theory* 36 (2): 153–165.

Macedo, Donaldo. 2006. *Literacies of power.* Cambridge, MA: Westview Press.

McLaren, Peter. 1989. *Life in schools: An introduction to critical pedagogy in the foundations of education.* New York: Longman.

————. 1994. Foreword: Critical thinking as a political project. In Kerry S. Walters (Ed.), *Re-thinking reason: New perspectives in critical thinking* (pp. ix–xvii). Albany: SUNY Press.

————. 1997. *Revolutionary multiculturalism: Pedagogies of dissent for the new millennium.* Boulder, CO: Westview Press.

————. 1998. Revolutionary pedagogy in post-revolutionary times: Rethinking the political economy of critical education. *Educational Theory* 48 (4): 431–462.

Mitsikopoulou, Bessie. 2007. The interplay of the global and the local in English language learning and electronic communication discourses and practices in Greece. *Language and Education* 21 (3): 156–170.

Pennycook, Alastair. 2001. *Critical applied linguistics: A critical introduction.* Mahwah, NJ: Lawrence Erlbaum.

Peterson, Robert E. 2003. Teaching how to read the world and change it: Critical pedagogy in the intermediate grades. In Antonia Darder, Marta P. Baltodano, and Rodolfo D. Torres (Eds.), *The critical pedagogy reader* (pp. 365–387). New York: RoutledgeFalmer.

Searle, Chris. 1977. *The world in a classroom.* London: Writers and Readers Publishing Cooperative.

Shor, Ira. 1992. *Empowering education: Critical teaching for social change.* Chicago: University of Chicago Press.

Silverstone, Roger. 2007. *Media and morality. On the rise of the mediapolis.* Cambridge: Polity

Simon, Roger I. 1992. *Teaching against the grain: Essays towards a pedagogy of possibility.* London: Bergin & Garvey.

Stanley, William B. 1992. *Curriculum for utopia: Social reconstructionism and critical pedagogy in the postmodern era.* Albany: SUNY Press.

Steinberg, Shirley R. 2007. Hollywood's curriculum of Arabs and Muslims in two acts. In Donaldo Macedo and Shirley R. Steinberg (Eds.), *Media literacy: A reader* (pp. 299–315). New York: Peter Lang.

Street, Brian. 1995. *Social literacies: Critical approaches to literacy in development, ethnography and education.* London: Longman.

Usher, Robin, and Richard Edwards. 1994. *Postmodernism and education. Different voices, different worlds.* London: Routledge.

Weiler, Kathleen. 1994. Freire and a feminist pedagogy of difference. In Peter McLaren and Colin Lankshear (Eds.), *Politics of liberation: Paths from Freire* (pp. 12–40). London: Routledge.

Zavarzadeh, Mas'ud, and Donald Morton. 1994. *Theory as resistance: Politics and culture after poststructuralism.* New York: Guilford Press.

Chapter 3

Apple, Michael W. 2000. *Official knowledge. Democratic education in a conservative age* (2nd ed.). New York: Routledge.

Bacini, Simon Curzio. 2008. "This is my pain." Agency and individuality in the experience of an Italian woman with chronic illness: A linguistic approach. In Chryssoula Lascaratou, Anna Despotopoulou, and Elly Ifantidou (Eds.), *Reconstructing pain and joy: Linguistic, literary, and cultural perspectives* (pp. 177–194). Cambridge: Cambridge Scholars Publishing.

Bernstein, Basil. 1990. *The structuring of pedagogic discourse.* London: Routledge.

Chilton, Paul. 2002. Do something! Conceptualising responses to the attacks of 11 September 2001. *Journal of Language and Politics* 1 (1): 181–195.

———. 2004. *Analysing political discourse.* London: Routledge.

Chouliaraki, Lilie. 2006. *The spectatorship of suffering.* London: Sage.

Fairclough, Norman. 2003. *Analysing discourse.* London: Sage.

———. 2005. Blair's contribution to elaborating a new "doctrine of international community." *Journal of Language and Politics* 4 (1): 41–63.

Grabe, William, and Robert Kaplan. 1996. *Theory and practice of writing.* London: Longman.

Graham, Phil, and Allan Luke. 2005. Militarising the body politic: New mediations as weapons of mass instruction. *Journal of Language and Politics* 4 (1): 11–39.

Halliday, Michael A. K. 1998. On the grammar of pain. *Functions of Language* 5 (1): 1–32.

Inglis, Fred. 1985. *The management of ignorance: A political theory of the curriculum.* New York: Basil Blackwell.

Kövecses, Zoltán. 2008. The conceptual structure of happiness and pain. In Chryssoula Lascaratou, Anna Despotopoulou, and Elly Ifantidou (Eds.), *Reconstructing pain and joy: Linguistic, literary, and cultural perspectives* (pp. 17–33). Cambridge: Cambridge Scholars Publishing.

Kress, Gunther. 1989. *Linguistic processes in sociocultural practice.* Oxford: Oxford University Press.

Lascaratou, Chryssoula. 2003. *Language in pain: Expression or description? The case of Greek.* Athens: Parousia Journal Monograph Series.

————. 2008. The function of language in the experience of pain. In Chryssoula Lascaratou, Anna Despotopoulou, and Elly Ifantidou (Eds.), *Reconstructing pain and joy: Linguistic, literary, and cultural perspectives* (pp. 35–57). Cambridge: Cambridge Scholars Publishing.

Machin, David. 2007. Visual discourses of war: Multimodal analysis of photographs of the Iraq occupation. In Adam Hodges and Chad Nilep (Eds.), *Discourse, war and terrorism* (pp. 123–142). Amsterdam: John Benjamins.

Scarry, Elaine. 1985. *The body in pain: The making and unmaking of the world.* New York: Oxford University Press.

Silberstein, Sandra. 2004. *War of words: Language, politics and 9/11.* London: Routledge.

Silverstone, Robert. 2007. *Media and morality.* Cambridge: Polity Press.

Van Dijk, Teun. 1998. *Ideology: A multidisciplinary approach.* London: Sage.

————. 2005. War rhetoric of a little ally. Political implicatures and Aznar's legitimatization of the war in Iraq. *Journal of Language and Politics* 4 (1): 65–91.

Van Leeuwen, Theo. 1996. The representation of social actors. In Carmen-Rosa Caldas-Coulthard and Malcolm Coulthard (Eds.), *Texts and practices* (pp. 32–70). London: Routledge.

Williams, Raymond. 1976. Base and superstructure in Marxist Cultural Theory. In Roger Dale, Geoff Esland, and Madeleine MacDonald (Eds.), *Schooling and capitalism: A sociological reader* (pp. 202–210). London: Routledge and K. Paul, in association with Open University Press.

Chapter 4

Apple, Michael W. 1993. The politics of official knowledge: Does a national curriculum make sense? *Teachers College Records* 95 (2): 222–241.

————. 1996a. *Cultural politics and education.* New York: Teachers College Press.

————. 1996b. Being popular about national standards: A review of National standards in American education: A citizen's guide, by Diane Ravitch. *Education* Policy Analysis Archives 4 (10). http://epaa.asu.edu/epaa/v4n10.html.

————. 2001. *Educating the "right" way: Markets, standards, God, and inequality.* New York: Routledge/Falmer.

Ballman, Terry L. 1996. Integrating vocabulary, grammar, and culture: A model five-day communicative lesson plan. *Foreign Language Annals* 29 (1): 37–44.

Boikhutso, Keene. 2010. The theory into practice dilemma: Lesson planning challenges facing Botswana student-teachers. *Improving Schools* 13 (3): 205–220.

Borko, Hilda, and Carol Livingston. 1989. Cognition and Improvisation: Differences in mathematics instruction by expert and novice teachers. *American Educational Research Journal* 26 (4): 473–498.

Carter, Kathy, Donna Sabers, Katherine Cushing, Stefinee Pinnegar, and David C. Berliner. 1987. Processing and using information about students: A study of expert, novice, and postulant teachers. *Teaching & Teacher Education* 3 (2): 147–157.

Clark, Christopher M., and Penelope L. Peterson. 1986. Teachers' thought processes. In Merlin C. Wittrock (Ed.), *Handbook of research on teaching* (pp. 255–296). New York: Macmillan.

Davis, Elizabeth A., and Joseph S. Krajcik. 2005. Designing educative curriculum materials to promote teacher learning. *Educational Researcher* 34 (3): 3–14.

Dendrinos, Bessie. 2001. European discourses of homogenization in the discourse of language planning. In Bessie Dendrinos (Ed.), *The politics of ELT* (pp. 30–42). Athens: University of Athens Publications. Reprinted in Donaldo Macedo, Bessie Dendrinos, and Panayota Gounari. 2003. *The hegemony of English* (pp. 45–59). Boulder, CO: Paradigm Publishers.

Doyle, Marie, and Daniel T. Holm. 1998. Instructional planning through stories: Rethinking the traditional lesson plan. *Teacher Education Quarterly* 25 (3): 69–83.

Eick, Charles J., Frank N. Ware, and Penelope G. Williams. 2003. Coteaching in a science methods course: A situated learning model of becoming a teacher. *Journal of Teacher Education* 54 (1): 74–85.

Farrell, Thomas S. C. 2004. *Reflective practice in action*. Thousand Oaks, CA: Corwin Press.

Fernandez, Clea. 2002. Learning from Japanese approaches to professional development: The case of lesson study. *Journal of Teacher Education* 53 (5): 393–405.

Friend, Marilyn, and Lynne Cook. 2007. *Interactions: Collaboration skills for school professionals* (5th ed.). Boston, MA: Allyn & Bacon.

Gunn, Cindy L. 2010. Exploring MATESOL student "resistance to reflection." *Language Teaching Research* 14 (2): 208–223.

Halbach, Ana. 2002. Exporting methodologies: The reflective approach in teacher training. *Language, Culture and Curriculum* 15 (3): 243–250.

Hirsch, E. D. 1988. *Cultural literacy: What every American needs to know*. New York: Vintage.

Ho, Belinda. 1995. Using lesson plans as a means of reflection. *ELT Journal* 49 (1): 66–71.

Hodge, Robert, and Gunther Kress. 1988. *Social semiotics*. Cambridge: Polity.

Holly, Mary L. 1984. *Keeping a personal-professional journal*. Geelong, Victoria, Australia: Deakin University Press.

Hughes, Bob. 2004. The opposite intended effect: A case study of how over-standardization can reduce efficacy of teacher education. *Teacher Education Quarterly* 31 (3): 43–52.

James, Charles J. 1992. What TAs need to know to teach according to the new paradigm. In Joel C. Walz (Ed.), *Development and supervision of teaching assistants in foreign languages* (pp. 135–152). Boston: Heinle & Heinle.

John, Peter D. 2006. Lesson planning and the student teacher: Re-thinking the dominant model. *Journal of Curriculum Studies* 38 (4): 483–498.

Kagan, Dona M., and Deborah J. Tippins. 1992. The evolution of functional lesson plans among twelve elementary and secondary student teachers. *Elementary School Journal* 92 (4): 477–489.

Keefe, Elizabeth, Veronica Moore, and Frances Duff. 2004. The four "knows" of collaborative teaching. *Teaching Exceptional Children* 36 (5): 36–42.

Kinchin, L. M., and M. Alias. 2005. Exploiting variations in concept map morphology as a lesson-planning tool for trainee teachers in higher education. *Journal of In-service Education* 31 (3): 569–591.

Kirst, Michael W., and James W. Guthrie. 1994. Goals 2000 and a reauthorized ESEA: National standards and accompanying controversies. In Nina Cobb (Ed.), *The future of education: Perspectives on national standards in America* (pp. 157–173). New York: College Board.

Knop, Constance K. 1982. Overview, prime, drill, check: An approach to guiding student teachers in lesson planning. *Foreign Language Annals* 15 (2): 91–94.

Koutsogiannis, Dimitris. 2004. Information and communication technology and language education: Towards an alternative critical approach. In Bessie Dendrinos and Bessie Mitsikopoulou (Eds.), *Policies of linguistic pluralism and the teaching of languages in Europe* (pp. 382–393). Athens: National and Kapodistrian University of Athens and Metaichmio Publications.

Lave, Jean, and Etienne Wenger. 1991. *Situated learning: Legitimate peripheral participation.* Cambridge: Cambridge University Press.

Linne, Agneta. 2001. The lesson as a pedagogic text: A case study of lesson designs. *Journal of Curriculum Studies* 33 (2): 129–156.

Luke, Allan. 1996. Genres of power? Literacy education and the production of capital. In Ruqaiya Hasan and Geoff Williams (Eds.), *Literacy in Society* (pp. 308–338). London: Longman.

Mallows, David. 2002. Non-linearity and the observed lesson. *ELT Journal* 56 (1): 3–10.

Martin, David J. 1994. Concept mapping as an aid to lesson planning: A longitudinal study. *Journal of Elementary Science Education* 6 (2): 11–30.

McDonough, Jo, and Steven McDonough. 1997. *Research methods for English language teachers.* London: Edward Arnold.

McLaren, Peter. 1995. *Critical pedagogy and predatory culture. Oppositional politics in a postmodern era.* London: Routledge.

McLoughlin, Linda. 2000. *The language of magazines.* London: Routledge.

Morton, Tom, and John Gray. 2010. Personal practical knowledge and identity in lesson planning conferences on a pre-service TESOL course. *Language Teaching Research* 14 (3): 297–317.

Perry, Rebecca R., and Catherine C. Lewis. 2009. What is successful adaptation of lesson study in the US? *Journal of Educational Change* 10 (4): 365–391.

Ploessl, Donna M., Marcia L. Rock, Naomi Schoenfeld, and Brooke Blanks. 2010. On the same page: Practical techniques to enhance co-teaching interactions *Intervention in School and Clinic* 45 (3): 158–168.

Posner, George J. 1985. *Field experience: A guide to reflective teaching.* New York: Longman.

Pridmore, Pat. 2007. Adapting the primary-school curriculum for multigrade classes in developing countries: A five-step plan and an agenda for change. *Journal of Curriculum Studies* 39 (5): 559–576.

Rhoads, Melanie, Ron Sieber, and Susan Slayton. 1996. Examining national standards. http://horizon.unc.edu/projects/issuespapers/National_Standards (accessed November 6, 2003).

Richards, Jack C. 1990. The dilemma of teacher education in second language teaching. In Jack C. Richards and David Nunan (Eds.), *Second language teacher education* (pp. 3–15). Cambridge: Cambridge University Press.

Richards, Jack C., and Charles Lockhart. 1996. *Reflective teaching in second language classrooms.* Cambridge: Cambridge University Press.

Rifkin, Benjamin. 2003. Guidelines for foreign language lesson planning. *Foreign Language Annals* 36 (2): 167–179.

Roskos, Kathleen. 1996. When two heads are better than one: Beginning teachers' planning processes in an integrated instruction planning task. *Journal of Teacher Education* 47 (2): 120–129.

Santagata, Rossella, and Giulia Angelici. 2010. Studying the impact of the lesson analysis framework on preservice teachers' abilities to reflect on videos of classroom teaching. *Journal of Teacher Education* 61 (4): 339–349.

Sardo Brown, Deborah. 1988. Twelve middle-school teachers' planning. *Elementary School Journal* 89 (1): 69–87.

———. 1990. Experienced teachers' planning practices: A US survey. *Journal of Education for Teaching* 16 (1): 57–71.

Schön, Donald A. 1983. *The reflective practitioner: How professionals think in action.* New York: Basic Books.

———. 1987. *Educating the reflective practitioner.* San Francisco: Jossey-Bass.

Shkedi, Asher. 2000. Educating reflective teachers for teaching culturally valued subjects: Evaluation of a teacher-training project. *Evaluation and Research in Education* 14 (2): 94–110.

Spear-Swerling, Louise. 2009. A literacy tutoring experience for prospective special educators and struggling second graders. *Journal of Learning Disabilities* 42 (5): 431–443.

Standerfer, Stephanie L., and Lisa R. Hunter. 2010. Square peg for a square hole: A standards- and repertoire-based curriculum model. *Music Educators Journal* 96 (3): 25–30.

Street, Brian V. 1995. *Social literacies: Critical approaches to literacy in development, ethnography and education.* London: Longman.

Swales, John. 1990. *Genre analysis: English in academic and research settings.* Cambridge: Cambridge University Press.

Tasker, Thomas, Karen E. Johnson, and Tracy S. Davis. 2010. A sociocultural analysis of teacher talk in inquiry-based professional development. *Language Teaching Research* 14 (2): 129–140.

Thornbury, Scott. 1999. Lesson art and design. *ELT Journal* 53 (1): 4–11.

Tyler, Ralph W. 1950. *Basic principles of curriculum and instruction.* Chicago: University of Chicago Press.

Tyler, William. 1999. Pedagogic identities and educational reform in the 1990s: The cultural dynamics of national curricula. In Frances Christie (Ed.), *Pedagogy and the shaping of consciousness* (pp. 262–289). London: Cassell.

Volosinov, Valentin Nikolaevich. 1986. *Marxism and the philosophy of language.* Trans. by Ladislav Matejka and I. R. Titunik. Cambridge, MA: Harvard University Press.

Wallace, Michael J. 1998. *Action research for language teachers.* Cambridge: Cambridge University Press.

Yinger, Robert J. 1980. A study of teacher planning. *Elementary School Journal* 80 (3): 107–127.

Zahorik, John A. 1970. The effect of planning on teaching. *Elementary School Journal* 71 (3): 143–151.

Chapter 5

Askehave, Inger, and Anne Ellerup Nielsen. 2005. Digital genres: A challenge to traditional genre theory. *Information Technology & People* 18 (2): 120–141.

Bernard, Michael, Spring Hull, and Barbara Chaparro. 2005. Examining the performance and preference of embedded and framed/non-framed hyperlinks. *International Journal of Industrial Ergonomics* 35 (2): 139–147.

Bolter, Jay David. 2001. *Writing space: Computers, hypertext and the remediation of print.* Hillsdale, NJ: Lawrence Erlbaum Associates.

Burbules, Nicholas C. 1998. Rhetorics of the Web: Hyperreading and critical literacy. In Ilana Snyder (Ed.), *Page to screen: Taking literacy into the electronic era* (pp. 102–122). New York: Routledge.

Dalal, Nikunj P., Zane Quible, and Katherine Wyatt. 2000. Cognitive design of home pages: An experimental study of comprehension on the World Wide Web. *Information Processing and Management* 36 (4): 607–621.

Djonov, Emilia. 2007. Website hierarchy and the interaction between content organization, webpage and navigation design: A systemic functional hypermedia discourse analysis perspective. *Information Design Journal* 15 (2): 144–162.

Finnemann, Niels Ole. 1999. Hypertext and the representational capacities of the binary alphabet. http://www.hum.au.dk/ckulturf/pages/publications/nof/ hrc.pdfb (accessed January 20, 2011).

Gee, James Paul. 1996. *Social linguistics and literacies: Ideology in discourses.* London: Taylor & Francis.

Jewitt, Carey. 2002. The move from page to screen: The multimodal reshaping of school English. *Visual Communication* 1 (2): 171–195.

Koszalka, Tiffany A., Jeroen Breman, and Malena K. Moore. 1999. Sharing lesson plans over the World Wide Web: Important components. *Education and Information Technologies* 4 (2): 143–151.

Kress, Gunther. 1989. *Linguistic processes in sociocultural practice.* Oxford: Oxford University Press.

———. 2000. Multimodality. In Bill Cope and Mary Kalantzis (Eds.), *Multiliteracies* (pp. 182–202). Melbourne: Macmillan Publishers.

Kress, Gunther, and Theo van Leeuwen. 2001. *Multimodal discourse: The modes and media of contemporary communication.* London: Arnold.

———. 2006. *Reading images: The grammar of visual design.* London: Routledge.

Landow, George. 1997. *Hypertext 2.0: The convergence of contemporary critical theory and technology.* Baltimore: The Johns Hopkins University Press.

Lemke, Jay. 1998. Metamedia literacy: Transforming meanings and media. In David Reinking, Michael C. McKenna, Linda D. Labbo, and Ronald D. Kieffer (Eds.), *Handbook of literacy and technology: Transformations in a post-typographic world* (pp. 312–333). Mahwah, NJ: Lawrence Erlbaum.

———. 2002. Travels in hypermodality. *Visual Communication,* 1 (3): 299–325.

Mitsikopoulou, Bessie. 1999. Linguistic hegemony in the discourses of applied linguistics and English language teaching. In A. F. Christidis (Ed.), *"Strong" and "weak" languages in the European Union: Aspects of linguistic hegemony* (Vol. 2) (pp. 729–736). Thessaloniki, Greece: Centre for the Greek Language.

Nielsen, Jakob, and Marie Tahir. 2001. *Homepage usability: 50 websites deconstructed.* Indianapolis: New Riders Publishing.

Snyder, Ilana (Ed.). 1998. *Page to screen: Taking literacy into the electronic era.* New York: Routledge.

Sosnoski, James J. 1999. Configuring as a mode of rhetorical analysis. In Steve Jones (Ed.), *Doing Internet research* (pp. 127–144). London: Sage.

Spool, Jaret, Tara Scanlon, Will Schroeder, Carolyn Snyder, and Terri DeAngelo. 1997. *Web site usability: A designer's guide.* North Andover, MA: User Interface Engineering.

Spyridakis, Jan H., Kathryn A. Mobrand, Elisabeth Cuddihy, and Carolyn Y. Wei. 2007. Using structural cues to guide readers on the Internet. *Information Design Journal* 15 (3): 242–259.

Swales, John M. 1990. *Genre analysis: English in academic and research settings.* Cambridge: Cambridge University Press.

van Leeuwen, Theo. 2005. *Introducing social semiotics.* London: Routledge.

Wei, Carolyn Y., Mary B. Evans, Matthew Eliot, Jennifer Barrick, Brandon Maust, and Jan H. Spyridakis. 2005. Influencing Web browsing behaviour with intriguing and informative hyperlink wording. *Journal of Information Science* 31(5): 433–445.

Zammit, Katina, and Jon Callow. 1999. Ideology and technology: A visual and textual analysis of two popular CD-ROM programs. *Linguistics and Education* 10 (1): 89–105.

Chapter 6

Apple, Michael W. 1993. The politics of official knowledge: Does a national curriculum make sense? *Teachers College Records* 95 (2): 222–241.

———. 2002. Pedagogy, patriotism, and democracy: On the educational meanings of 11 September 2001. *Discourse: Studies in the Cultural Politics of Education* 23 (3): 299–308.

Bennett, William J. 1998. The place to harvest patriots. *School Administrator* 55 (5): 38–40.

Bernstein, Basil. 1996. *Pedagogy, symbolic control and identity. Theory, research, critique.* London: Taylor & Francis.

Centre for Public Policy Research. 2002. Faith-based schooling and the invisible effects of 11 September 2001: The view from England. *Discourse: Studies in the Cultural Politics of Education* 23 (3): 309–317.

Chiodo, John J., and Leisa A. Martin. 2005. What do students have to say about citizenship? An analysis of the concept of citizenship among secondary education students. *Journal of Social Studies Research* 29 (1): 23–31.

Chouliaraki, Lilie, and Norman Fairclough. 1999. *Discourse in late modernity. Rethinking critical discourse analysis.* Edinburgh: Edinburgh University Press.

Freire, Paulo. 2005. *Pedagogy of the oppressed* (30th anniversary ed.). New York: Continuum.

Giroux, Henry. 2004. Pedagogy, film, and the responsibility of intellectuals: A response. *Cinema Journal* 43 (2): 119–126.

Gounari, Panayota. 2009. Rethinking critical literacy in the new information age. *Critical Inquiry in Language Studies* 6 (3): 148–175.

Hickey, Gail M. 2002. Why did I get an 'A' in citizenship? An ethnographic study of emerging concepts of citizenship. *Journal of Social Studies Research* 26 (2): 3–9.

Hyslop-Margison, Emery J., and James Thayer. 2009. *Teaching democracy: Citizenship education as critical pedagogy.* Rotterdam: Sense Publishers.

Koutsogiannis, Dimitris. 2004. Critical techno-literacy and "weak" languages. In Ilana Snyder and Catherine Beavis (Eds.), *Doing literacy online: Teaching, learning and playing in an electronic world* (pp. 163–184). Cresskill, NJ: Hampton Press.

Lankshear, Colin. 1997. *Changing literacies.* Buckingham, UK: Open University Press.

Martin, Leisa A., and John J. Chiodo. 2007. Good citizenship: What students in rural schools have to say about it. *Theory and Research in Social Education* 55 (1): 112–134.

Muspratt, Sandy H., Allan Luke, and Peter Freebody (Eds.). 1997. *Constructing critical literacies.* Cresskill, NJ: Hampton Press.

Pennycook, Alastair. 2001. *Critical applied linguistics: A critical introduction.* London: Lawrence Erlbaum Associates.

Shor, Ira. 1992. *Empowering education: Critical teaching for social change.* Chicago: University of Chicago Press.

Westheimer, Joel. 2003, March-April. Citizenship education for a democratic society. *Teach Magazine,* 17–20.

———. 2004. The politics of civic education. *PS: Political Science & Politics* 38 (2): 231–235.

Westheimer, Joel, and Joseph Kahne. 2004a. What kind of citizen? The politics of educating for democracy. *American Educational Research Journal* 41 (2): 237–269.

———. 2004b. Educating the "good" citizen: Political choices and pedagogical goals. Political Science & Politics 38 (2): 241–247.

———. 2006. The limits of political efficacy: Educating citizens for a democratic society. *PS: Political Science & Politics* 39 (2): 289–296.

Wodak, Ruth, Rudolf de Cillia, Martin Reisigl, and Karin Liebhart. 1999. *The discursive construction of national identity.* Edinburgh: Edinburgh University Press.

Index

About the Author

Bessie Mitsikopoulou is Associate Professor at the Department of Language and Linguistics, Faculty of English Language and Literature, University of Athens, Greece. Her research interests are in the areas of critical discourse analysis, educational linguistics, and digital literacies. Recent projects she has coordinated include English Literacy in Second Chance Schools in Greece, digital enrichment of the English textbooks in the Digital School Project of the Greek Ministry of Education, and the e-school for the State Certificate of Foreign Language Proficiency.

Her publications include *Policies of Linguistic Pluralism and the Teaching of Languages in Europe* (Metaihmio Publications), *The Periphery Viewing the World* (Parousia), *Literacy in English: Curriculum, Methodological Suggestions, Educational Materials* (Greek Ministry of Education), and several articles in academic journals such as *Language and Education, Journal of Language and Politics, Language Learning and Technology, Journal of Computer Mediated Communication*, and *Journal of Applied Linguistics*.

Printed in Great Britain
by Amazon

38920831R00129